THE MYSTERIES OF MACHU PICCHU

What ancient culture built the Throne of the Sun, one of the most magical sites in the world, and the Temple of the Moon, a triumph of human daring? Who quarried to perfection and transported the gigantic monoliths weighing several tons? Strangest of all, why are there no inscriptions of any kind at Machu Picchu?

It appears they had no written language. But how could a culture that didn't even have an alphabet possess the sophisticated technology to build aqueducts and hanging gardens? Did they have another form of communication, perhaps telepathic, unknown to us? These are just a few of the intriguing ideas that Simone Waisbard explores in this startling account of Machu Picchu.

THE MYSTERIES OF MACHU PICCHU is one in a series of Avon Books dedicated to exploring the lost secrets of ancient peoples and earlier times . . . secrets that challenge mankind today—and may hold the key to our own future.

Other books in this series

THE MYSTERIES OF MACHU PICCHU

Simone Waisbard

AVON
PUBLISHERS OF BARD, CAMELOT AND DISCUS BOOKS

THE MYSTERIES OF MACHU PICCHU was
originally published in French as
Machu Picchu, Cité Perdue des Incas.

AVON BOOKS
A division of
The Hearst Corporation
959 Eighth Avenue
New York, New York 10019
Copyright © Robert Laffont, S.A., 1974
Published by arrangement with Éditions Robert Laffont.
Library of Congress Catalog Card Number: 79-50430
ISBN: 0-380-43687-6

First Avon Printing, April, 1979

AVON TRADEMARK REG. U.S. PAT. OFF. AND IN
OTHER COUNTRIES, MARCA REGISTRADA, HECHO EN
U.S.A.

Printed in the U.S.A.

Contents

Foreword

Machu Picchu! . . . A great petrified mystery.
—Jacques de Lacretelle

Ululating *quenas*, the raucous sound of the *pututus*, the eerie pounding of drums made of human flesh set the pace for the hieratic procession of thousands of Indian warriors, decked out in feathers and armed with shields and spears of gleaming gold, who are escorting the supreme Inca, carried aloft on a golden litter.

Behind them, the band of noble *curacas* in shimmering tunics, the Orejones with earlobes distended by heavy cylinders of chased gold, the perfumed cortege of the beautiful Chosen Women, the solemn procession of the Virgins of the Sun, the high priests wearing gold masks encrusted with turquoise, the richly adorned ancestral mummies, the golden idols and fabulous treasures borne by the slow caravan of russet llamas trail off in the maze of a magical city which touches the sky of the pre-Columbian gods . . .

Hiram Bingham watches the entire procession pass by in a dream. This vivid, enveloping dream would one day, at the beginning of this century, launch him into a thrilling search for the "Lost City" of the Incas.

In the very heart of the Andes, 100 kilometers from Cuzco (the ancient capital of the Inca Empire of the Tahuantinsuyo, but already on the threshold of the "green ocean" of the Amazon Basin), there stretches, as far as the eye can see, the colossal cosmic chaos of a bluish, granitic cordillera, notched by monstrous abysses and crowned with glaciers and immaculate snowy peaks—the abode, since the earliest times, of the fierce Apus, revered spirits of the ancestors.

Against this sumptuous background, in the shadow of a vertiginous peak which emerges from the fringed clouds

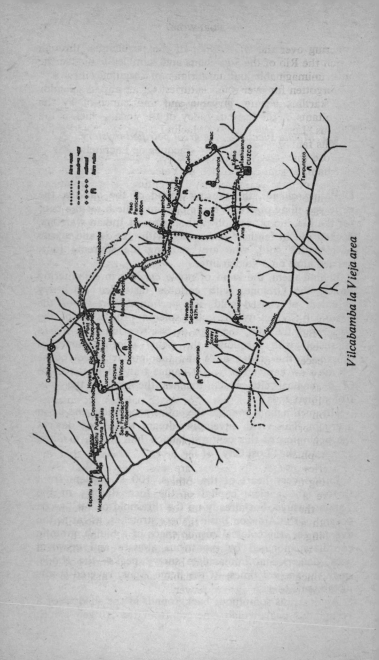

Vilcabamba la Vieja area

hovering over the wild *cañon* of the Urubamba, through which the Rio of the Sun winds and rumbles, is hidden the most unimaginable and mysterious of forgotten cities.

Forgotten for over four centuries! Of an unreal splendor and startling beauty, invisible and undreamed-of by the inhabitants of the Sacred Valley of the Incas—such is the famous "Lost City" atop the Machu Picchu, the "Old Peak," with its fantastic secrets.

More than sixty years have passed since the day Hiram Bingham, a young professor at Yale, discovered it in the course of an extraordinary adventure (the complete account of which has yet to be published), yet most of the mysteries that enshroud this monument of ancient Peru still remain and still seem impenetrable. Quite unlike the archaeological rebuses that intrigue investigators of Mayan ruins in Mexico, Egyptologists at the foot of the pyramids, or scholars confronted with the giant statues of Easter Island, the "unknowns" of Machu Picchu have thus far discouraged the avid pens of authors claiming to demystify the obliterated history of legendary vanished civilizations.

Why this incredible silence concerning such prodigious ruins? Because nothing is known about their history. No engraved column or stele informs the visitor, as in Rome or Greece. Nor are there any monumental statues to point the way to temples, as in Memphis or Thebes. Nor vivid frescoes or haunting friezes adorning the walls, such as those in Assyrian sanctuaries or Aztec palaces. No inscription on the tombs. No runes, hieroglyphs, pictographs, tablets, or code revealing the esoteric knowledge of the Andean masters. The complete lack of written or ideographic messages, however cryptic, suggests that the mysteries of Machu Picchu are even deeper and more puzzling than those posed by other ruins of antiquity.

Like a gigantic petrified sarcophagus, Machu Picchu stifles the otherworldly cries of the Incan phantoms. Smooth as an angel's skin, the stone of the monoliths—weighing several tons and quarried to perfection by who knows what Titans capable of overcoming an inhuman terrain—is the only mark left by the mysterious god-men who conceived Peru's imperishable, age-old masterpiece—proof of their supernatural power.

Nor do the numerous and baffling mysteries of the "Lost City" pertain only to past eras. Some are much more recent.

Among the thorniest problems in Peru's hermetic prehistory is that of the absolute dating, which gives rise to heated controversies. Is Machu Picchu pre-Inca, or should it be included in the list of conquests by Pachacutec, the great restorer of the Inca Empire, whom historiographers compare to the "King of Kings"?

Starting with the brutal dissolution of the Empire of the Tahuantinsuyo, before the intrepid thrust of Pizarro's mercenaries, historical questions abound. Though their bushy beards and light skin fooled the Indians, who took them for "messengers" of Viracocha, the traditional postdiluvian creator of the Sun, the Moon, and the Andean peoples (an ancient legend predicted his return at some future time, which had apparently arrived), it seems the secret refuge of the last Incas and the last virgins of the solar cult was totally forgotten after the Spanish Conquest of Peru.

Today another question mark punctuates the long list of mysteries surrounding Machu Picchu: Can Hiram Bingham, in all justice, be rightfully considered the first to have discovered the marvelous "Lost City"?

And finally—even though the fact is generally unknown, even in Peru—was the majestic "skyscraper" attributed to the Incas ever really "lost," in the proper sense of the word, as the American explorer claimed?

Now cleared, the perilous trail that Hiram Bingham followed on muleback in 1911 is traveled by thousands of fascinated tourists every year. However, there is still no road from Cuzco to Machu Picchu! Only a minuscule, wobbly *autocarril* and a picturesque and very slow sierra train packed with natives wearing the typical rainbow-colored costumes ventures into the impasse of the terrifying Urubamba Cañon. And it is not until the end of the journey that an acrobatic minibus vertically scales a track consisting of lightninglike zigzags.

Everywhere the lush jungle storms the steep flanks of the Salccantay, one of the major peaks of the Vilcabamba Cordillera, which reaches over 6,000 meters in altitude. On every side the tropical forest extends its green tentacles,

submerging ruins that cling to summits. How many has it
devoured that remain unexplored? For countless centuries
torrential rains have been washing away the ancient paved
roads, carrying off the fragile liana bridges thrown like
hammocks across ravines, and eroding the mountainside.

Short of breath, one reaches solitary heights where the
rarefied air restrains the movements of an organism not
acclimated from birth to the unusual environment of the
altitude.[1] However, at various times there lived here ingenious "jewelers" in rock—builders of palaces, fortresses,
sanctuaries in the cyclopean style. We know not when or
whence they came, how or why they left or disappeared.

But where are the ruins? From the recesses of a gorge
so narrow that the sunlight scarcely penetrates to the
bottom, to the peaks of the apocalyptic wave of granite
frozen at the beginning of the world, one's eyes seek in
vain the slightest trace. And then, around a bend in the
path, there suddenly looms, like a mirage or a vision
summoned by a magic wand, an entire city, so far from
"dead" that it would suffice, it seems, to raise new roofs of
golden rushes atop the colossal walls spared by countless
telluric tremors and centuries of erosion, and to adorn the
enormous parabolic Torreón with the splendid golden disk
of the Sun once again, in order to bring back to life the
incomparable artists who, in defiance of the laws of gravity
and equilibrium, constructed—with an admirable science
and artistic sense—this "Eighth Wonder of the World"
which today is plunged in a silence that extends worldwide.

What was the real name of this celestial city? Who built
it, and when? Who lived here? Who inhabited it last? Was
it abruptly abandoned, and for what obscure reason? Was
it a sacred city, forbidden to all but the imperial elite?
What strange rites were celebrated here? Are we standing
before the gynaeceum of the beautiful Acllas consecrated
to the exclusive love of the Inti, women upon whom no
man dare lay eyes except under penalty of death? Is this
the supreme acropolis of the Sun, reserved for the Amautas,

---

[1] The Indian of the Andes has *two more liters of blood* than
most mortals have. I discuss high-altitude biology in my book
Masks, Mummies, and Magicians (Edinburgh: Oliver & Boyd,
1965).

ancient sages and astronomical scholars who studied here
the signs of the heavens in order to orchestrate the periods
of sowing and harvesting? Or was this, rather, the impregnable "strongbox" of the Amazons of the Moon and
the Sun, who were barricaded within the Andes and
brought to light by a curious rumor during the mad search
for El Dorado?

Did the watchtower perched on the pointed summit of
the Huayna Picchu, or "Young Peak," protect the magnificent city from potential invasion by the tribes of barbarians
who sprang like painted demons from the nearby virgin
forest?

At the height of an empire expanded to the point of
imprudence,[2] did the Inca perhaps come here, returning
from victorious but exhausting campaigns, to seek in his
dark-skinned seraglio the warrior's rest and to consult,
atop this deified mountain, with the ancient deities?

But in point of fact—and this is not the least of the
mysteries of Machu Picchu—were the Incas themselves
aware of the "Lost City"?

All these doubts gnaw at the mind of the researcher.

For half a century, each tentative step amid these
fabulous ruins has only served to augment the number of
mysteries, rather than to solve any. Americanists themselves also run up against the inexplicable muteness of the
texts written since the sixteenth century, in which, logically,
they should find some allusion to the "Lost City." This
silence is all the more troubling in view of the fact that
the archival documents, ancient anonymous manuscripts,
conventual and military chronicles, viceregal ordinances,
and Quechua and Aymara vocabularies are prolix as to the
nomenclature of the places said to be Incan—all as a

_____

[2] The frontiers of the Tahuantinsuyo (the ancient name of
the Incan Empire, which was not called Peru until after the
Conquest) reached from the Rio Ancasmayo in southern Colombia to the Rio Bio-Bio in the center of Chile, covering the present countries of Ecuador, Peru, and Bolivia, and extending into
northwest Argentina, the impenetrable jungles of Brazil, and
the savannas of the Orenoque —encompassing, that is, an area
of about 2 million square kilometers.

function of the treasures that the Spaniards coveted and
the idolatrous practices that the Inquisitors tried fanatically
to extirpate in order to indoctrinate the Indians in the
Christian faith.

But nowhere do we find the name anxiously sought by
Hiram Bingham and, after him, a host of prominent
Americanists. And six decades after the American explorer's sensational find, this gem of pre-Columbian Andean
architecture continues to guard the secrets entrusted to it.

Bingham himself strove in vain all his life to decipher
those enigmas which he considered most fascinating. He
converted his personal hypotheses into imprudent theories,
and this brought upon him, after his initial success, a good
number of harsh criticisms:

• The three trapezoidal windows of the great temple
(which, opening on the void, are so remarkable that no
other ruin, among the *50,000* archaeological ruins of
ancient Peru catalogued by UNESCO in 1968, contains
anything similar): are they, as Bingham tried desperately
to prove, the legendary *toccos* of Pacaritampu, the mythical
cave from which the founders of the Cuzco dynasty
emerged?

• Or is the temple, as Bingham held as persistently, the
elusive Vilcabamba la Vieja, the forbidden lair of the great
sorcerers and seers of the abominable "University of
Idolatry" vehemently condemned by two Spanish evange-
lists who, despite their wiles, never succeeded in reaching
it?

• Or, if not, is it Viticos, the refuge hastily fortified by
Manco Inca and his rebel sons, who heroically resisted the
soldiers of Charles V and Philip II for nearly forty years?—
for the Conquest, begun in 1532 and not completed until
1572, was nowhere near as easy and brief as too many
careless writers have suggested.

• Or is it, rather, the Casa del Sol, the supreme "House
of the Sun"?

• Do the 150 shriveled mummies found in the funerary
caves of the Old Peak—all of them young women who
must have been particularly pretty, according to the findings of Dr. George F. Eaton, an osteologist with the Yale
Peruvian Expedition—belong to the last Virgins of the
Sun, who, escaping from the Acllahuasi in Cuzco in the

nick of time, fled with the Inca to this lofty, impregnable place, sheltered from the lechery of men such as Pizarro and his acolytes?

Is it possible to clear up the mysteries of Machu Picchu and to reconstruct the plot of so confused a preliterary story? One of the worst difficulties impeding investigation lies in the faithful interpretation of texts which were handwritten or printed in a medieval Castilian and an outmoded alphabet, on the basis of "confessions" extorted from Indians who understood nothing of the language of the foreign invader. Added to this difficult problem, the cessation of archaeological excavations (which, since 1915, have never been resumed at Machu Picchu) explains both the dearth of worthwhile literature concerning the intriguing "Lost City" and the mysteries that enshroud it.

For nearly fifteen consecutive years I delved into almost incunabular archives, working on the site, interviewing Peruvian historians and archaeologists, collating and comparing their opinions. Finally, I tracked down the *last living eyewitnesses* who, with Bingham, participated in the resurrection of Machu Picchu and who, out of respect for his memory or because of ignorance, had never spoken out publicly.

The secrets I thus garnered and the painstaking research finally enabled me to pick up the thread—which had *truly* been lost—of an extraordinary, fascinating story.

PART ONE

Hiram Bingham in Search of the "Lost City" of the Incas

Go and look behind the Ranges—something lost behind the Ranges. Lost and waiting for you. Go!

—Rudyard Kipling

CHAPTER ONE

The "Cradle of Gold"

> *History tells us that after the siege of Cuzco the Inca Manco . . . withdrew into the inaccessible mountains, on the right bank of the Rio Apurimac.*
> —Vicomte Eugène de Sartiges, 1834

TOWARD CHOQUEQUIRAO

Hiram Bingham,[1] who gets his taste for adventure, he says, from his forebears, takes as a leitmotif a passage of Rudyard Kipling's which pushes him irresistibly toward discovery. As early as 1905, he follows the glorious route of Simón Bolívar across the Andes from Venezuela to Colombia, and in 1908, traveling the old Spanish Trade Route to Lima on muleback, he discovers "the fabulous land of the Incas."

When he arrives in Cuzco, the ancient symbolic "navel" of the Tahuantinsuyo, the honorable Don Nuñez (prefect of the Apurimac, the province located in the steepest part of the cordillera) urges that they explore together the region where once there was "a marvelous city." Its name conveys all sorts of promises: Choquequirao, the "Cradle of Gold."

According to local legend, it was here that Manco Inca, the last of the unfortunate legitimate sovereigns, lived after the Conquest.

Pioneers had traced a path, but in a hundred years three attempts had met with only partial success.

---

[1] Born in Honolulu on November 19, 1875, Hiram Bingham was elected a senator, then governor of Connecticut in 1924. An intrepid mountaineer, aviator, and traveler, he died in Washington on June 6, 1956.

The prefect of the Apurimac had formed a company of treasure-seekers in Cuzco, mestizos grown rich by having the poor natives in their employ cultivate immense sugar-cane plantations. The members had subscribed several thousand dollars. Bingham soon realized, however, that the official's interest in the ruins of Choquequirao had very little to do with the heroic history of the Incan resistance. Don Nuñez was hoping, more prosaically, that the famous "lost treasure of the Incas" would be found there, having been buried for four centuries.

According to rumor, the "Cradle of Gold" was so vast that it may have contained 15,000 inhabitants. There were reports of temples, palaces, "baths," a great sanctuary with idols, and even prisons.[2]

The expedition leaves Cuzco on the first of February—the worst season—under a flooding rain that will fall relentlessly throughout the four-day journey, through steep mountains notched with narrow gorges. They must circumvent swamps bathed in chill mists, skirt waterfalls of a terrifying beauty, and wear themselves out on stairways carved, Inca-style, into the living rock, in order to descend vertiginously, by hundreds of stairs, into a verdant valley before reascending, as far as the summit, toward a snowy peak. The climate varies brutally. The polar cold of the desolate high peaks suddenly gives way to an equatorial heat, a lunar vista of scrub bamboo bristling with thorns, mimosa, and gigantic candle cacti.

THE FAMOUS LIANA BRIDGE
OVER THE "LORD RIVER" APURIMAC

Does the fabulous treasure not justify taking risks?

Learning from his predecessors' failure, Don Nuñez has a new path cleared in the direction of the majestically meandering torrent, whose roaring voice echoes in every direction, earning it its Quechua name of Capac Mayu, the

---

[2] The existence of an ancient Incan city was known in the eighteenth century, but the first scientific exploration dates back to de Sartiges in 1834, followed by Léonce Angrand, Samañez Ocampo in 1853, then Hiram Bingham and Max Uhle. Popular opinion held at the time that Manco Inca had taken refuge there.

"Sonorous Prince," the "Laughing Monarch," or "he who speaks like a chief," the powerful "Lord River" venerated by the Incas.

Embanked by two steep slopes and flowing so abundantly that, hundreds of kilometers farther north, it is one of the principal affluents of the Amazon, the wild current of this "great speaker" (in Bingham's words) has sculpted in the cordillera a gorge thought to be larger and deeper than the famous Grand Canyon of Arizona.

"Praised by the poets, crossed by the Incas and the Liberators, witness to the wars and dissentions of the Conquest, axis of our entire history, it is the giant voice of the country, the sacred rio of the oracles, born among peaks saturated with legends and memories," writes the great Peruvian historiographer José de la Riva Aguero.

The *cañon* of the upper Apurimac is one of nature's fantastic spectacles, but also a pitiless murderer, the "river that kills," sweeping away the famous liana bridges that span it. Apparently, Mayta Capac, the fourth Inca, conceived the design of the first work of this sort himself, inventing it and supervising the construction, then marching across the interminable suspended footbridge, made of twisted maguey fibers, with 12,000 warriors.

These acrobatic bridges long served the Spanish soldiers, arousing their fear as well as admiration. It is said that when Pizarro rode off in search of coveted treasures, he came to a fragile liana bridge that swung in the wind. Unable to persuade his men to venture onto the footbridge with pleas or threats, he spurred his horse and crossed it "with lightning speed"; his troup followed. But this ingenious bridge was often swept away by the river or burned by the Indians.

Cieza de León, the well-known chronicler, described the way he had to cross the torrent, upon his return to Lima, after having fought Gonzalo Pizarro and his rebels: in a basket that slid on ropes. In the sixteenth century, cutting or seizing the *oroya*—this pulley cable—was a matter of life or death for the conquistadors.

"Reconstructed with ropes as thick as one's calf, 122 common paces long," the Apurimac bridge was crossed in 1579 by Montesinos, the other great chronicler, and later, in 1834, in the course of his "Voyage to the Republics of South America," by the Vicomte de Sartiges. But "Each week an accident occurred. The river is so wide," he writes, "that it [the bridge] forms a formidable curve and the weight of a single person is enough to make it sway like a swing!"

Some years later, François de Castelnau also hesitated to set foot on the fragile assemblage of wicker and sticks, "amid a tempest of bird calls." But the most famous of Incan bridges ended up rotting for lack of maintenance, and all that remains of it is the extraordinary drawing made by George Squier in 1877.

How, then, are Bingham and his party to reach the opposite bank, nearly 300 meters away? The white water roils furious waves, but, foreseeing the difficulties, Don Nuñez has brought along a Chinese diver accustomed to diving into Andean torrents in search of possible treasures. The latter, by swimming across with a coil of telegraph wire, enables the Indians to improvise a footbridge which they consider "death-defying." The mules refuse to venture onto it. They have to be unloaded, and the equipment must be transported by hand.

Once they reach the other side, they must climb up the side of a ravine. They have to stop every fifty paces, hearts and temples pounding like drums, to catch their breath; but as they go higher, the panorama of the valley acquires an enchanting magnificence.

The next morning, Bingham and his companions at last enter the fantastic "Cradle of Gold."

A MESSAGE FROM
THE DEPTHS OF TIME

The Peruvian *huaqueros* dynamite the ruins in order to pillage freely. They gut palaces and temples, sending venerable mummies up in dust, but the search disappoints the prefect and his accomplices.[3] Indifferent to their letdown, Bingham measures the scattered bones of a skeleton. Extremely superstitious, the Quechua carriers assume that

[3] One of the expedition guides found a *macana* (club) made of an alloy of 3 kilos of gold, as much copper, and 1 kilo of an unidentified metal. Don Nuñez apparently let Bingham have the antique weapon for about 20,000 soles.

the disturbing blond giant is communing with the spirits of the departed Incas, who will revenge themselves on the natives. Do the ghosts of the Sons of the Sun perhaps mysteriously disclose to him that Choquequirao is not the true "Lost City" of the Incas?

Upon Bingham's return to Lima, Carlos E. Romero confirms this fact. At this time, at the beginning of the twentieth century, the Peruvian historian is the only one to have acquainted himself with the ancient chronicles (thus far ignored) that were written during the Conquest by the Inca Titu Cusi and the Spanish captain Baltazar de Ocampo, and which suggest that these ruins are not—as Romero's colleagues still believe—the final refuge of Manco and his sons.

Romero thinks that Choquequirao was a frontier fortress defending the upper Apurimac Valley, one of the natural approaches to Cuzco, from the surprise attacks of a powerful enemy nation, the Chancas, who placed the Incan capital in grave danger during the reign of Viracocha Inca —or perhaps from the barbarity of the savage Amazonian Antis.

It is highly probable, however, that Manco Inca used Choquequirao as a base camp for punitive expeditions which he ardently waged against the Spaniards for eight years. Cieza de León and Garcilaso pointed out, at the time, that the route used most frequently by the conquistadors passed through Huamanga (now Ayacucho). In 1912, José Gabriel Cosio, the administrator of the University of Cuzco in charge of supervising the second Yale Peruvian Expedition, noted that the ancient road (outlined by stone markers, as were all the imperial highways of the Incas), which rises 3,500 meters to the *apacheta* of Chuquiton, continued to be used by innumerable caravans of commercial traffic between Ayacucho and Pampaconas (a historic site that will be treated in later chapters on "the end of the Incas").

Nothing tallies, Bingham declares, with an Incan "capital": "neither the site, nor the poor architecture, crudely constructed." This statement causes some surprise, because Cuzco's authorities place the last hideout of the Incas on the right bank of Apurimac, that is, exactly the site of the explored ruins—which doesn't jibe with what de Sartiges wrote either; he stayed at Choquequirao for a week and described "a triumphal wall pierced by an Egyptian-style door, which supports the altar of the Sun."

For Bingham, the "Lost City" of Manco is "*much farther*, no doubt in the heart of mountain ranges that are still unknown. Hidden. One must look for it, and one ought to find it, in a labyrinth of high granitic peaks, hidden under the thick green curtain of the jungle, protected by the mystery of four centuries of oblivion and the secret religiously kept by the Quechua Indians."[4]

We shall soon see that, if he does not identify the source of this information, it is no accident. And how well Bingham's description fits Machu Picchu! Does he have any proof? "A hunch," he will confess, supported by his studies.[5]

No chronicle of the Conquest escaped him. Catechists, captains, ordinary Spanish soldiers, corregidors, viceroys— all had heard, from the mouths of very old Incan Amautas, splendid history lessons preserved on *quipus,* intriguing mnemonic knotted cords, for which their descendants forgot the "sesame." Forced to accept the fact that their last masters lived in exile in an impenetrable Andean stronghold, the *quipucamayocs* nonetheless never divulged—even under torture—the precise location of the bastion.

[4] According to disclosures by Gustavo Montoya and Dr. Alberto Giesecke, both friends and confidants of Bingham, in the Peruvian newspaper *El Comercio* (Lima) in 1961.

[5] The Peruvian historian Luis E. Valcarcel believes that Bingham's trip through the Urubamba Cañon was inspired by a document attesting to the existence of a mysterious city, which he found among some ancient archives in Spain. I shall provide further proof of this.

CHAPTER TWO

In the Sacred Valley of
the Rio of the Sun

*The Sacred Valley, dominated by middle
stretch of the Urubamba, some 20
kilometers northwest of Cuzco, is located in
the heart of the Inca Empire . . . On the
left bank of the river looms the inextricable
massif of Vilcabamba, refuge of the last
Incas . . . On the right bank rises the
immense eastern cordillera, beyond which
stretches, mysterious, the world of the forest.*
—Nathan Wachtel, 1971

THE YALE PERUVIAN EXPEDITION

In June 1911 the first Yale Peruvian Expedition is ready.
Like the following expeditions, which will occur in 1912
and 1915, it is under the patronage of Yale University,
which Hiram Bingham attended, and the National Geographic Society. All the material has been furnished by
businesses in New York; the Peruvian government will see
to the transportation of the explorers from the port of
Mollendo, located 1,000 kilometers south of Lima, to Cuzco.

The expedition includes (in addition to Bingham, the
leader) Isaiah Bowman, geologist-geographer; Harry Foote,
naturalist; topographer Kai Hendrickson; surgeon William
G. Erving; engineer H. L. Tucker; and Paul B. Lanius,
assistant. They all disembark at Mollendo with several tons
of luggage, which is soon transferred aboard an archaic but
picturesque little train worthy of the Wild West. The loco-
motive chews up the rails with its enormous cowcatcher;
Indians and llamas wander onto the track, unmindful of
the din made by the well-polished copper bells which adorn

9

the roof of the machine and the jets of steam that shoot from its flanks to dislodge them.

The Mollendo-Cuzco route performs a tightrope act, rising from sea level to the heart of the Andes. After having circumvented a chain of volcanoes powdered with fresh snow, crossed vast, sandy, desertlike pampas populated by rare, elusive vicuñas, and clung to desolate rocky *punas,* the train reaches—at 300 kilometers as the crow flies, but 813 by means of the Ferrocarril del Sur—a high plateau sprinkled with numerous typical Indian hamlets.

Tired and dust-covered, Bingham and his companions at last discover, in the hollow of a valley, the sacred city of the Incas, the monumental Cuzco, built, it is estimated, in the eleventh or twelfth century, at an altitude of 3,500 meters. Since the Spanish Conquest, the ancient city no longer dozes beneath roofs made of rushes threaded with gold, but under red tiles and in the shade cast by a few eucalyptus trees imported from Spain. The bald, rounded peaks surrounding it have witnessed the birth of one of the most marvelous and advanced world civilizations ever to arise on the South American continent.

The multicolored, animated sight of the small Cuzco station takes the Americans' minds off their fatigue. A crowd of people the color of patinated bronze, dressed in brightly striped ponchos and voluminous felt skirts, come and go with little skipping steps, their voices sharpened by the altitude. Wearing the traditional flat round hat made of black felt lined with red and trimmed with golden braids in the form of a cross, the Indians cook on the very ground, in bulging earthenware pots. A ragged little girl with shiny crimson cheeks hands the travelers bowls of spicy soup; its steam burns their eyes.

"These pariahs," Bingham notes, "are nevertheless the legitimate descendants of those who formed the legions of the Empire of the Incas!"

There is no one who has not heard of a legendary city paved with pure silver, with gardens full of animals, birds, trees, flowers, and life-size statues made of solid gold incrusted with precious gems. Some say they could guide the expedition on the path to these ancient ruins. Others display fragments of ancient parchments gnawed by insects and rats. Are they sincere or deluded? Hiram Bingham listens to no one. Even before he sets out, are the Inca gods perhaps his most dependable allies?

IN CUZCO, ANCIENT CAPITAL
OF THE INCAS

First of all, the Americans must procure beasts of burden capable of transporting their heavy equipment across the jumble of mountains. Llamas—animals exclusive to the cordilleras, with their languorous regard and hieratic walk —seem likely, despite their slowness, in view of their known resistance to the harshest climates, to altitude sickness, and to privations. But their hooves are extremely fragile and allow them to carry only a bundle carefully bound to their flanks, of a weight never exceeding 20 kilos. If the load shifts even slightly, the llamas—which are sensitive and capricious anyway—will lie down across the trail. Nothing can make them get up—neither flattery nor blows—and the *llamero* who drives a caravan knows the touchy nature of these beasts so well that he will try not to cross them.

Made for an oxygen-scarce atmosphere and for long Indian excursions, Andean mules are better carriers, stronger and easier to drive. But they are not as immune to the powerful attraction of the void. And there is nothing to prevent them from taking a rider along with them on a fatal leap.

Several days pass in Cuzco, in anticipation. Then an Italian merchant long established in Quechua country, a man as infatuated with archaeology as is Bingham, offers his assistance. Don César Lomellini has made his fortune dealing in coconuts harvested in the hot *selvas* of La Convención, at the bottom of the Sacred Valley of the Sun, at the very edge of the mountains where, according to some rumors, Manco Inca may have once retreated.

Like a character in a novel, the Italian lives in the sumptuous historic palace of the Marquis de Valle Umbroso, a grandee of Spain and a conquistador; he has converted the restored first floor into an Incan and colonial museum. He has even more fantastic possessions: the pre-Columbian ruins of Colcampata, nothing less than the imposing palace of the first Inca, Manco Capac, atop a hill overlooking the entire city.

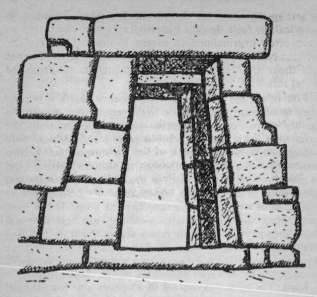

Monolithic portada *with double frame,*
Calle Tullumayo, Cuzco

César Lomellini provides the Yale expeditionists with
fourteen sturdy mules and his best *arriero*, the Indian
Rodriguez Carpio, who is intimately acquainted with the
region to be explored, both its inhabitants and its hazardous
topography.

What is Hiram Bingham actually seeking in the jumble
of the proposed trails, so little or so poorly known? A mysterious city named Viticos,[1] all trace of which has been
totally lost; Carlos E. Romero has told him it should be located—according to a sixteenth-century chronicle—"about
100 miles from the *cuzqueño* palace of the Spanish viceroy."
Extremely vague directions, to be sure! Nevertheless, Bingham doesn't hesitate a second in choosing his direction.

The only possible landmark, provided by Father Calancha
(whom Bingham trusts implicitly), is "a great white rock

[1] Misunderstood by the chroniclers, the orthography of
Quechua names is so imprecise or distorted that one may read,
alternately, Viticos, Vitcos, Uiticos, Bitcos, Vicros, Witq'os, etc.

over a spring of water." But Lomellini, when consulted, is skeptical; he feels that the historiographers of the Conquest were often overinclined to invent theories that were the product both of their desires and of the lies that the Indians told them in order to lead the conquistadors far from the secret refuges.

The few maps drawn between 1535 and 1572 do not offer much more information. Viticos appears on none of them! Nor does it appear on the more recent and more detailed map of the naturalist Antonio Raimondi, who, around 1865, penetrated the interior of the Vilcabamba Cordillera, farther than anyone had proceeded in three centuries. Cordoned off from the rest of Peru by giant mountain ranges, this region is still virtually unknown to the inhabitants of Cuzco, even though it is only 200 kilometers away and is the most opulent region in Peru by virtue of its rich mines, its pasturelands, and its tropical crops covering 300 square leagues of surface area.

Calancha indicates only that Viticos was "two or three days' journey from Vilcabamba la Vieja," and that it constituted "the principal capital of the rebel Manco and his sorcerers." Thus it is in this mysterious religious sanctuary that Incan princes and princesses, Virgins of the Sun and imperial mummies, stupendous idols and treasures, must have been safeguarded. But where should one seek this completely forgotten place, a place that has disappeared from maps and memories? Right from the start, Hiram Bingham seems to know perfectly well—better than the Peruvian explorers—where to go!

ON THE TRAIL OF MANCO INCA

One morning in July 1911 the Yale Peruvian Expedition starts out on the same route that Manco Inca took when he succeeded, by means of a ruse, in escaping maltreatment at the hands of Pizarro and in fleeing with the imperial treasure, the enormous golden disk of the Sun which adorned the great temple of the Coricancha, and a quantity of valuable clothing made of artfully woven wool.

The Peruvian government cleared the mule trail in 1895 so that coca and aguardiente (an alcohol made from sugar cane, which the cuzqueños regard highly) could be transported more economically and rapidly than they had been

by way of the snowy peaks, rising to 5,000 meters, that had
been the only possible route previously. The new trail follows the sinuous course of the Vilcanota, otherwise known
as the Willkamayo, the Rio of the Sun, the ancient sacred
river of the Incas, which today is called first the Yucay
River, then the Vilcanota, and finally, at the entrance to the
grand *cañon*, the Urubamba, until it merges at last with the
Apurimac and forms the Amazon.

The Peruvian gendarme Carrasco prances at the head of
a picturesque caravan, followed by Bingham, who is dressed
like a Boy Scout and mounted on a dwarfish mule, his
boots scraping the red earth in the same rhythm as his
mount's shoes. This outlandish Don Quixote, pale and
blond, with eyes like pale water, sets off gales of laughter
among the natives of the valley, who ordinarily are dis-
trustful and taciturn in the presence of the few strangers
who venture onto their lands. (Undoubtedly Bingham had
no idea, but they called him "the Man with Six Legs," and
the old Quechuas with whom I spoke referred to him by
this nickname.)

Two hours away from the brisk cold of Cuzco, the temperature becomes much milder. The natural setting changes
visibly, quickly growing lush. Tiered fields climb the slopes
of the cordilleras on both sides, bursting with stalks of
wheat, barley, or corn, of a size that astounds the expeditionists. With some pride, the guide Carpio informs them
that the *choclos*, the ears of the Sacred Valley, have "the
largest grains in the world, as large as hazelnuts." Nevertheless, this prodigious earth was not found on these peaks
originally. The pre-Columbian peoples—the Andenes, whose
name inspired that of these mountains—hoisted it up themselves onto the agricultural terraces. They carved the sides
of the Andes, from top to bottom, into interminable steps,
like monumental pyramids which surpass the famous "hanging gardens" of Semiramis. After countless millennia, the
obstacles encountered in these places are on the giant scale
of the inhuman landscape.

The magnificent Eden of Yucay has a climate so mild
that it is always referred to as "the Garden of the Incas."
All the Incas spent their yearly vacations here, hosting
sumptuous feasts and leaving their regal cares behind.

It seems fitting to point out a unique feature of Incan
history, because it in fact suggests an explanation for the

profusion of ancient cities perched on summits, well concealed and, like Machu Picchu, showing the subtle mark of the architects of the Incas: *The Sacred Valley of the Rio of the Sun was the exclusive property of the sovereigns of the Tahuantinsuyo*. It is the only area in the enormous empire of the four quadrants that belonged to no *suyo*.[2]

Garcilaso de la Vega, the son of an hidalgo and the Inca princess Chimpu Occlo, claims that this valley "surpasses all the other valleys in Peru in excellence." Mariano and Tschudi, who traveled through it around 1850, describe the superb edifices fortified by walls decorated with sculpted pumas holding victory trophies. They write that, to commemorate noteworthy conquests, the Incas would erect monoliths, as the Romans did, and cement them with molten gold—a hypothesis that contributed to the dismantling of fabulous palaces.

The Inca Viracocha spent his childhood in one of the imperial residences of Yucay. His mother, Mama Chicya (famed for her slender waist, as well as for her large nose, hooked like a condor's beak), was the daughter of Tokay Capac, king of the Tampus—a name to remember, for, from the dawn of the Incan dynasty, this famous chief may have played an important part in the obliterated history of Machu Picchu.

Fond of feasts and dances, and a friend to animals, Mama Chicya lived, it is said, surrounded by green parakeets, multicolored macaws, wild pigeons, and all sorts of small animals, monkeys, and other creatures of the virgin forest, installed in a veritable zoo.

When very old (many Incas lived past a hundred), Viracocha retired to this magical palace, where he must have plotted an ambush to murder one of his sons, the Inca Yupanqui—the future Pachacutec—for the benefit of Urco, his favorite. The enemy brothers gave battle in the

[2] To the east, the Antisuyo, a region of tropical forests and primitive tribes; in the heart of the Andes, the Contisuyo, a region of guanacos, between 3,000 and 5,000 meters in altitude, the birthplace of the Quechua race and the potato; at 4,000 meters, around Lake Titicaca, the Kollasuyo or Altiplano of the ancient Aymaras; on the Pacific slope, the Chinchaysuyo of the seacoast pampas and desert sands, interspersed with verdant oases where the Andean rios descend.

vicinity of Yucay, and Urco perished; the old Inca died of grief shortly thereafter.

I heard that some of his direct descendants have survived down to the present, in the neighboring mountains. In 1968, Andeanists were surprised to discover, clinging to the slopes of the San Juan glacier, several villages not listed on any Peruvian map, and the rumor swept through the Sacred Valley that "the last Incas" were hiding there.

During the Conquest the paradisial region became the marquisate of Oropesa, granted to the Inca Sayri Tupac, the son of Manco the rebel. Opposite the rio, one can discern the path by which the young prince, followed by a glittering cortege, descended in a litter (or *usnu*), and, at the site of the present village, his house, where he lived for three years before dying suddenly in 1560, probably poisoned. Built at the beginning of the Spanish colonization, of adobe brick atop a monolithic foundation, the palace retains the Incan structure (walls "receding toward the top," trapezoidal doors and niches), whereas the entrance is crowned by a coat of arms that looks curiously European.

Out front, crumbling under the weight of four centuries, two trees crammed with history are finishing out their lives. In their shade, the Inca emperors attended civic festivals held in their honor. These ornamental trees—*pisonay* in Quechua (*Erythrina falcata Benth*)—are always planted in pairs, very close together, symbolizing the two sexes. The Indians eat their brilliant red flowers, which fall in bunches, earning them the name of "blood trees." And these particular trees indeed witnessed a bloody drama! Gonzalo Pizarro, the younger brother of the famous Francisco, ordered that forty-five insurgents, whom he had had his cavalry trample, be buried, up to the waist, at their feet. Because these trees, centenarians four times over, are stooped over like old people, the Quechuas are convinced that the roots, having once been drenched with Spanish blood, will not let them die standing.

THE SALCCANTAY, TOTEMIC MOUNTAIN

As one approaches the town of Urubamba, an ebullient vegetation spreads its green tentacles across lowlands and high up toward the peaks. Hairy, reddish lianas entwine trees embroidered with rose and mauve orchids. The huge white bells of daturas scent the air, intoxicatingly.

High up in the sky glitter marvelous glaciers: the notches of the Salccantay, the Media Luna, the Huayanay, the Nudo Esquina, the Hatun Orcco, which all rise to about 6,000 meters. A good many legends are told in the valley about these deified mountains, kept inviolate by the Apus, the guardian spirits of the Quechua, and about the Salccantay in particular, the giant that watches over them; the Quechua are filled with fear and respect at the sight of it. The hermetic soul of the Indians sees this mountain— whose name means "the most savage"—as the totem originally created by Inti Sun. Its ledges are among the most gigantic in the world, hemming the peaks and suspending sharp ridges. The great French mountain climber Lionel Terray, for whom I served as impromptu guide on the high plateaus of Lake Titicaca, told me that these ledges "are the specialty of the Vilcabamba Cordillera."[3]

Slashed with ravines and bottomless gorges, covered with a jumble of rocks, bordered by monstrous seracs, the Salccantay stands out against the clouds, "insulting the skies with the haughtiness of its tapered ridges, an enormous diamond crystallized since the cosmic era, as inaccessible and arcane as the Godhead," writes Paz Soldan.

The story of the Salccantay, the two-headed mountain, was told to me by an Indian guide. One of the two "heads," China-Salccantay, represents the "savage female." The other, Orcco-Salccantay, is the "male" of the couple. They are both irascible deities quick to avenge themselves on anyone who disturbs their age-old peace. This is why, according to popular belief, our approach set off "fiendish laughter"—which was actually tons of snow vaporized into

[3] Several mountain-climbing expeditions have tackled the Salccantay. The first, led by the Italian Piero Ghiglione, failed. The Swiss climbers Broeniman and Susana Heller and Felix Marx made it up to the lower peak, by two different routes, in 1952. A Franco-American expedition led by Bernard Pierre reached the main peak. There remained the eastern peak, inviolate and considered one of the most dangerous peaks in the Andes; it was conquered by a Franco-Dutch expedition composed of Lionel Terray, Raymond Jenny, Tom de Booy, and Egeler on June 11, 1956.

a fine iridescent rain in a very strange effect, falling from the "Trident of the Damned" with an infernal din, audible for many leagues around.

THE FORBIDDEN LOVE
OF OLLANTA AND JOYOUS STAR

After a brief visit with the alcalde of Urubamba, Bingham sets off in the direction of Ollantaytambo (a site popular with tourists today for its impressive Incan ruins). In a landscape that recedes into the distance, everywhere are tiered hundreds of agricultural terraces, their containing walls jutting with unusual flat stones arranged on a diagonal, on successive levels. These *sarutas*, or "flying staircases"—an ingenious means of connecting different heights—enable one to climb very rapidly from one *anden* to another.

The rio itself is choked between two megalithic walls. High up one sees, like a sentinel guarding the pass, the effigy—painted in red, white, and black on the very rock— of an Indian warrior about to shoot an arrow. This *incapintay* must have been executed by the order of Tupac Inca Yupanqui to commemorate the surrender of the rebel prince Ollanta, former ruler of these lands.

The news has spread throughout the Sacred Valley that strangers are coming in search of the "Lost City." But which lost city? There are so many! The summits of Vilcanota are a vast graveyard of ruins.

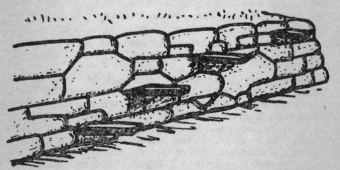

Anden *with* sarutas, *or agricultural terrace with "flying staircase"*

A veteran of the Sacred Valley, the gendarme Carrasco knows Ollantaytambo very well, but he is unaware of its origins, which date back to before the Incas. Nothing is known for certain about the time preceding the glorious reign of Pachacutec, who conquered the country in the thirteenth century, earning himself comparisons with Ramses, Genghis Khan, Alexander the Great, and even Napoleon.

Located at the entrance to a mythological valley, Ollantaytambo witnessed many wars, which were still, under the Incas, "a ritual act that was carried out according to ancestral tradition, which was obeyed out of fear of the gods and spirits," according to Frédéric Engel in his recent detailed study, *Le Monde précolombien des Andes.*

Sinchi Ollanta, military leader of the Tampus, the ancient lords of the valley of the Rio of the Sun, leads the Incan armies that control the Antisuyo into battle. His earlier prowess has earned him the glorious rank of general of the empire, and he will figure in Peruvian history as the first popular hero, "the Titan of the Andes." However, this honorific title, due solely to his courage, does not give him the right to look upon the very beautiful Cusi Coylor, the favorite daughter of the omnipotent Inca. Although he greatly appreciates the merits of Ollanta's superior strategy, Pachacutec is overwhelmed with a mad, blind fury when he learns, from the high priest of the Sun, of the guilty pleasures that the princess Joyous Star has enjoyed with this plebeian. By his order, the sacrilegious girl is entombed in the dark dungeon of the House of the Chosen Women at Cuzco. Ollanta flees rather than stand trial before the imperial court, although he is determined to free the divine princess who has violated the ancestral laws.

The Sinchi musters all his supporters at Ollantaytambo in order to confront Pachacutec's legions, which are pursuing him. A terrible battle is waged against them on the banks of the rio. Firmly retrenched in the colossal fortress that defends the rocky gorge, Ollanta's warriors tear Pachacutec's army apart. This unusual reversal for the Inca's soldiers incites to insurrection all the tribes for 60 leagues around. Two hundred caciques, who rule over the thousands of Indians conquered by the Incas more by force than good will, soon form a confederation of the tribes of

Vilcanota. The allied chiefries rise up to cast off the yoke of the Orejones from Cuzco.

The battle of the man of the earth versus the Sons of the Sun—the fight of telluric man versus sidereal man—lasts several years. Pachacutec dies without seeing the outcome. His son, Tupac Yupanqui, perceives the danger of this interminable rebellion, which is compromising the security of the Tahuantinsuyo. What his father was unable to achieve with force, he will attain through guile. His ablest captain, Rumi Nahui, "Stone-Eye," suggests a cunning plan. He will allow himself to be captured by Ollanta's warriors and will complain to them that the Inca mistreated him, ostensibly as punishment for the defeats they have suffered. The stratagem works. Ollanta, pitying Rumi Nahui, allows him to enter the fortress, where, after nightfall, great feasts are held to celebrate his capture. Taking advantage of the general drunkenness, and following a plan formulated ahead of time, Stone-Eye admits Inca soldiers through a secret entrance.

Ollanta is led in chains to Cuzco, where he must undergo the torture prescribed for traitors. How does the story end? I prefer the ending provided by the Peruvian poets, who wish it to be happy. Tupac Yupanqui, confronted with the product of the love between Cusi Coylor and Ollanta, the young and very lovely Ima Sumac,[4] who informs him of the sad fate of her mother, pining away in the prison depths, proves magnanimous and pardons the lovers.

What is worth remembering, above all, about this passionate drama, which has become legendary in Peru, is that it introduces the fortress of Ollantaytambo and of the great Tampu lords, which therefore must have been *already built during the reign of Pachacutec*—a detail that

---

[4] Revived recently by a famous Peruvian singer, the name Ima Sumac is in fact a Quechua exclamation that can be translated as "How beautiful!"—whether the object in question is a woman, a flower, or any other thing worthy of admiration. Also, the love story of Ollanta was the subject of a Quechua play whose author is unknown. The best-known version was transcribed and performed in 1780. It is attributed to the priest Valdez.

may also play an interesting role in terms of the mysteries surrounding Machu Picchu.

Another episode closely links Ollantaytambo with the Incas who rose up against the conquistadors. It was, in fact, the first place where Manco stopped on his way to an exile from which he would never return. It is at Ollantaytambo that the Inca halted with his court, his seraglio, and his treasures when he gave Pizarro the slip, and here— "from lofty terraces (with lava stairways still intact), which striate the horizon like the tiers of a stadium," as described by Paul Morand—he would inflict a bitter defeat on the Spaniards. It is from Ollantaytambo that Manco, his Chosen Women, the vestals of the Sun-Punchao, the sacred llamas, some 60,000 loyal followers, and the imperial army would set out into the labyrinth of the sierras, after having caved in mountainsides to block passages, destroyed the paths, and severed the liana suspension bridges.

THE CYCLOPEAN FORTRESS OF OLLANTAYTAMBO

On the trail of the Inca, in the shadow of the fortress located at an altitude of 2,750 meters, Hiram Bingham and his escort come across *the only pre-Columbian city in Peru*, whose ancient palaces are still, to this day, inhabited by the descendants of the mysterious builders. Though the centuries have eroded the paving stones of the road, it still leads to the vast rectangular plaza of Manyanraki, with its surface of trodden earth, surrounded by imposing houses which exude the inexpressible sadness of bygone days. The doorways with their lintels of massive stone, the trapezoidal niches (a row of one hundred excellent niches adorns one of the walls of the entrance to the fortress), the walls made of granite blocks smoothly polished and fitted without the slightest interstice—all retain an extraordinary majesty, despite the neglect evident in the facades.

One perceives, through a monumental double-frame *portada* of light-colored granite, *4 meters high*, the interior arcades and the llama park of a palace that was once impressive. An Indian man is weaving a poncho with broad brown stripes on an old wooden loom hooked to *ahuanas*, a type of ring carved in the stone for this purpose.

Squared off like a checkerboard, the narrow streets of

the town have retained the names they had during the Incan epoch. The little Rio Patacancha has been canalized and divided into *acequias*, or gutters, which distribute the water throughout the various districts. In order to protect his desperate retreat, Manco had the course of the rio diverted, so that it flooded the bottom of the valley.

Once, during Pachacutec's reign, there was a particularly prolonged dry spell which created a water shortage in Ollantaytambo. The Inca had the one hundred golden idols of the *huacas* brought to the square and challenged them to make it rain within three days. Since the miracle did not occur, he ordered that the idols' heads be cut off—as the Indian crowd howled with fright.

THE SIX MIRRORS OF THE SUN

In the middle of the village, in the garden of a dismantled palace, is found one of the most remarkable "ritual baths" of ancient Peru, that of the Nusta, or Inca princess. Was it that of the joyous Cusi Coylor? The owner of the property does not know, but he notes: "The bath of the Nusta is one of the foremost masterpieces not only of Ollantaytambo but of all Incan art." A jet of water falls into the rectangular canal carved atop a huge monolith, on top of a large flat paving stone set in the floor. Hiram Bingham considers the work "as worthy of our admiration as the Roman baths." He discovers the presence of the classical scalar symbol of Tiahuanaco[5] (an elevated site now located in Bolivia, far from the Sacred Valley), as well as a puma head, also linked with the mythology of this pre-Incan civilization.

Zamorra, the owner of "Coya's Garden" and a descendant of both the imperial nobility of Cuzco and a conquering hidalgo, shows the scholars from Yale seats carved in the granite, "for the Inca queen's ladies-in-waiting to sit on," he pretends to know, "during the lustral bath of the Venus of the Rio of the Sun." He pictures her gleaming bronze body, her long, flowing black hair, and her silken clothing woven of vicuña wool, worked with threads of

---

[5] See my book *Tiahuanaco, 10,000 ans d'énigmes incas* (Editions Robert Laffont).

gold and silver—similar to the priceless cloth found in mausoleums, covering mummies.

As for the age of the monuments of the Tampus (the name "Ollantaytambo" is relatively modern, and the inhabitants of the town do not know it by its older, authentic name, "Tambo"), although from all evidence they bear the mark of the Incan style, Zamorra suggests that they date from well before the dynasty begun in the tenth or eleventh century by Manco Capac. As proof, he shows Bingham the megalithic substructure of the palace that he inhabits, the upper floor of which, added after the Conquest, is composed of monoliths taken from the walls of the fortress and joined by whitewash. A heavy wooden gate studded with silver nails is set in a monumental trapezoidal doorway which is typically Inca—and thus, for Zamorra, *posterior* to the substructure. A single slab of granite, 2 meters long, constitutes the lintel. It is a form of architecture designed to last for all eternity.

After examining the fortress briefly, Bingham comes away convinced. The cyclopean walls, the airy bastions, the immense "hanging gardens" outlining a majestic amphitheater, and, above all, the fantastic "mirrors of the Sun" attest to a past of inspired grandeur.

As if crowned at the horizon by enormous glaciers, the mysterious "mirrors," aligned along a narrow ceremonial platform, are composed of six gigantic masses of roseate porphyry, carved into slightly irregular rectangles, erected vertically and measuring nearly 4 meters high by 1.75 meters long and nearly the same width. Zamorra calculates that these juxtaposed slabs weigh at least 20 tons each.[6] Few people in any other area of the known world, he says, have succeeded in transporting to a similar altitude such heavy blocks of stone.

A few protuberances, no doubt hammered out by the sixteenth-century extirpators of idolatry, probably represented puma heads or the entire totemic animal.

These "mirrors" may date from an era long before that

[6] The Bolivian archaeologist Carlos Ponce Sangines estimates the weight of the largest slab at about 40 tons and that of a great "tired stone" left in the middle of the road (6.70 X 3.60 X 1.67 meters) at over 100 tons!

of the Incas. "When the brilliant sun, upon rising, struck the sacred symbols, the sight of them surely filled the monarchs, the high priests, and believers with a profound mysticism, faith, and hope," writes the archaeologist Luis A. Pardo of Cuzco. Other enormous blocks, abandoned a short distance from the "mirrors of the sun," reveal, according to this same observer, "either that the work was halted before it was completed or that the entire edifice was in the process of being dismantled."

How were such blocks of porphyry raised to the highest part of the fortress? It is a mystery, one of the abiding enigmas of pre-Columbian Peru; scattered about between altitudes of 3,000 to over 4,000 meters, these cyclopean masses and monstrous anthropolithic statues, at incredible distances from the quarries from which they were taken, must have been transported—one can think of no better explanation—by anonymous Herculeses.

It was easy to find the quarry of Choquetacarpu (or Cachi-Catta) located on the opposite slope, at the foot of the high *cerro* Yanaccata, where there still remains a quantity of blocks that have only been detached and others that have already been cut, carved, polished, and placed on hardwood logs. Without any possible doubt, it was necessary to lower these pieces of the mountain as far as the river and then to get them across—but by means of what "magic"?

Zamorra knows the answer. It is a rather simple means, if one gives the matter a little thought: by diverting the course of the torrential waters during dry spells—a practice perfected by the Incas. Still, how many human arms were necessary to carry off such an enterprise? How many bodies were crushed by the *saysuccarumi*, the "tired stones" which litter the *huayrancalli*, the road for hauling, which is 1 kilometer long, 4–6 meters wide, and stretches from south of the agglomeration to the Sacred Rio? I've counted a hundred of these carved stone blocks on this road! Proof of these dramas are the caves and the funerary *chupas*, semicircular or quadrangular mausoleums in which lie the remains of roadmenders and master builders who fell victim to these very heavy monoliths.

The quarry is located at a distance of about 2 leagues from the fortress and about 700 meters higher than the river. Five terraces support it. A broad, sloping causeway extends from the lowest of these and extends to the river. Opposite the Rumira hacienda, an islet splits the waters into two branches. The maneuver used by the Incas was to divert first the left branch of the rio, in order to move the blocks as far as the island, and then divert the waters in the other direction, to complete the operation.

The renown of Machu Picchu now overshadows that of the magnificent ruins of the romantic Ollantaytambo, described in the nineteenth century in dithyrambic terms by intrepid voyagers such as Marcou, Castelnau, Wiener, Squier, and others, when the famous "Lost City" was still unknown.

Bingham, who has read all these accounts, devotes to what he assumes is "the capital of an ancient principality," equipped with a fortress and a garden for the Incan nobility, only a brief description of the storehouses, prisons, and monasteries perched here and there, above the village, on inaccessible slopes. He neglects to mention the impressive *nustac-tianan*, thrones carved directly into fallen boulders, near a solar observatory whose prism projected to a height of 30 centimeters. He does not describe, moreover, what would seem to have been a great sarcophagus located nearby, nor the arrangement in tiers of the funerary chambers built against the mountainside (on certain feast days it was the custom to line up the notable mummies in front of these chambers), nor the Incamisana, the altar on which the reigning Inca would celebrate who knows what secret rites after having undergone ritual ablutions in a nearby basin.

The hybrid names of several other archaeological ruins are not designed to clear up their mystery. For instance, the name "Hospitalniyoc" given by the Indians to a series of sixteen compartments lined up along some 100 meters, provided with niches, and each divided into three equal parts: popular tradition has made it out to be a kind of pre-Columbian sanitarium. Or the "Inca-Huatana" carved with four tall trapezoidal niches, where certain prisoners of noble descent apparently were tied up before being thrown into the abyss. One can discern clearly from afar, on the flanks of the Pinculluna Cerro, two groups of monolithic cells literally "hung" over the abyss below— about 50 meters below for the cells reserved for men, and

20 for the women. It is difficult to delude oneself as to the function of these *despeñaderos*, beneath which there in fact lies a great quantity of human bones.

The magnificent Yachayhuasi, or "School for Virgins," sits atop a pyramid of five platforms and is reached by way of ten monumental *portadas*. But was this merely a "school," or was it rather a hideaway for erotic rendezvous? The name of the place, "Pinculla," causes the confusion, for, according to the authorized statements of the Quechua linguists whom I consulted, *ullu* should be translated as "male member."

CHAPTER THREE

The Grand Cañon of the Urubamba

THE OLD COLONIAL ROUTE

Before the path that the Yale Peruvian Expedition would follow was opened by dynamite in 1895, travelers who wanted to go from Cuzco toward the lower end of the Sacred Valley had a choice of only two routes, equally difficult. Therefore, the travelers who ventured there during the four centuries of Spanish colonization were very few.

One route, followed by the Vicomte de Sartiges, still passes between the ice-covered peaks of the Salccantay and the Soray before descending only a few miles from Machu Picchu.

The other, well known to the conquistadors who doggedly pursued the fugitive Incas, crosses the snow-covered Pass of Panticalla, then rapidly descends the peak of the Padre Eterno and later runs alongside the warm gorge of the Rio Lucamayo.

The Vicomte de Sartiges describes the first route. A secretary at the French embassy in Rio de Janeiro (he describes himself as "a Parisian abroad, curious about everything"), the young diplomat embarked in 1834 on board the sloop *La Favorite* to undertake perilous study trips that today we would call ethnographic. He made two explorations through the Andes and the Amazonian jungle, also pursuing in vain the mysterious "capital of the last Incas."

The pioneer tourist de Sartiges actually defied the icebergs of Cape Horn and the Chilean volcanoes, lived among the savage, cannibal Antis, visited the silver mines of Potosí, and toured Lake Titicaca (at an altitude of 4,000 meters), examining the sacred islands of the Sun and the Moon before finally returning to Cuzco. Then, as Bingham would later do (but in the viscount's day there was no tourist's itinerary through the Urubamba), de Sartiges organized one of the first expeditions in search of a sort of Peruvian Herculaneum whose unknown marvels he had heard extolled on every side.

The Peru of the Incas attracts this explorer as irresistibly as it will the professor from Yale, and the extraordinary account of an antiquarian-priest in Curahuasi, a small town in the Apurimac Cañon, compounds his curiosity. Thus, he cannot resist the temptation to explore the ancient city of Choquequirao before returning to Lima.

We find him, therefore, before Bingham, on the pathways of a high cordillera, with fifteen Indians and a seasoned guide. He bivouacs at Soray, in a native hut, then climbs "toward the high pasturelands that here mark the limits of vegetation . . . Beyond commence the *nevados* of the great chain of the Andes. The mules are obliged to stop every ten paces to catch their breath and to shake off the flakes of ice that blind them." When he finally redescends by the other slope, "the pasturelands reappear, then the briars, the woods . . . At the bottom rung of this ladder, each level of which marks a new vegetal zone, enormous lianas, banana plantations, pomegranates, sugar cane, pineapples, and coffee plantations transport the traveler into the torrid zone, when only a few hours earlier he might have thought himself amid the polar ice!"

Today it is difficult to retrace the inexplicably rambling course taken by the French viscount, which finally ends up at the Huadquiña hacienda, after having overcome a challenging saddle at an altitude of over 5,000 meters. Huadquiña . . . this detail is particularly striking, for it is not only in the opposite direction from Choquequirao, but practically at the foot of the Machu Picchu.

What is de Sartiges doing here, if he has not heard about the "Lost City" of the Incas? And in that case, one wonders why he has left the gorge of the Apurimac (and the treasures that the priest in Curahuasi imagined were in the "Cradle of Gold") to pick up the trail of the warriors of Manco Inca, Sayri Tupac, and Titu Cusi, who—as all the historical traditions attest—ran up and down the slopes of the Salccantay, again and again, as rapid as their arrows, to take by surprise and massacre the Spanish reinforcements that Francisco Pizarro sent from Lima to rescue his brothers besieged in Cuzco by rebelling Indians.

Why this leap into so Dantesque an environment, which forces him to turn his back on the coveted ruins and to complete an exhausting five-day circuit instead of trying to trace a much more direct route, starting from the famous bridge over the Apurimac, as all the other expeditionists had done?

In carefully rereading the account rendered by the Vicomte de Sartiges, I had the impression that he was not telling all, when it came to his bizarre itinerary. The "nearby ruins" that he mentions, without elaborating further—weren't these perhaps Machu Picchu? Was he perhaps the victim of a guide who, for secret reasons shared at the time by all the Quechuas in the Sacred Valley, led him away from these mysterious ruins, which he did wish to visit, since he makes another long detour around Lares, above Ollantaytambo, before giving up for good?

A "SESAME" FOR BINGHAM

In charge of an archaeological and ethnological mission to Peru under the auspices of the Ministère de l'Instruction Publique, Charles Wiener describes in turn, in 1875, the circuitous journey that he undertook in these same inhospitable altitudes.

"In the name of French exploration," Wiener travels through Inca territory for two years, clearing prospective or unknown paths in every direction, working in a field "then little developed," gathering "exhibits," and taking back to Paris's Museum of Natural History a magnificent collection comprising 4,000 archaeological specimens.

"In Ollantaytambo," he goes on, "I was told there were ancient ruins on the east slope of the cordillera, whose principal names I knew—Vilcabamba and Choquequirao . . . and other cities as well, *Huaina Picchu and Matcho Picchu.*"

Here, then, is the great revelation made by Charles Wiener, who, for the first and only time in all the works devoted to Peru before the present century, wrote down in black and white—and included in his map of the Sacred Valley—these two magic names which Hiram Bingham would carefully note three decades later.

Intrigued by this hearsay, Wiener resolves to undertake one last excursion, but the path, which follows the imperial route of the Incas, stops at Ollantaytambo at this time. To penetrate the Urubamba Cañon would in fact require a series of tunnels carved in the rock, and there are a thousand other difficult obstacles which the voyager cannot even guess at. Therefore, he also sets out from Ollantaytambo, heading for the Pass of Panticalla, only to end up in the tropical region of Lucumayo, turning away from the goal and turning his back on the Sacred Valley. However, he must be aware that—on the other slope, near the confluence of the Urubamba and Vilcabamba rios, after crossing the historic bridge of Chuquicacha (key-post of the Incan resistance against the mercenaries of Charles V)—he could retrace his steps all the way to the Huadquiña hacienda and from there succeed in climbing the Picchus: while in Ollantaytambo, *he had been informed of their exact location.*

Unfortunately for Wiener, the river has set off a big landslide in the Lucumayo gorge, blocking the path. Therefore, he wanders off to the far end of the Santa Ana Valley, among the savage Piros—that is, farther and farther from Machu Picchu.

ON THE ANDEAN PEAKS, RUINS EVERYWHERE

Beyond Ollantaytambo, where the caravan is augmented by four Indians from the town, who are well acquainted with the region, Bingham *knows* he is approaching the ultimate goal. He orders Carrasco to question every native they come across. But each time, the answer is evasive. The likelihood is infinitesimal that a "pure-blood" Quechua would give away ancestral secrets for the benefit of a mestizo, let alone a white. The natives fear the vengeful wrath of the mummies huddled up in the folds of the sierras more than they do the constabulary.

The caravan progresses very slowly in the hollow of the valley, a dramatically magnificent site. Gifted with an instinct for danger which often smacks of divination, Carpio's mules never set out on the thread of a path without first testing with a hoof the solidity of the ground or the branches thrown down in the guise of a footbridge. Raising his eyes, Bingham can make out sections of ancient walls clinging to narrow, rocky ledges. Carrasco knows that these are the foundations of an ancient imperial highway leading to Salpunca, the true gateway to the province in pre-Columbian times.

On all sides, ruins cling to the peaks. A battered fortress, remains of bastions, watchtowers, *tambos,* and temples succeed one another without interruption, plastered to the vertical sides of the *cañon* like creeping ivy. The names of the cyclopean ruins which hang from nearly inaccessible walls? Forgotten! Neither Carrasco nor Carpio, the guide, nor the Indians who live there know the names. But, using their imagination, they have given these places other names, inspired by their outlines, the color of the earth or rock, an animal that frequents them, the trees that engulf them. However, Bingham's intense desire remains both frustrated and whetted. Never do the natives pronounce the names he so wants to hear: Viticos, Vilcabamba la Vieja. Since the massacre of the Incas and the dissolution of their empire, it is as if Mama Pacha, Mother Earth, has swallowed up the two forbidden cities of Manco and his sons.

The agricultural terraces become scarcer as the American explorers advance along the majestic *cañon.* The ancient peoples, for whom thus far no herculean task had been too much, had to work here in a demonic natural setting masked in the dark, shadowy green of a tropical jungle so dense it seemed uninhabitable. In less that 30 kilometers, the Urubamba drops 1,000 meters in altitude to the bottom of the gorge. Bingham admires the courage of the ancient peoples who, by astounding means, stole from the rio and the mountains tiny plots of arable land, miraculously contained by low supporting walls. How did they manage to inlay these plots in vertical slopes above fierce abysses? How did they hoist up heavy, carved rocks by the thousands? How did they bottle up the rio in a notch so cramped that, in some places, the opposite slopes seem almost to touch? To climb these slopes, the Americans must follow a minuscule path which rises so abruptly that they are troubled by the altitude and suffer from vertigo. Overlooking a waterfall that fills the space with an unbearable racket, the ruins of a splendid palace are—in Carpio's words—impossible to reach. Who, then, built this "taboo" palace?

Much higher up in the clouds, on the right bank, stand the archaeological ruins of Corihuayrachina.[1] The Indian tradition holds that during Incan times gold was washed there, from a lode which cannot be found today. From the bank, between two parapets, there rises an acrobatic mega-lithic stairway. It was necessary to carve or set up *sixty-four steps* in a place where one could get only a toehold for support, in order to overcome the abrupt slope and end up on a rocky pedestal in the shape of a truncated cone. From this magnificent observatory, one can see the neighboring ruins of Quente—the "hummingbird" city—and watch over the most important bridge in the area.

THE THIRTY-SEVEN-FACETED STONE OF TORONTOY

With the end of the gardens tiered along the mountain-side, Torontoy marks the threshold of the Urubamba Cañon, 20 kilometers long and 1,000 meters deep, the color of burnished steel. This phenomenal geological progression will give Professor Bowman migraines; he is responsible for making an exact survey. The granitic cliff is broken here by the furious course of the Rio of the Sun, littered with half-submerged rocks, and intersected by seething rapids which burst into foam against the slopes. Even dur-ing the dry season, no Indian dares to swim across it, much less cross it in a canoe.

At a distance of 91 kilometers from Cuzco, the archae-ological group of Torontoy looms on a platform a little higher than the railroad tracks. The lower wall of the main building—undoubtedly a noble's residence—is composed of an extraordinary puzzle. Inlaid with thirty-seven angles into a monumental rock, upon which they have been mathe-matically fitted, twenty-five monoliths form a wall pierced by three trapezoidal niches, which must have had, accord-ing to Victor Angles Vargas, "a special significance in the world of beliefs of the Inca people." From the upper part emerge stone projections, which are too damaged today (cows are kept in this room!) for us to understand their

[1] The name "Corihuayrachina" is used for several places, all of them very high up, where winds blow at unusual velocities.

liturgical and ideographical significance, but perhaps they outlined "the stylized heads of two llamas."

The imposing *nevado* of the Veronica glistens in the distance, amid a translucent sky. The vertiginous flight of the waters of the Urubamba and its furious voice fill the *cañon*. Is it perhaps the voice of the ancient spirit of the sacred waters, raising its waves to trap the men who have ventured onto the mesh of branches thrown across the river? Carpio wants to stop before nightfall, which occurs almost instantaneously. Any Indian who hears the plaint of the god of the Willkamayo after dusk will come down with *susto*, the "disease of sadness," and die.

Disturbed by the grunting of guinea pigs and the chirping of crickets, the expeditionists sleep badly, in a hut full of ragged natives. The sun rises, washed by an iridescent mist which, curiously, stretches two rainbows across the gorge—perhaps in remembrance of the Incas, who used rainbows as emblems on their imperial banners.

Bingham would like to cross over to the other slope, but the guides refuse. One of them, whom I later traced, would tell me that Bingham forced one of the carriers to cross the torrent; he drowned, bearing valuable cargo. Once the cargo had been recovered, the American explorer had the body thrown back in the rio. "At once," the guide told me, "a shower of stones crashed down on the caravan like a burst of artillery fire"—hence the name, "Artilleruyoc," since given to the vengeful peak.

MANDOR PAMPA

Caught between the steep walls of the *cañon*, the explorers pass by the site known as La Máquina because of the rusted carcass of an engine that lies there; a rich Spanish settler tried to transport it as far as his *caña* plantations. Starting from this place is the *camino bravo*, a wild, increasingly constricted path which climbs toward the top of the gorge. Landslides and the precipitous slope force the riders to dismount from their trembling mules. Way below, night has engulfed the roaring river. To press on would be suicidal. However, not a single light announces the presence of the tiniest Indian village nearby. The Americans are nearly overcome with discouragement when

Carrasco tells them that, less than 100 meters away, they can set up a makeshift camp.

A few more twists along the waters glistening in the light of the moon, which has risen at last, and Carrasco announces Mandor Pampa. The song of the fluvial spirit harmonizes with the strange jungle noises that now pervade the entire *cañon* floor. Who, even among the least superstitious of travelers, could withstand the spell of the Andean night in such a setting?

The pampa of Mandor is just a small sandy plain, where the tents are quickly raised. Unmindful of his companions' exertions, Bingham takes out his logbook and records his impressions of this "land of matchless charm": "It has the majestic grandeur of the Canadian Rockies, as well as the startling beauty of the Nuuanu Pali near Honolulu, and the enchanting vistas of Koolau Ditch Trail on Maui, in my native land . . . I know of no place in the world which can compare with it!"

But their clothes are stiffened with dust and sweat, their hands slashed by brambles and bloody with poisonous insect bites. How long must Bingham's companions endure this torture? It has already been twelve days since they left Cuzco, and they have not found any ruins that would at last satisfy the fancy of the leader of the Yale Peruvian Expedition. Everywhere, after a brief once-over, he has declared that none of the ruins found corresponded, in terms of the site, to the accounts given by the chroniclers of the Conquest, whom he can quote by heart.

Suddenly, thunder rocks the *cañon*. A tempest breaks loose amid the ice-covered peaks of the Salccantay, at the foot of which they are camped. Lightning bolts and a torrential rain which collapses the tents streak across a landscape from another planet. The panic-stricken Indians believe that the ancient Apus of the Wild Mountain are demonstrating their anger at the approach of the intruders.

Overcome by exhaustion, Bingham yields to the need for sleep, obsessed once again by the voice which promises him a fabulous "Lost City." Does he perhaps possess, in addition to these magical words, the certainty of reaching his goal? Does he perhaps believe that within a few hours he will be the Prince Charming who will awaken this marvel, asleep under a canopy of tropical forest and still virgin?

CHAPTER FOUR

The Discovery
of Machu Picchu

> *Its location is fantastic, with the city cling-*
> *ing to the upper slope and crest of a narrow*
> *ridge . . . The sheer sugarloaf of Huayna*
> *Picchu rises like a rhinoceros horn . . . Its*
> *mystery is heightened by ghostly wisps of*
> *low cloud.*

> —John Hemming, 1971

THE LAST CENTENARY SLEEP

With the passing of the cold, damp Andean night, a new gray dawn smothers the *cañon*. Their tents dismantled, the explorers hastily break camp. But the previous evening they have passed by a ramshackle *choza* beneath a roof of rotted thatch, whose owner Carrasco has boasted he knows very well, a young mestizo whom he described as the "little king" of muleteer traffic through the Sacred Valley of the Incas. All the passing caravaneers stay with him, Carrasco says, whether they be rich *hacendados* traveling to their plantations or the occasional gendarme pursuing an outlaw Indian.

Under a lean-to, beasts laden with sacks of coconuts, ears of corn, coffee, cocoa, and tropical fruits find abundant fodder. In the inn travelers partake of local specialties: bean *chupe* in a devilishly spicy broth, *charqui* of smoked llama, *olluquitos* stew with red pepper, roast *cuy* with peanuts—all washed down with copious amounts of pale *chicha*, fermented to its peak. They sleep there as well, right on the ground, rolled up in ponchos—in a neighborly spirit that did not appeal to the Americans.

The gendarme maintains that the mestizos of Mandor

Pampa have, through hearsay, the best information concerning the surrounding area. Bingham therefore decides to send him out in search of information. The owner of the hut, annoyed that the Yale Peruvian Expedition has had the audacity to camp on his land, disregarding custom and without his permission, receives Carrasco coldly. However, he listens attentively when the gendarme mentions that he could get hold of some money for "seekers of Incan ruins."

Inca "houses"? But there is *a whole city*. And he grows excellent gourds, as well as the biggest *rocotos* peppers in the Sacred Valley, in the "hanging gardens" and in the very patio of "the Inca's palace." Is this mere braggadocio? Raising his eyes to the heavens, in the direction indicated by the mestizo's finger, which is pointed at the peak rising up like a gigantic pole, the gendarme cannot make out the slightest trace of a pre-Columbian city. But the mestizo insists: The entire mountain is covered with Inca ruins, between the two Picchus which pierce the clouds.

Brought before Bingham, the mestizo states his name: Melchor Arteaga, the very man the American was supposed to find! For even if he never gives it away, even if he will never say a word about it, Bingham has recently become the repository of a priceless secret—a secret I shall discover only a half-century later.

It takes a day to reach the "Lost City," provided it isn't raining. But a downpour is already dimming the vista of the high peaks, and before long it will be saturating the bottom of the *cañon*. Regrettably, the trip must be postponed until the next day. If the weather improves, the sun should become visible from the impasse at about 10:00 A.M., the time decided upon for leaving Mandor Pampa, despite the countless perils that lie ahead. That night, Machu Picchu enjoys the last of its ancient sleep.

A MAGICAL DISCOVERY

At daybreak on July 24, 1911, an icy drizzle bathes the Urubamba Cañon, from which rise, like so many evanescent wisps of smoke, mists that drape the tip of the Picchus in colors and unreal forms. Can it really be that one of the most fantastic cities in Peruvian antiquity lies asleep, on so high a perch? For the first time, Bingham is tempted to doubt the friend who, at Cuzco, had promised him it was. Tomorrow—thanks to this person, who will long maintain silence and anonymity—will Bingham meet with fame and glory?

The enthusiasm of the other members of the Yale Peruvian Expedition has been considerably dampened during the exhausting ride of the previous days. None of them believes any longer in the chimerical lost "capital" of the Incas. In any case it seems impossible that it could crown the steepest peak they've ever seen. Everyone finds an excuse for not participating in another disappointing venture.

Melchor Arteaga is late. The gendarme goes off to look for him and finds him still at the inn, sitting—with his teeth chattering—by a fire made of eucalyptus branches, which smokes up the tavern. To set out in such bad weather would be madness, he protests. Is he perhaps even more fearful of the reproaches of the Indian caravaneers if he betrays, for a paltry sum, the ancestral secret carefully guarded for several generations? Have they perhaps made him fear the wrath of the guardian Apus, who, the legends say, roam the forgotten city?

The mestizo obeys the gendarme reluctantly. Scowling, draped in an old red poncho, he precedes the American along the path by the rio. Suddenly, Arteaga leaps to one side, killing a fer-de-lance serpent with furious jabs of his machete. The "yellow viper," the most dangerous ophidian of the Amazonian jungle, infests this region. By means of great leaps, it can attack its prey up to waist height. This is the *chicotillo*, the "flying serpent" of pre-Columbian times which one sees represented on ancient pottery from the Andean area. One of the Indians with the small group says that in a single day he has seen fifty of these serpents killed on a plantation, and seen several of his fellow workers die of their bites.

The mestizo soon leaves the road parallel to the Urubamba and disappears into a thick fog. At this point the *cañon* is reduced to a gigantic fault which resembles the gateway to the "Green Hell." Arteaga makes his way through thorny briars before reaching the river, spanned by a half-dozen tree trunks of unequal length. The din of the water drowns out his voice. With gestures, he indicates to his companions that they should take their shoes off in order to set out, with bare feet, on the slender, spray-soaked logs. Like an acrobat, his face contracted, his eyes riveted on the wild current, his back hunched over, the mestizo, running with little steps, reaches the opposite bank, beckoning to the others and to Bingham, who is the last to cross, completing the journey on all fours.

The mountain will be increasingly *brava*, Arteaga warns, full of "yellow vipers." The tentacles of flowering lianas whip the expeditionists' faces and entangle their legs. With each step the tropical jungle becomes denser, carpeted with decaying humus. The ground, saturated with water, is so slippery that the men hold one another up and cling to one another, sinking in up to their knees. Ahead of them, out of sight, the mestizo and gendarme progress slowly, cutting their way through the mesquite brush, a shrub with wood like iron, armed with long hard thorns as dreadful as a sharpened steel point. A torrid heat succeeds the coolness that prevailed in the hollow of the emerald *cañon*. Drenched with humidity, the heat is all the more uncomfortable combined with the effects of the altitude.

At 2,500 meters the group wanders into the clouds that hover above the *cañon* and shroud the summits and the bottomless precipices grouped around the peak. Carpio, the official guide, is familiar with the area by sight, but has never been curious enough to climb the Picchus. On the other hand, two "treasure-seekers" who have joined up with Bingham, Monroy and Lizarraga, encourage him when he feels he can endure no more. They are nearing the goal, they assure him.

One last effort and the American explorer can't believe his eyes. Contrary to all expectations, this so-called impregnable peak is inhabited! His dream is crushed: instead of "the Inca's palace," he sees before him only a wretched hut built on a narrow promontory. Fearful, two natives emerge when Melchor Arteaga calls out to them. What are they doing there? Disenchanted, Bingham learns that Recharte and Alvarez and their families have been living on the Old Peak, the Machu Picchu, for four years, sheltered from the sergeants who recruit Indian "volunteers" for the Peruvian army, and free, as well, from subjugation by the hacienda *lugartenientes* responsible for enrolling, in the same way, workers for the vast agricultural enterprises down in the valley, and, finally, free from all taxes, restraints, and schedules. They are the absolute—

and unknown—masters of the intoxicating lost paradise of the Inca gods.

Amid one of the most majestic panoramas on the planet, these misanthropes peacefully cultivate an Eden that passersby in the hollow of the *cañon* would never suspect existed. Corn, potatoes, red peppers, *camotes* (sweet potatoes), fields of beans, rows of sugar cane grow a few steps from the hut. Two paths, they say, connect them with the so-called civilized world: the one taken by their unexpected visitors, clinging to the mountainside, and another, completely hidden and even more dangerous, on the opposite slope. Once a month they use one of the paths to descend into the *cañon* and valley to barter with the products of their harvest.

The wives of the two natives have brought the thirsty visitors a gourd full of cold water and now offer them roast sweet potatoes. Seated on a crudely quarried bench, Bingham takes in the fantastic kaleidoscope of the accordian-pleated Andes; the swath cut by the Urubamba, which snakes by below, amid a cloud of bluish vapor; the extraordinary richness of the virgin forest, which carpets the mountain right up to the summits capped with perpetual snow; the menacing darkness of the chasms, which puncture the culmens of the cordilleras; and the orgy of infinitely varied colors. The dazzling sight arouses an indefinable exhilaration, which Bingham has difficulty shaking before he can wonder once again, Where are the "Inca houses" promised by the mestizo? No pre-Columbian ruin appears in the vicinity. He perceives only a solitary peak, a granite arrowhead emerging hundreds of meters above the waters of the Sacred Rio.

Will Bingham give up in disappointment? He reviews his prospects one last time. No other region seems as propitious for a refuge unknown to the conquistadors. But could this lost peak, located over a gorge cut off to traffic for centuries, hide more than a few sections of dilapidated wall, of which he has already seen plenty? Will he discover here one of the mysterious lost capitals of Manco Inca?

Bingham places his trust in the *chiuche*, a Quechua boy (Bingham does not provide his name, and later, Peruvian researchers will try to relocate him, without ever finding a trace) who, taking him by the hand, says, laughing, that he knows where "the house of the Inca" is. Around the

promontory, an unhoped-for sight wrests an exclamation of
surprise from the American explorer: as if airborne, a
hundred agricultural terraces, supported by long walls of
solidly arranged stone blocks, stretch before him—the
work of funambulists, for each *anden*, he estimates, must
measure about 30 meters long and 3 meters high. The
jungle has been cursorily cleared; age-old cedars have been
partly burned, since it was impossible to fell them. Enormous red gourds decorate these "hanging gardens," which
fascinate Bingham because they remind him of the equally
admirable agricultural platforms of Ollantaytambo—which
were in fact constructed around a pre-Hispanic city.

Forgetting his exhaustion, Bingham comes running when
he hears Carrasco call out; the gendarme is accompanying
the little Indian boy. And Bingham will lack words with
which to express his enchantment: "Houses, dozens of
buildings . . . Inca temples, palaces! I've never seen such
well-constructed walls or such magnificently carved monoliths," he will note hastily. Touched by the golden finger of
a sunbeam, the incomparable "Lost City" at last emerges,
like a magical vision, from the camouflage of mists and
jungles that for four hundred years forbade access to it.
Reborn from the depths of time, an entire city arises,
resplendent.

THE MYSTERY OF MYSTERIES

Carpio will say he saw Bingham jump onto the ridge of
a thick wall and run toward the unknown sanctuary. A
huge overhanging rock temporarily halts the explorer's
feverish course. Under this rock is something phantasmagorical, the significance of which he does not grasp immediately. But once his eyes grow accustomed to the dark,
he distinguishes what he will name the "Royal Mausoleum,"
a strange cave whose inner walls were entirely lined with
the finest monoliths. Evoking the heralds of arms who
perhaps once stood there (unless these high niches were
installed for the use of high priests or imperial mummies
wrapped in sarcophagi of woven cloths and mantles), the
gendarme stands upright in one of the trapezoidal niches
that decorate the cave. Tiered benches carved in the rock
invite one to meditate or to observe secret rites. Fleeting

images haunt the mind of the young scholar from Yale. Bingham will relive this moment for years.

Leaving this cave, set up so "royally," Bingham raises his eyes, intrigued by the work that crowns the sacred den. What he then discovers seems to him to surpass in daring and sumptuousness all the Incan and pre-Incan ruins he has seen thus far. A horseshoe-shaped *torreón*—a type of tower in which the builders did not "buckle the buckle"— caps the boulder, which acts as its foundation. Inlaid in the base, adapting to its slightest irregularities, an impressive parabolic wall follows the natural curvature of the rocky promontory before extending it in height. Recalling the Coricancha, the famous solar temple in Cuzco so admired by Americanists the world over, Bingham instinctively decides that this *torreón* is a faithful reproduction of the latter, that it is "the work of a master artist." The rounding of this demi-tower is so flawless that, in his view, it constitutes the most successful example of pre-Columbian masonry in the two Americas. Visiting it, he observes that all it lacks are golden idols in the niches—also trapezoidal —which decorate the inner wall. Between these and those overhanging them, great rounded or quadrangular "stone-pegs," typical of the ancient architecture of the Sacred Valley, project from the wall. What could have been hung from them? Ceremonial robes, or wool *quipus* on which accounts and statistics were recorded by tying these cords a certain way? The question has not ceased to intrigue archaeologists; they are still unable to guess the true purpose of these pegs.

The ecstatic Bingham's eyes return to the graceful line of the curved wall, an assemblage so well conceived that neither the centuries nor earthquakes have affected its symmetry and solidity. From the base to the top, the rows of white granite parallelepipeds, which look as if they have been cut at right angles, progessively diminish in size. Far from affecting its balance, this receding slope, on the contrary, lightens the top of the building. In the force as well as the grace imparted by the Torreón of Machu Picchu, Bingham perceives the purest of the masterpieces attributed to the Incas. He finds "the flowing lines, the symmetrical arrangement of the ashlars, and the gradual gradation of the courses" more pleasing "than the marble temples of the old world." He notes, with emotion, that, joined without mortar, without the slightest gap, these monolithic walls "might have grown together."

Led by the *chiuche*, the explorer climbs a hill from which he can look out over the entire prodigious panorama of the "Lost City." He sees one surprise after another: The various groupings, which succeed one another at various levels on the rounded surface of the Old Peak, are connected, not by mere streets, but by stairways—stairways carved into the rock itself or inlaid by means of granite slabs set up in this breathtaking terrain. Hundreds of steps plunge to the depths of the *cañon* or rise up to the sky.

Overwhelmed by this transcendent vision, Bingham imagines that he can again overhear the dialogue of the Inca and the cosmic deities of the cordillera. In his mind he reconstructs the spectacle of the ritual processions of the virgins of Inti, the hieratic march of the high priests of Punchao, the advance of the Inca, his torso gleaming with a gold Sun, followed by the Chosen Women and the noble Orejones. How many of these phantoms did it take to carve these thousands of steps, polished like glass, and how many centuries did it take to erect such imperishable wonders?

Confronted with the limitless number of nearly intact palaces, Bingham feels as if Manco Inca, his gynaeceum, and his court could have left only yesterday. Bewitched, he follows the little Indian guide, who runs up a triumphal ramp to the top of the highest artificial pyramid in the city. In the middle of the upper platform there looms, in all its glory, the mysterious Intihuatana, where the Willac Umu must have symbolically tied Father Sun during the great solar festivals.

Bingham climbs back down, at the bronzed heels of the child, who leads him to the Temple of the Three Windows —three openings much larger and higher than those of all the other cities said to be Inca thus far discovered. Three gaping windows, unequaled anywhere, set opposite the rays of the rising sun, they pierce a massive wall made of the finest-grained light granite. They are so exceptional that from this moment forward Bingham will be convinced that nothing like them exists anywhere else in ancient Peru— and it must be noted that, so far, he has been right.

These three ageless windows overlooking the void will

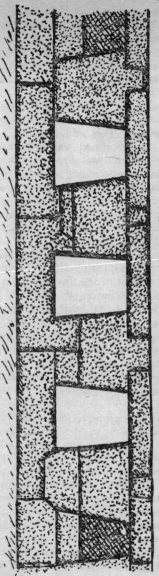

Sketch of the famous wall with three symbolic windows

prove both the answer to the Yale scholar's dreams and a nightmare. They will fascinate him and force him (him and all the historians and archaeologists who henceforth will hurl themselves into their megalithic embrace) to examine the chronicles of the conquistadors page by page—readings that are careful, but fruitless on the whole, and will lead him astray.

Melchor Arteaga has committed the sacrilege of planting beans and salad greens in the garden of the adjacent "Principal Temple"! This odd building without a front, composed of three polished walls (the two lateral walls reach out like unfurled wings), opens onto a ceremonial plaza. It encloses an astounding trinity of impressive monoliths, which probably constituted the great altar that was used for sacrifices, unless it was designed for displaying venerable mummies to the leading personages of the empire who visited this certainly totemic site—or perhaps for a triad of gold idols.

In the haze of the fleecy mists that ascend from the Sacred Rio, concealing the chasm of the *cañon*, Bingham's last vision will be that of the tiny silhouette of the *chiuche*, profiled against the crimson sky. His only memory of the Quechua child will be a burst of triumphant laughter, before the child disappears into the void. The American runs after him, calls out, looks for him, but does not find him; he will never see him again. Has Bingham still been dreaming? Was the child but a miraculous sprite who stepped out of the pre-Columbian legends to take him by the hand and lead him to glory?

A GHOST TOWN WITHOUT A HISTORY OR A NAME

Actually, after the Expedition of 1911 Bingham will take back with him to the United States only a brief glimpse of the "Lost City" atop Machu Picchu. When he sees it again a few months later, cleared by the team that stayed at the site, he will find it even more splendid than he hoped. But for the moment the impression that this could not be either Viticos or Vilcabamba la Vieja impels him to move on again, *following an itinerary carefully mapped out in advance*, to the bottom of the next valley, the Vilcabamba,

there to seek, of course, the true lost "capital"—there
where, in fact, it ought to be!

Still burning with enthusiasm upon returning from this
fantastic leap into the Inca past, Bingham contemplates—
with legitimate pride—the valuable booty obtained: precious
topographical, geographical, and geological surveys of an
area that, before he came along, had never been scientifi-
cally explored or studied in any detail; studies of the flora
and fauna, illustrated by magnificent collections; documents
on the anthropology, sociology, and archaeology of the
Urubamba and Vilcabamba valleys. The Yale Peruvian
Expedition brings back, moreover, numerous boxes of
pottery, textiles, ornaments, and Incan weapons. Over
7,000 photographs are gathered in thick albums. Informed
of the discovery of Machu Picchu, the world press of the
time calls it "the greatest event in the New World since the
odyssey of Christopher Columbus."

Bingham, one reads, sank his entire fortune into the
venture and cut into his inheritance. But in exchange he
had acquired undying fame and given modern Peru the
most fantastic of "lost cities."

Has he perhaps also forfeited his peace of mind? Indeed,
the question looms larger than ever for him: What is this
mysterious city which he has discovered? Now, everything
he had anticipated and carefully prepared is again subject
to question, because of this very discovery. Years of reading and research and nights of insomnia lead him to a bewildering conclusion: Having set out to unearth from
oblivion the last capital of the Incas who rebelled against
Spanish colonization, here he is, the godfather of a ghost
town without a history, without an age, without any
memories—indeed, without a name!

Is this really what he was looking for? Viticos or Vilcabamba la Vieja? Or is it some other place? Bingham
doesn't know—he no longer knows! He feels as incapable
of expressing an opinion as he is of deciding. In view of
the greater mystery that he has just involuntarily brought
to light, what will he—or what can he—decide since
nothing is known about these ruins, which are thousands of
years old, but newborn in terms of Peruvian prehistory?

Once again he will reread—word by word—the ancient

sixteenth-century chronicles recounting the agony of the last four Inca reigns of Vilcabamba. And between the lines he will try to reconstruct, four hundred years later, the path of a long exile.

Does this path pass by Machu Picchu—or not? Herein lies the entire mystery.

PART TWO

The End of the Incas

The Conquest . . . strictly terminates with the suppression of the Peruvian revolt, when the power, if not the spirit, of the Inca race was crushed for ever.
—William Prescott, 1863

CHAPTER FIVE

The Rebellion of Manco Inca

When he saw the Spaniards divided, Manco Inca revolted and waged a cruel war against them, with the intention of exterminating them or chasing them from his land.
— Father Bernabe Cobo, 1653

THE PREDICTION OF THE ORACLES

Although at first glance the known history of the end of the Incas may seem to have no direct connection with that of Machu Picchu, it is, on the contrary, so tightly bound to the latter, as we shall see, that one is forced to retrace it in detail, as Hiram Bingham did. However, as he presented it, the history is incomplete or distorted, either because new documents have surfaced since the discovery of the famous "Lost City" which modify what was known at the beginning of the twentieth century, or because he omits or garbles certain passages. My initial task, therefore, was to reconstruct, based on references, this history accurately and without taking sides.

The year 1536 heralds one of the most heroic epochs in the history of Peru. Francisco Pizarro, his brothers Gonzalo, Juan, and Hernando, his young cousin and page Pedro Pizarro, his half-brother Martín de Alcantara, and a few dozen bold adventurers undertake a fantastic enterprise for the glory of Charles V, king of Spain (and their own): the conquest and subjugation of the monumental Empire of the Incas.

Ever since the Ayar Manco Capac, the traditional founder of the Incan dynasty, who came from the elevated Lake Titicaca near Cuzco, the great Indian chieftains (who pride themselves on being the Sons of the Sun) have so enlarged the Tahuantinsuyo that when the Spaniards arrive, two brothers who are enemies, Atahualpa and Huascar, are fighting over their inheritance—that is, an enormous portion of a continent nearly twice as large as Europe, which, heretofore unknown to the rest of the world, has seen the successive development of glorious civilizations. The Incas had a rare genius for reviving and perfecting all the discoveries and inventions of their predecessors, who had first appeared in the country at least 10,000 years earlier,[1] unifying the territory and universally imposing strict but wise laws.

Confronted with the Spaniards cased in armor and metal helmets, the Incas—dressed in wool tunics and feathered headdresses—are misled by an ancient prophetic legend[2] and take the Spaniards for messengers of Viracocha, the supreme creator of the postdiluvian genesis. They realize their tragic mistake too late. The excesses, the atrocities committed by the invaders, who pillage, rape, and murder as they go along, remove the scales from the Incas' eyes and revive their fighting spirit. A long *guerrilla* will soon break out amid an apocalyptic terrain, between pale soldiers who have crossed two oceans to conquer a world without parallel in Europe, and fierce, swarthy warriors, the masters of the tutelary high Andes.

Francisco Pizarro is warned of the fire that smolders in the breast of the Indian peoples. In a shrewd move, he offers to recognize Manco Inca as the Capac Inca—the Quechua synonym for "emperor." This sham coronation enables him to enter Cuzco unresisted.

From the Inca's point of view, is it too late to change the course of destiny?

His elder brothers assassinated,[3] Manco Inca Yupanqui, the legitimate heir of the great Capacs of the Tahuantin-

---

[1] See my book *Tiahuanaco, 10,000 ans d'énigmes incas* (Editions Robert Laffont).

[2] The arrival of the conquistadors on the shores of the Inca Empire occurred shortly after the priests of the sun made extensive invocations to the idols, opposing Atahualpa, a bastard usurper, and requesting that divine justice accede the throne to Huascar, one of the legitimate descendants of Huayna Capac.

[3] A "fictional" Inca named earlier by Pizarro, Tupac Hualpa, died suddenly while accompanying the conquistadors to Cuzco.

suyo, paces like a cornered puma in the iron cage where, in his brothers' absence, Pizarro has him imprisoned, under the pretext of safeguarding him, while he himself travels to Lima. But before the jail was locked up, Manco was put in chains!

Through the prison bars, the young Inca observes the legendary "navel" of the Incan world, a capital so vast that the first three Spaniards to arrive here were unable in a week to see all of the "holy city" and the 333 *huacas* or *adoratorios* surrounding it.

Manco watches the four royal roads which branch out from a cross in the center of the city toward the four *suyos*. He listens to the horseshoes clattering on the pavement previously traveled only by silent, haughty llamas. From the fortress of Sacsahuaman, where he is a captive, Manco traces the gigantic shadow of the three sawtooth-notched walls that defend it. Carved and set in place by herculean hands, the megaliths of this phenomenal military masterpiece—many of which weigh at least 20 metric tons —resist the efforts of the Spanish workers who try to dismantle them in order to build churches on the sites of the ancient temples. The Inca reflects that since the dawn of time, his race has possessed the immutable force of these stones, which has defied the centuries and earthquakes before flouting the oppressor, before whom they now refuse to bow.

Of the 200–odd children that his father—the brilliant Huayna Capac—had by the Coyas and Chosen Women, Manco is certainly one of the most intelligent. He was troubled by the unreasoning rivalry of his two older brothers. Atahualpa, the bastard son of Quito, emptied the monumental pyramids of the coastal deserts, the solar temples of the high peaks, and 1,000 Andean palaces to offer the treasures contained in them to Pizarro in payment for an illusory, Aladdinesque ransom that did not save his life. But first Huascar had been killed by his orders! This shameful, fratricidal hatred opened wide the doors of the Empire of the Sun to the whites.

Nevertheless, this handful of foreigners would not have had much effect, before the well-disciplined Indian militia, had the two rivals, when faced with danger, allied themselves. But Huayna Capac's strange behavior divided the country,[4] just as his bizarre statement sowed confusion in the minds of his people. When he heard that the Spaniards had debarked on the northern coast of the empire, the old sovereign appeared convinced that the ancient predictions of the oracles were coming true: "The Viracochas who have come by the sea on which our ancient god, our civilizing hero, once set forth," he said, "will one day be the masters of the Tahuantinsuyo. We shall be forced to obey them."[5]

Like Atahualpa, Manco at first yielded. He received with dignity the presents that the Spanish Julius Caesar had sent him: sweet Spanish wine, brocades, velvets, silks, mirrors, almonds, and raisins. Of all the objects that were unfamiliar to him, he most appreciated a pair of scissors! He also accepted the shaky throne of his ancestors, on which the conquistador diplomatically placed him. For a while, Manco even fought by his side. Pizarro thus conquered the famous Quizquiz and his army of Cañari warriors (Indians from Ecuador who had sworn to kill the Inca and all his family—and would succeed) and then saw to the execution of the great general Atahualpa, to whose memory half the empire would remain faithful.

From their very first encounter, Pizarro and Manco measure each other up: one with the advantage of extensive experience as a conquering soldier (Pizarro was over sixty when he arrived in Peru), the other an Indian with an overbearing arrogance, that of a god and master in his own country. They embrace. They will form an alliance, Pizarro assures Manco, to wipe out the Incas of Quito, their com-

---

[4] Regardless of what a lot of historiographers have written about it, this rivalry was not the first of its kind, and it is not really known whether Huayna Capac actually divided the immense empire between two of his sons. There is nothing that would prove this fact or permit it to be established. All through the Inca saga, we see a series of conflicts of succession, which are generally brought to an end, if not by arms, then by poison.

[5] Huaman Poma reports that the oracles questioned by Huayna Capac did not want to "answer anything at all," and that he ordered that all the priests of the *huacas* be put to death and these idols destroyed. Only the Pariacaca *huaca* dared answer him "that it was no longer the time to speak of any government, for men called Viracochas would soon be arriving, during his reign, to govern in the name of an all-powerful lord."

mon enemies. However, since the abrupt execution of
Atahualpa rouses Manco's suspicions, Pizarro, to prove his
good faith, also hands over to him the general Chalcuchima,
whom Manco orders burned alive—a barbarous act that
should be noted, like many others which Manco would later
commit. He would not hesitate, in fact, to order the
murder of several of his brothers and other relatives who
side with the conquistadors, as well as all the Indians—
women, children, and entire families—in their service. His
cruelty would inspire fear in the people, and, in conjunction with a number of mistakes in military tactics, would
explain in large part the ultimate failure of the Incan
resistance. For not only would great numbers of Indians
henceforth fight alongside the Spaniards, they would provide them with food and with fodder for their horses, the
"sinews" of this war.

Moreover, the Quechuas would not understand why
Manco, enlightened as he was by the heinous assassination
of Atahualpa by Pizarro's order (after a verdict that was
worse than summary and unfounded), then became the
enemy's accomplice, instead of fighting to the death. When
he realizes at last that he is thus losing a great number of
partisans, Manco is quick to inform the people of his
hidden intentions. His alliance is only apparent, he proclaims, designed to inspire confidence in the whites so that
they will stop distrusting him. Its immediate purpose is to
get them to grant him his liberty, without which he can do
nothing. The Willac Umu and his best captains are assigned
the task of revealing his secret plan, surreptitiously, to all
the Indians in the empire.

THE LURE OF THE GOLDEN STATUES

In his cage, having recapitulated these dramatic events,
Manco admits that he was duped, his plans have been
thwarted. The Cañaris have become his pitiless guards.
They harass him mercilessly, urinating in his face, raping
the Chosen Women in front of him.

The Inca knows that the Christians have been sent
extensive reinforcements from Spain, as well as thousands
of Indians from Central America and Negroes from Africa.
The cavalry and their firearms terrify his legions, who flee
or switch over to the service of those better-armed. Out

of fear or vanity, his own brothers are plotting against him, hoping to steal from him the illusory crown.

Manco is now convinced that the oracles and Huayna Capac were wrong in preaching submission. He will not continue much longer to respect the last request of the old emperor, who died shortly after the whites appeared in South America. To escape from the trap into which he has fallen, Manco will use the cunning that characterizes his race. Did his ancestors not conquer hundreds of hostile tribes more by clever words than by force, which was used only when their persuasive diplomacy had been exhausted? It was not for nothing that the hidalgos taught him trickery! He has been informed that one of his generals has Francisco cornered in Lima; that Gonzalo and Juan are in the sierra, waging war against the Quechua warriors who are massacring Spanish soldiers and miners; that Diego de Almagro is traveling toward Chile, guided by the Willac Umu. He himself has given the high priest of the Sun (his uncle) orders to abandon the conquistador as soon as they are far enough away, and to regroup while en route the forces that have remained loyal to the young sovereign.

The Inca also has another trump card up his sleeve: Hernando, who has shown some regard for him, has just returned from Spain, where he has delivered to Charles V the priceless booty of early seizures. In his absence, the situation has changed considerably. The Indian revolt has intensified. Separated from his brothers, disturbed by the continual disappearances of Spanish contingents (whose fate is never learned), Hernando is perhaps vulnerable. Why not suggest to him that, by helping each other, they might be able to restore order, which has been dangerously compromised? Dazzled by the glint of gold (the "sacred tears of Father Sun," the flood of which he must continue to channel into the coffers of his king), Hernando will be easily lured. He scarcely needs to be entreated to release the Inca; in return he demands more and more gold. But Cuzco's vast reserves have been exhausted.

Manco suggests to Hernando Pizarro that Pizarro let him travel to the Sacred Valley of the Willkamayo, where sumptuous commemorative feasts are to be held in honor of Huayna Capac. He will bring back the effigy of his father, "a golden man of his size, made in his likeness." The Inca keeps his word. However, the statue is hollow.

No problem! If he could return to Yucay—this time with an escort of 3,000 Indians, necessary to transport a solid idol—he will bring back "an *orejon de oro* with insides and everything of gold," which weighs, he claims, over 2 hundredweights!

Hernando falls for the bait. Manco sets out in April 1536, brandishing the standard of the rebellion. He will never return—or rather, he will soon reappear to besiege Cuzco with tens of thousands of armed warriors.

And if a miraculous happenstance, still unexplained, had not come to the Spaniards' aid, no doubt the Inca's attack might have changed the face of this New World.

THE INCA'S FLIGHT TO YUCAY

At least 100,000 warriors followed Manco, who stole some hundred horses from the Pizarros. Many of his captains, like the Inca himself, mount them with pride. The rest, aides who transport supplies and water, prepare arrows and slingstones, and pile up rocks at the top of ravines to be toppled onto hidalgos passing by below. Innumerable Indian women also follow the Inca—picturesque *rabonas* who make meals, corn *chicha*, and love, and engage in combat so spiritedly that when one of these swarthy provisioners is captured, the mercenaries of Charles V, imitating Caesar's legionaries, cut off her right hand.

Behind Manco march his archers, his stone-slingers, porters bearing the ancestral mummies bedecked with jewels, the Orejones, high priests, sorcerers, and magi, some 1,000 Chosen Women, and the Virgins of the Sun, watched over by the Mamacunas. A hundred thousand llamas have been laden with treasures that the Indians had hidden in the *chinkanas*, the secret underground galleries of Cuzco and Sacsahuaman. The Inca is also carrying with him the object of everyone's desires, the extraordinary anthropomorphic idol of the Sun, the Punchao, which contains a heart of gold molded with the ashes of the hearts of the great deceased emperors.

Hernando Pizarro is furious. The influence that Manco, once free, is still capable of exerting on his people is a menace that cannot be ignored. A conquistador overlooked by the historians, Alonso Enriquez de Guzman, the bastard cousin of Charles V and a brazen adventurer, pirate, forger,

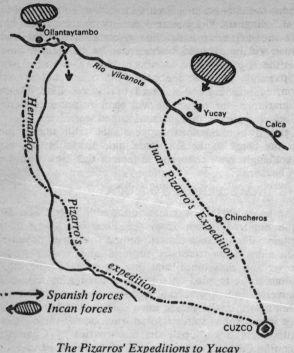

*The Pizarros' Expeditions to Yucay
and Ollantaytambo
(according to General Felipe de la Barra)*

heretic, and blasphemer (he parodied Christ by having himself attached, naked, to a cross during Holy Week!), wrote that "the young Inca, about twenty years old, was served and worshipped by his Indians as if he had saved their bodies and would save their souls. Thus, they take him truly to be a god, because they say that he is the Son of the Sun which they worship."

Juan Pizarro, the youngest of the four brothers, hastily musters sixty cavalrymen to rush after the Inca encumbered with an extensive escort. But outside of Cuzco, 10,000 Indians block their path. While they are giving battle, Manco is already far away in the Andes, amid the gigantic mountains closed off by very difficult passes where horses can proceed only at great risk; here he will take refuge—

"without the hidalgos' being able to discern his mysterious retreat," Bingham will comment. But he will be wrong.

The Inca first retreats to Ollantaytambo. Suspecting that the ruse will be exposed before long, he stands firm and awaits the Spanish forces, sacrificing to the Sun each dawn two Spanish prisoners and a horse.

Gonzalo and Hernando decide to attack him in his headquarters; they expect to take him by surprise there, relatively unguarded. They know that many of his troops are fighting in distant provinces.

All the Spaniards, black slaves, and sound horses are mustered, along with several thousand auxiliary Cañaris and Chachapoyas, who are under orders from members of the *cuzqueño* nobility whom dynastic rivalries have estranged from Manco. Gonzalo leads the small army, flanked by twenty horsemen who are to "liquidate" the Inca sentinels posted along the banks of the Sacred Rio, who might sound the alarm. A useless precaution! Manco has already been warned, and the Spaniards are forced to engage in exhausting skirmishes before they reach the formidable ramparts of the fortress. Its pyramidal terraces are covered with fierce Anti archers; the mountaintop is swarming with a befeathered human mass.

The great Indian chieftains present a singular mien beneath their helmets, which represent monstrous animals and can be opened in front by means of a sort of spring, or masks that are equally frightening. Countless banners made of cloth and glistening feathers float above these strange beings.

The arrogant Hernando charges as far as the first tier of this "Cyclops' mosaic." But he is forced back by a downpour of arrows and slingstones, accompanied by savage howls. The battle wavers for a long time.

Manco then has the river diverted and floods the bottom of the valley, where the melee is intense. Stuck in the mud, caught in the current, great numbers of horses and Indian provisioners in the Spaniards' service will drown.

The Pizarros will never be able to take this fortress manned by unchained Titans. Knowing that the Indians customarily do not fight at night, they retreat in the darkness, leaving their tents up in the hope that their retreat will go undetected. But for the first time in Incan history, Manco goes against tradition rather than let the enemy escape, and he has the paths strewn with thorns and long cactus spears, which tear at their mounts' hocks. With much difficulty the Spaniards manage to flee; the Indian auxiliaries fall victim to the carnage.

The chroniclers present will report that the Incas were "so victorious that it seemed to them as if they could take on the entire world, and that when they saw the conquistadors routed, overwhelmed with fear, they burst out laughing." However, Manco seemed disturbed by the fact that Pizarro's troops had slipped through his fingers. If they had waited until the next day to retreat, no one would have escaped alive.

A "WAR OF NERVES," INDIAN-STYLE

The Peruvian historiographer Juan José Vega has retraced the vicissitudes of the Indians' "true war of reconquest." Manco, he notes, will try repeatedly to recapture Cuzco. When he sees the Spaniards divided into two clans ready to kill one another, he thinks that if, as an enemy of the "Pizarrists," he joins with the "Almagrists," he may have a chance. Hence, he sends a message to Almagro. Its tone is not that of one defeated: "By God, yes, I do not lie! I swear to you on the cross that if I rebelled, it was more because of the terrible treatment to which I was subjected than because of the gold that was taken from me. I gave Juan Pizarro 1,300 gold bricks, 7 jars of gold and silver, 2,000 objects made of pure gold, and even more to Hernando. 'Dog!' he said to me. 'Give me more, or I'll have you burned.' Almagro, if you punish them, I shall make peace with you. . . ."

A rendezvous is arranged at Yucay, and the hidalgo sets forth in that direction. But he falls into an ambush, in which those escorting him all perish. What has happened? Perhaps Manco was sincere, preparing to receive Almagro, right up to the moment when a runner arrived with word from Pizarro: "Do not place any trust in Almagro's promises. He has no power to govern. He is lying to you."

Angered, Manco insults the emissaries of the two rival factions. He hurls at their feet the heads of 200 Spaniards and his most precious war trophies: the tanned hides of

150 horses. Then he sends the horrified messengers back. This will be Manco's last contact with the invader for a long time. Everything he does from now on will inexorably backfire. The ground will give way beneath him.

No longer knowing whom to trust, the Inca finally chooses exile, after having consulted the magical oracles.

THE GREAT RETREAT OF THE INCAS

Crossing the high Andean peaks (located at an altitude of 5,000 meters) beyond Ollantaytambo, Manco beats a second retreat into the Lucumayo Valley. He stops over at Amaybamba, convinced that no one can catch up with him in this region protected by mammoth peaks. The Inca wants to celebrate here his victory over the Chachapoya Indians, allies of the Spaniards who tried to block his path. He has their chief, Chuqui Llasax, decapitated; then he hosts a banquet and gets drunk with his troops. Paullu Inca (whom the Spaniards have just "coronated" in Manco's place), Captain Rodrigo Ordoñez, and hundreds of Indian auxiliaries—the efficacious agents of all the victories of the Conquest—take them by surprise here, undefended. It is a complete disaster for Manco.[6]

The conquistador will take back to Cuzco, as prisoners, the young prince Titu Cusi and his mother, and several Coyas, along with venerated mummies, marvelous jewels, and a great golden Sun. They also seize "20,000 llamas and alpacas" from the imperial preserves. And they free some captive hidalgos, shaved and shorn. The Inca, alas, has handed ten others over to the cannibals of the nearby jungles. If Manco succeeds in fleeing, it is thanks to the winged feet of his faithful bearers from the Lucana tribe.

Despite this reversal, Manco, having exhausted the peaceful means of recovering the ancestral throne, does not

[6] Some doubt remains as to the exact site of this dramatic night of festivities. Some chroniclers will hold that this costly defeat for Manco took place in Viticos; Titu Cusi, a participant in and victim of this reversal, will, in a *relación* dictated to the mestizo Martín Pando, place it much farther away—proving that the Spaniards penetrated one of the "lost capitals" later sought by Hiram Bingham very early on.

have any intention of giving up the fight. He will first throw the Spaniards off the scent. By what mysterious paths do his troops descend from the mountains of Vilcabamba to set upon the Spaniards? The latter suffer such grave losses that in Madrid Charles V is angered: This rebel must be dealt with, by whatever means are necessary! The king repeats his orders to a series of viceroys, who travel to Peru to govern in his name.

At his hideout in Viticos, Manco receives, in succession, fabulous proposals of peace and threats of terrible reprisals. This time he will not let himself be tempted, or intimidated, or moved. He simply waits, perfecting a tactic which his three sons will later revive: Every time matters are such that he is on the brink of ruin, he asks to negotiate. He promises to turn himself in if his conditions are accepted. But since his demands are intentionally exaggerated, they involve interminable negotiations, which enable him to gain month after month.

In September 1539, as the threats are predominant, Manco proposes a meeting with Pizarro. If he comes in person, Manco will surrender—but only to him. From Lima, Pizarro hastens to Cuzco, where he is advised not to trust the Inca. Hence, the conquistador sends ahead a company bearing gifts—including a beautiful mare led by a mestizo—to coax the Inca. Assuming that Pizarro is among the group, Manco sets a trap for him, which is described by Alonso Borregan, an obscure soldier involved in the Conquest:[7] "We were headed for a tampo that is behind Biticos, beyond Ollantaytambo, between sierras," he says. "Thank God, we saw the Indians go by and take the *paso*. We avoided the ruler and fled. The Inca killed the beast with a rock." And Pizarro narrowly escaped death.

---

[7] Dated 1533, Alonso Borregan's chronicle was not discovered until 1940, in the archives of the Society of Jesus in Cuzco; the historian Rafael Loreda was informed of its existence that same year. Alonso Borregan came to Peru with the conquistador Alvarado. He relates that some blacks in revolt cut a finger off his right hand and that he lost an eye "because of women." He acted as a mediator and conciliator in the conflict between the Pizarrists and the Almagrists, while belonging to the latter group.

THE ASSASSINATION OF MANCO AT VITICOS

The years pass. From the lower Andes, Manco has watched the Pizarros stagger beneath the blows of Almagro, Sr., and his son; they too soon fall into disfavor. At the slightest sign of weakening in his enemy, the Inca once again takes courage. However, one last time his luck will be tragically against him.

Several Spaniards show up one day at the gates of the secret capital. Fugitives who joined in a plot against Pizarro contrived by Almagro, they all participated in his murder. These five men (or seven, in some versions of the story) are certain they are done for, unless the Inca takes pity on them. They beg Manco to hide them until the situation takes a turn for the better. The Inca consents to harbor them. Out of the goodness of his heart? No, to perfect his Castilian and to learn from them how to make powder for the European firearms he has confiscated, how to use harquebuses, and how to shoe the horses in his possession—and perhaps also because these fugitives got rid of his principal enemy for him, the men responsible for the fall of the empire.

The refugees teach the Inca to play chess and checkers, and to bowl. Manco is soon advising his teachers. While he treats them in a princely fashion (showering them with precious gifts, eating and talking with them at length, providing them with Indian women), he nonetheless is constantly on the alert that they do not give him the slip. In the beginning he even has them guarded. The young prince Titu Cusi will comment that Manco kept these fugitives by his side "as his servants," a phrase which might explain the resentment that one senses smoldering in their hearts, which will later affect their behavior.

In May 1544 an interesting bit of news reaches Viticos: Blasco de Nuñez, the bearer of "new laws" favoring the Indians, has just debarked at the port of Callao-Lima, assigned by Charles V to pry the Inca from his inaccessible "condor's nest."

Diego Mendez, Gomez Perez, Francisco Barba, Cornejo, and Monroy explain to Manco that an opportunity for all of them seems to be presenting itself. If they go to Lima to offer their help to the new viceroy, they will be in a better position to negotiate an amnesty, not only on their own behalf, but also for the Inca's benefit. Diego Mendez, who has authority over his friends, assures him that after ten years of deadly fighting without results, the time is ripe to secure the indulgence of the Spanish plenipotentiary, and that he will be able to negotiate with an eye toward reestablishing peace; he offers to restore Manco to the throne.

What Diego neglects to mention is that he will take advantage of the situation to wangle an honorific reward in exchange for this undertaking. As for Manco, he yearns to see the Cuzco of his forefathers once again. Why should he not attempt to regain his rightful dominion, through the entreaties of one of his protégés?

Diego Mendez goes to Lima and returns, bearing promising news: The viceroy will pardon everyone. He awaits the Inca.[8]

It is then that, in a manner as unforeseeable as it is dramatic, the last act of Manco's life is played out. Unforeseeable, unless, during his trip to Lima, Diego Mendez was advised (that is, ordered) to do away with the Inca. This was, from all evidence, the most effective way to put a stop to the Indian uprising.[9]

[8] The versions differ here as well, depending on the informant. Gomez Perez, some claim, was the intermediary, and it is he who, during a bowling match, felled the Inca with a blow to the head. Others hold that the tragic incident occurred over a game of chess, and Manco, unarmed, was transfixed by the swords and daggers of his opponents, or else that he was killed during a game of quoits played with horseshoes. What has not been revealed is that Diego Mendez was the half-brother of Rodrigo Ordoñez (famous for having halted François I at Pavie), who will pursue Manco until his own death.

[9] The great Peruvian historian Raul Porras Barrenechea has pointed out that the refugees wrote to Lieutenant-General Alonso de Toro to ask for a pardon. According to the testimony of one of Pizarro's servants, de Toro promised to pardon them on the condition that they do away with the Inca, because, as the owner of a vast coca plantation capable of bringing in ten thousand pesos a year, he was unable to draw profit from it "because of the war against the Inca."

According to Cieza de León's version, when the fight broke out between Manco and the renegades, the Inca gave his men

Imprudently, Manco, having just learned that one of his vassals, Carhuay Ayso, lord of Cotamarca, is contriving a plot against the state of Vilcabamba, sends his personal guard—1,000 armed men—in search of the traitor. Meanwhile, he decides to hold a feast in honor of his Spanish guests, whose departure for Lima is imminent, in order to show them his gratitude. The feast concluded, they engage in a bowling match—his favorite diversion. Diego Mendez wins from the Inca a gold piece, which the Inca is quick to take back. When the conquistador, who has a violent disposition, loses his temper, Manco tells him, mockingly, "that he can certainly keep the gold piece and that if he wants more, he will see that it is given him."

Mendez becomes so incensed at the idea that the Inca is offering him charity that the party is called off. But he insults Manco so rudely that the Inca rebuffs him with a blow.

The others have gathered to one side. Have they long since decided to do away with their host? Have they been awaiting this opportunity, or did they provoke it?

When, in order to celebrate the return of Captain Rimachi Yupanqui with the Indian conspirator and to erase the disagreeable memory of the quarrel, Manco drinks to their reconciliation from a cup of chased gold, Diego Mendez sneaks up behind him and stabs him before any of his companions can intervene. The young Titu Cusi wishes to go to the aid of his father, who is lying on the ground, but he is pursued by lances and javelins into the bushes, where, in their hurry to leave, the Spaniards do not find him.

The regicides—who have kept their horses saddled—soon rush off full speed in the direction of Cuzco, burning the liana bridge of Chuquichaca behind them. But they lose their way at night and take shelter in a hut, where

---

orders to kill the Spaniards. Diego Mendez then hurled himself at the Inca and riddled him with a dagger.

It is fitting to recall that, for the Incas, unlike the Spaniards, games were not only for amusement but an activity linked to myths and divinatory magic: The game in question assumed the form of a good or bad omen. Manco's opponents were unaware of this fact. Did the Inca perhaps read, in this magical act, the advice to eliminate his adversaries?

Rimachi Yupanqui surrounds them. He has the hut set on fire, and there the Spaniards meet with a cruel death.

At Viticos, Manco survives his wounds for five days. He has the final pleasure of seeing, impaled on arrows, the bearded heads of his murderers, curing in the frosts and sun of the Andes. To his son, his captains, and his faithful followers, who, according to the custom, are lamenting at his bedside, the dying Inca murmurs: "Do not grieve that they took my life in this remote spot. They killed my brother Atahualpa when he was at the apogee of his power, and at the peak of the empire. Therefore, feel no sorrow over my death."

Manco's nobility amid disgrace will earn him comparisons with Hannibal and Pyrrhus, "for the irony and pettiness of the manner of his death," by Luis Alayza y Paz Soldan. Before dying, the Inca finds the strength to order his followers not to allow the Christians to defile his lands, and to accept as their lord and master his eldest legitimate son, the very young Sayri Tupac, whom he entrusts to the noble Orejon Atoc Supay ("the Wild Fox"), regent of Vilcabamba.

Embalmed, Manco's body is transported, with all due honors, to the solar temple of the "lost capital."

CHAPTER SIX

Poison for Sayri Tupac
and Titu Cusi

> *Because it seemed to me of the utmost im-*
> *portance that Sayri Tupac step forward*
> *without delay to pledge allegiance to His*
> *Majesty . . . I suggested to one of his uncles,*
> *Cayaotopa, that he might persuade him to*
> *come forward of his own accord, rather than*
> *by force.*
>
> —La Gasca, 1548

THE SURRENDER OF SAYRI TUPAC

While he has inherited from his ancestors a taste for
ostentation, Sayri Tupac, heir to a sceptor now chimerical,
has none of their combative qualities. From birth, according to the imperial genealogical laws, this Inca—who bears
the curious name "Rich Tobacco"[1]—is destined for the
supreme sacerdotal rank of Willac Umu, or "sacred head,"
high priest of the Sun. As a young prince, he orders that
the age-old rites be perpetuated in the city of Viticos, where
his father, at the beginning of his exile, ordered a new
palace built, since the ways and customs forbid him to live
in the residences of the preceding Incas, Pachacutec, Tupac
Yupanqui, and Huayna Capac, whose mummies have been
brought there because he did not dare leave them in Cuzco
or Ollantaytambo. Everything in the Incas' palaces is supposed to remain as it was on the day of their death, with

---

[1] Eugenio Alarco notes that tobacco (*sayri* in Quechua),
harvested in the Vilcabamba region, constituted an element of
great importance magically: it was used to counteract the evil
influence of sorcerers.

numerous servants continuing to attend to the mummies as they did to the Incas when alive, as much in terms of daily tasks as for the great yearly demonstrations—and especially the famous procession of the Mallquis, celebrated at the beginning of the month of Ayamarca, which, curiously, coincided in ancient Peru with the All Souls' Day of the Catholic Church.

In the reflection of the colossal golden Sun which adorns the wall of the great temple, a court that is still sumptuous surrounds Sayri Tupac. His goldsmiths work fabulous jewelry for the ravishingly beautiful Coya Cusi Huarpay, daughter of Huascar, whom Sayri Tupac will marry, according to the custom. Charles V has been replaced by Phillip II, who hopes that the Inca of Vilcabamba will come to him out of diplomacy and not require the costly violence employed until now. The viceroy Hurtado de Mendoza is assigned to draw up "an agreement of peace and good will" with Sayri Tupac. He will use as "appointed liaison agents" the Inca's friends, and particularly the women—above all, Beatriz Coya, Sayri Tupac's aunt, whom he is known to "trust and respect more than anyone else."

On the long road to Viticos, the cacique Tarisca, a relative of the Inca, precedes the bearers of the truce, Juan de Betanzos and Juan Sierra, husband and son of princesses of the Sun.[2] These two Spaniards bear presents and "a royal provision of pardon for everything in the past."

They will argue cleverly that all the sisters and daughters of the Incas are now married to hidalgos, with whom they have had children, thus giving birth to a new mestizo race of Peruvians. What good is it, therefore, to persist in wars that are as pointless as they are bloody? Are the Spaniards not the absolute rulers of the empire, which has even lost the name Tahuantinsuyo and assumed that of Peru? Would

---

[2] Juan de Betanzos married Angelina Yupanqui, the sister of Atahualpa and Manco who had been Francisco Pizarro's mistress. Juan Sierra is the son of Beatriz Coya Manco Capac Yupanqui (another daughter of Huayna Capac), who was seduced by the famous Captain Mancio Sierra de Lequizamo, who "bet the [golden] Sun before it rose," after having won it in a game, and lost it that same night.

it not be better to come to an understanding, as the king of
Spain wishes?

The viceroy promises to be magnanimous. Sayri Tupac
will be treated amicably. Surrounded by his court and the
luxury of which he is fond, he can return to his palace in
Yucay. But the young Inca's advisers describe to him the
risks he may run if he allows himself to be tempted by the
offer. Did not Atahualpa, Manco Inca, and so many other
members of his family perish because they placed too much
faith in the conquistadors?

Sayri Tupac sends the emissaries and presents back to
the viceroy, adding a few rare animals from the tropical
jungles so as not to insult him too greatly. But the Inca
soon changes his mind: If the lands that Pizarro confiscated
from his father and his grandfather Huayna Capac's
palaces in the Sacred Valley are restored to him, he will
sign the desired peace treaty. His terms are accepted, and
the viceroy sends him a sword from Toledo and gold
stirrups. In addition, Miguel de Estete, one of the "heroes"
of that dark day in Cajamarca when the empire dissolved
in treachery, hands Sayri Tupac the famous gold headdress
with scarlet fringe that he tore from the head of the unfortunate Atahualpa. So that he does not have to put it on,
Sayri Tupac will pretend that he no longer rules. The truth
is that the crown, inherited from a "traitor" who handed
his country and the imperial treasures over to the European
invaders without a fight, disgusts him. He will never wear
it; in fact, he will leave it behind at Vilcabamba when he
departs.

But the Inca lingers on. His advisers continue to temporize. It is impossible, they tell him, to travel during the
rainy season. They must wait for the dry season. However,
spring 1549 comes and still Sayri Tupac does not make his
departure: it is postponed by the sudden death of Paullu
Inca, confirming his worst suspicions.

"CONSULTING THE ORACLES"

The situation drags on into September 1557, when the
viceroy, growing impatient, starts to exert pressure. But it
is not until after an extraordinary divinatory ceremony—
of which Diego Fernandez de Palencia will provide a full

account—that a decision is finally reached. The high priests of the sun have resolved to consult Father Sun, Mama Pacha, and the sacred *huacas*, offering "ritual sacrifices" to the age-old deities of the Quechua Olympus so that they will speak and advise the Inca. He is subjected to a strict fast (as are the magi, seers, and nobles in his entourage), which is to last until the morning set for "consulting the oracles."

All the fires have been extinguished the moment the *pututus* (loud war conches) were sounded. A solemn procession ascends toward a high peak, where the incantations take place and young creatures are burned before the idols.

The propitiatory rites completed, Sayri Tupac returns from the sierra, his face beaming: The auguries have proved favorable! "The Sun, Mother Earth, the Sky, and all our *huacas* advise me to leave," he announces. "Do not tell me that it is out of fear or pusillanimity that I am going," he adds. "We have never been so well fortified and so well prepared for war. Nevertheless, consider the response given and how fitting it is to go visit our neighbors and friends, since we do so want to see the lands where we were born!"

Does the Inca perhaps harbor, despite all, some apprehension? "Of course," he concludes, "here I am lord of all I could possibly want. But you must consider the fact that the sun wishes me to leave . . . even if it must cost me my life."

Eighteen days and nights of drunken feasting mark the verdict of the gods, even though the Inca's old captains appear overcome with grief and worry throughout. Nevertheless, after having fastened around Sayri Tupac's forehead the *borla* of scarlet wool fringed with gold tassels and adorned with three *coriquenque* feathers (the *coriquenque* is a mysterious sacred bird), the majority determine to accompany him on his daring return to his birthplace.

It is October 7, 1557, when Sayri Tupac, his sixteen-year-old wife, his captains and his court, 300 Indian nobles, and his guard of savage Antis leave the little independent "empire" of Vilcabamba forever. Not only will the Inca see the magnificent Cuzco once again, the viceroy will invite him to visit Lima, the brand-new capital of colonial Peru, founded twenty-two years earlier by Francisco Pizarro. The Inca makes what is almost a triumphant entrance on the evening of Epiphany, January 5, 1558. He is welcomed by the Marqués de Cañete, who regally guarantees him an annual income of 18,000 *castellanos* and makes him a gift of all the lands he is reclaiming. A chronicler who attends the ceremony, struck by the ironical remark that Sayri Tupac then makes (he does not lack for bitterness!), tells us that the Inca pulled a thread from the fringe bordering the tablecloth for the banquet given in his honor by the archbishop of Lima, and showed it to all the guests gathered. "In relation to the entire tablecloth," he declared, "this thread represents no more than the lands that are being given me, compared to the immense empire of the Tahuantinsuyo which my ancestors once conquered and ruled."

Let us note the fact that Sayri Tupac was the only Inca ever to look upon Lima, the "Pearl of the Pacific," where he proudly rode about in a golden litter, borne by his befeathered Antis. He traveled its narrow streets, with their long, overhanging balconies made of lacelike openwork cedar and closed up like cupboards—streets crowded with carriages and black slaves.

Still quite dazzled by this strange life he has discovered, traveling amid great pomp, acclaimed and feted on his way by the people, Sayri Tupac returns to his Andean peaks. He takes up residence in Yucay, in the heart of the imperial garden of the Sacred Valley, where he will live sumptuously for a few years. Then he too will pass away in a suspicious manner.

"As soon as I heard of the death of Sayri Tupac, I was deeply troubled, and I thought that the Spaniards had killed him, just as they caused my father's death," Titu Cusi Yupanqui will say. Various rumors about this sudden death circulated at the time. At first an attempt was made to convince people that the "unhappy Inca" had died of melancholy. Some people thought that the dissidents of Vilcabamba, unable to forgive one who had yielded to the conquerors' demands, had perpetrated the crime. Others blamed Paulla Inca's son, who wished to reclaim the crown worn by his father, Manco's brother and rival. But the great chronicler Huaman Poma de Ayala makes a formal accusation: "It is a Cañari—once again!— named Francisco Chilche who poisoned Sayri Tupac," he asserts. This parvenu, a leading Indian in Ecuador, was not exactly

pleased to see the Inca reclaim the property with which
Francisco Pizarro had rewarded him for his services. Having joined forces with the Spaniards since the beginning of
the confrontation between the two inheritors of the empire,
Atahualpa and Huascar, Chilche reigned as a tyrant over
the fief of Yucay, showered with substantial tributes and
women, which the former vassals of the Inca offered him
in order to ally themselves with this new formidable master.
The Cañari, Huaman de Poma adds, owned "all the plantations of the emperors and of the Sun, as well as the best
cornfields"—whence his hatred and his recourse to poison
to get rid of the intruder.

This Cañari "Borgia" was imprisoned for a year, then
released "for lack of evidence." In truth, the Spaniards
exhibited more concern than satisfaction when they learned
of the death of the acculturated Inca. Even though he had
prudently left his brothers in Vilcabamba, his belated submission allowed them to predict that the latter Incas and
the last rebels would finally accept the peace so laboriously
arranged. Now they had to begin all over again.

Thus, the death knell sounded once again in 1561 in the
heart of the Andes, while in Lima and Spain the news of
Sayri Tupac's sudden demise inspired a pessimism as profound as his successor's attitude was problematical.

TITU CUSI, BASTARD AND APOSTATE

After being captured during the night of festivities, Titu
Cusi remained a prisoner in Cuzco for scarcely two years.
His father had him released in turn and called him back to
his side in Viticos.

Titu Cusi rules over much fertile land and people, who
obey him and pay him tribute, and if he repeatedly makes
raids, seizing quantities of Indians and livestock, "he has
never killed a Spaniard or burned a church," as the judge
Juan de Matienzo informs the king.

Because he was the product of the love of Manco for
a Chosen Woman, the hidalgos call Titu Cusi a "bastard
and apostate." This does not prevent him from donning
the *mascapaicha*, the imperial symbol, even though the
Spaniards feel that actually the ornament rightfully belongs
to his half-brother, who is legitimate: Tupac Amaru, "the

Bright Serpent." As soon as he is coronated, Titu Cusi, observing the ancient customs, places his younger brother in the care of the Mamacunas of the god Punchao, who will raise him—still in accordance with the rules of conduct established many centuries ago—among the Acllas, or Virgins of the Sun. Where?

Baltazar de Ocampo specifies "in the Casa del Sol, the House of the Sun, located on an impregnable peak of the cordillera where stands the fortress of Pitcos dedicated to the god of day." The chronicler does not hesitate to accuse Titu Cusi of keeping Tupac Amaru "secluded and imprisoned . . . usurping the government for himself."[3]

As for where, exactly, the new Capac Inca resides, the secret will be so well guarded that Titu Cusi will travel 40 leagues through a Dantesque gorge each time he is visited by Spanish emissaries, rather than let them come to the mysterious "forbidden capital" of Vilcabamba la Vieja. Perusal of the chronicles shows him, in fact, regularly shuttling between Viticos and Pucyura, Hurancalia, Choquepalpa—and, who knows, Machu Picchu?

Titu Cusi must be about thirty-three years old. Fairly large, he has a dark complexion, and his face is pitted by smallpox; his mien is severe. Bursting with pride, a rousing speaker, wordy, occasionally boastful, appearing impulsive but sensitive, he makes an impression on all who meet him. Shrewdly, the Inca realizes that, for the moment, the enemy is unbeatable. He will therefore also temporize interminably. He boasts of having, in the warmer regions, so many allies among the savage cannibals that they could populate "twice the territory from Quito to Chile."

Rodriguez de Figueroa, who writes a colorful account of a dangerous mission involving Titu Cusi which he carries out, encounters at Viticos an extremely macabre surprise: The heads of his compatriots who twenty years earlier assassinated Manco Inca are still impaled on lances and exposed to the contumely of the Indian warriors.

Titu Cusi, wearing his crown and magnificently decked

---

[3] Americanists are greatly intrigued by the name "Pitcos"; for a long time they believed it to be an alteration of the spelling of Viticos. But isn't Pitcos closely related to Machu Picchu? I shall return to this subject later.

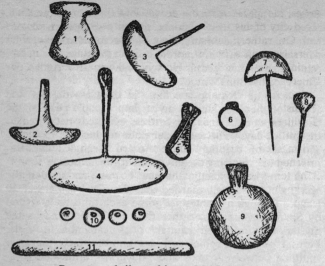

Bronze and silver objects, Machu Picchu
1. Hatchet. 2–4. Tumis. 5. Tweezers.
6. Ring. 7–8. Tupus (shawl-pins).
9. Mirror. 10. Spangles. 11. Champi (crowbar).

out in multicolored feathers, his chest gleaming with a large silver disk, meets with Rodriguez de Figueroa on May 11, 1565, at Bambacona (Pampaconas). The Inca is carrying a shield, a dagger, and a lance, all made of gold. His blue tunic is set off by a fine woolen mantle. His thighs and calves are circled by garters with feathers and small wooden bells. Twenty or thirty fairly good-looking women surround him, serving him food on a reed mat, from silver dishes.

This historic interview, like those which will follow, does not bring concrete results. As Manco and Sayri did before him, the Inca reiterates offers of peace coupled with conditions that require some thought. Titu Cusi is trying desperately to safeguard the independence of his neo-Inca domain, by means of interminable diplomatic dealings.

All of a sudden he is demonstrating an astonishing "good Christian" spirit. He was baptized at Cuzco during his captivity. Have the decorum of the church, the apostolic devotion of the missionaries, the incense of the chanted masses, the spectacle of the processions through the ancient sacred city of his forefathers made a strong impression on him? Or, rather, knowing the religious fanaticism of his adversaries, does he intend to take advantage of it by feigning a pious attitude? He allows Diego Rodriguez de Figueroa to set up a cross on the red clay esplanade where the Inca sits enthroned on a *tiana* of chased gold. But the conquistador relates that he must then spend several days attending Incan rites and festivities, while subjected to the insolent looks and sarcastic comments of one or two thousand masked warriors, who, stimulated by great quantities of fermented *chicha*, sing and dance to the haunting sound of the tom-toms, for nights on end, howling and gesticulating like demons.

Rodriguez ventures to call in a second "ambassador." But when the new emissaries unfortunately show up with harquebuses, Titu Cusi angrily sends him back with his escort and then orders the suspension bridge at Chuquichaca torn down, before withdrawing deep into the labyrinth of the Vilcabamba Cordillera. Nevertheless, he keeps with him the mestizo Martín Pando, an interpreter who speaks Castilian as well as he does Quechua.

THE PAGAN UPRISING OF TAQUI ONGOY

Viceroys, intendants, Spanish counselors will succeed one another and parley endlessly with Titu Cusi to get him to specify his demands. An agreement seems underway when suddenly alarming rumors spread through Peru and as far as Chile. Large stores of bows, arrows, and provisions have been discovered. Several Spanish governors have apparently disappeared without a trace.

Incredible news breaks. Urged on by the powerful sorcerers of Vilcabamba, the Inca has attempted to reestablish idolatry! If one is to believe the avowals of the vicar Luis Olivera, who advises the royal court of Lima, his magi preach "the resurrection of the *huacas*" as in the glorious age of the Tahuantinsuyo.

The demonic preachers of heresy, the priest asserts, are insidiously infiltrating the Andes, in order there to celebrate purifying rites, as of old. They impose fasts and demand offerings for the pre-Columbian deities.

This heretical movement, dubbed Taqui Ongoy,[4] is all the more alarming since, before Rodriguez, the Inca boasted that he was "as great as the pope of the Catholic Church in the spiritual domain," and he ratified the peace treaty of Acobamba "before the creator Sun and the Earth, which he worships as a mother that gives to men all that they need in order to live."

This pagan uprising proved, therefore, that he had never abjured the ancestral religion, and the movement might arouse the amorphous Indian masses, inciting them to rebellion beneath the banner of the gods which, once banished, had now returned.

The intervention of the judge Matienzo makes Titu Cusi realize that he has gone too far. He rescinds the pact he made with the rebel Caracas with a view to a general uprising, at a date that, he admits, he himself was ultimately to set. As proof of his good will, he consents to let two Augustinian monks come and settle in his territory; they will evangelize the Indians of Vilcabamba.

Is this a new ruse? Does he hope that the monks will give up along the way, discouraged by his followers? Nothing daunts Friar Marcos Garcia, who arrives in Pucyura and stands before the Inca surrounded by his court; Titu Cusi quite annoyed that one of his hiding places was so easily found. Does the secret revealed not render dangerously vulnerable the position of Vilcabamba la Vieja, where

---

[4] Named for the magical chants and dances performed in honor of the Stars, the sect of Taqui Ongoy lasted at least a dozen years. The movement took root in the belief that the Spaniards used a form of magic to put the Indians to sleep and to extract from them human fat, which alone could heal them of an otherwise incurable disease. Father Cristobal de Molina notes, "This false information was designed to arouse hatred between the Indians and the conquistadors." He reports, "The natives believed that all the *huacas* in the realm that had been destroyed and burned by the Christians would be resurrected to defend them." They all would join together in the renowned *huaca* of Pachacamac and in the equally famous *huaca* of Titicaca, the Sacred Lake, whence they would "take flight to give battle to God and conquer Him. The Spaniards would be wiped out, and the ocean would swell and drown all their cities, so that no memory of them should remain."

rites are celebrated of which the servants of the foreign God (whom they wish to impose on Indians) so disapprove? Especially since the city is only at two or three days' distance?

Titu Cusi will do everything in his power—successfully —to make sure that the Spanish monks never cross the threshold of the forbidden sanctuary, whose doors Marcos Garcia will try to break down.

Infuriated by the apostolic sermons that the monk delivers with more blows with the stick than sprinklings of holy water, Titu Cusi wishes to defy God personally. Although, while baptized under the name Diego Castro Titu Cusi Yupanqui, he had already married one of his sisters, the Inca takes a second wife, who has also been converted.

In 1569 another Augustinian monk comes to Pucyura (where the Inca maintains his court and his army) and builds another church nearby, in Huarancalla. With his jovial, compassionate nature, the newcomer is welcomed by the Indians, whom he clothes, teaches, and heals. Diego Ortiz thus becomes a close friend of Titu Cusi; however, he cannot curb the excesses of Marcos Garcia, who gathers the inhabitants of the villages and forms a procession to go burn one of the sacred shrines of the solar cult, the *huaca* Yurac Rumi (the deified "White Rock"), located near Viticos, at Chuquipalpa, where the oracle of Inti speaks above a dark pool of water.

The monk's audacity will not go unpunished. But, warned in time by an Indian woman, Marcos Garcia avoids the "deadly herbs and powders" intended for him. How will the Inca get rid of the troublesome monks?

THE "DEVOTEES OF LUST"

Neither gold nor silver tempts either monk. Would women, perhaps? Following the counsel of the idols and deities consulted by the sorcerers of Vilcabamba, Titu Cusi selects the most beautiful and dissolute of his Chosen Women, from among the light-skinned Yungas. Naked beneath black or white *cushmas* modeled after the missionaries' cassocks, the bold Acllas get as far as the friars' beds; the friars' "angelic virtue" repudiates all the erotic temptations and the "infernal fires." These false novices, "devotees of lust," will give up after three weeks of fruitless provocations and be baptized by Diego Ortiz and Marcos Garcia!

Since the monks persist in their desire to desecrate "the University of Idolatry" of Vilcabamba la Vieja, where the "professors of witchcraft, teachers of the abominations" carry on their sinful activities, Titu Cusi contrives another "diabolical" stratagem: he will pretend to take these madmen there himself!

Carried on his golden litter, the Inca heads toward the principal seat, followed by the two barefoot priests. He has had the road flooded! Slipping, falling waist-deep in freezing water, covered with mud, shivering and praying, Marcos Garcia and Diego Ortiz regain solid ground only after three days of trials, which are especially exhausting at this altitude. When they imagine that their ordeal is at an end and that they will soon be entering the fabulous sanctuary of the Sun at last, Titu Cusi tells them that this trip was intended solely to discourage them. He orders that they be given lodging outside the sacred city, in order that they not see the worship, ceremonies, and rites conducted by his sorcerers, in which he and his captains participate daily. The two monks will never succeed in getting a glimpse of the mysterious city.

Abandoning all caution, they curse the pagan idols all the more zealously and hunt them down, dashing them to the ground, thus arousing the anger of the priests of the solar cult.

THE MARTYRDOM OF DIEGO ORTIZ

The time has come for Titu Cusi to make a pilgrimage to the *mochadero* ("place of prayer") where Manco, his father, was assassinated, near Viticos. The Inca drowns his sorrow in great quantities of *chicha*. The glacial night falls on the high peaks of the cordillera where the chapel is located. What happens then? What drama unfolds in private, among the Inca and the ministers of God?

Horrified, Angelina Llacsa and the Coya Polanquilaco, the Inca's two wives, watch as he suddenly swells up, turns purple, and coughs up blood. Has he perhaps caught a chill? By his bedside, the good friar Ortiz prepares an empirical remedy: an egg beaten with some sulfur and red pepper. At first the Inca pushes the glass away; then he heeds the mestizo Pando, who urges him to drink it. A few seconds later, struck by paralysis, Titu Cusi dies amid frightful spasms.

No sooner has the Inca expired when the interpreter is slaughtered. Like a fury, the Coya Polanquilaco, who has always been the monks' worst enemy, accuses Diego Ortiz of having poisoned Titu Cusi. In front of all the captains and nobles in his entourage, she orders the priest to "revive the Inca with a mass." Since Ortiz fails, he is stripped, then placed on a cross, his arms broken. There he passes the night in the freezing cold. He is scourged and forced to endure an abominable torture. With a rope running through his jaw, for three days he is dragged before Tupac Amaru, the new heir to the rebel empire of Vilcabamba, who will have to decide his fate. Is it Tupac Amaru who orders that the unfortunate monk be put to death—that he be impaled on a bamboo pike and trampled by the exacerbated Indian mob? This multitude believes that Titu Cusi's demise was due to the expulsion of the oracle of the sun, driven by fire from the temple of Yurac Rumi.[5]

Diego Ortiz is finished off by a club, with a blow to the neck, after five nights of horrible agony, accompanied by the sinister pounding of drums, the lugubrious wailing of the Indians, and the rending cries of the Inca's women. The martyred monk will be buried vertically, upside-down. All the chapels and churches built by the two missionaries, as well as the wooden crosses that they set up, will be burned. Little pouches for coca, the magical leaf, are cut from their sackcloth robes.

It must be emphasized once again that while the tragic

---

[5] Gomez de Tordoya states that Tupac Amaru "had the Augustinian monk killed because he reproached Titu Cusi for his vices." Juan Perez de Prado, mayor of Cuzco in 1582, related that "the Inca who succeeded Titu Cusi caused a friar named Diego Ortiz to be martyred and killed . . ." Father Calancha confirms that "Tupac Amaru ordered that he be killed because he blasphemed against the idols . . . who detested him, and because he was the principal enemy of the Sun Punchao and of the *huacas*." In truth, it was not because he might have poisoned the Inca.

events just related were taking place in the far reaches of the Andes, the Spaniards knew absolutely nothing about them. The Incas in fact went to great lengths—even to the point of crime—to cover up the death of Titu Cusi, whom for a long time the viceroys would go on trying to appease.[6]

In 1569 a heavy curtain of silence again descends over the fief of Vilcabamba—a silence that gradually begins to seem strange to the hidalgos. Several emissaries are sent to the Inca, who does not respond as he did previously, and the messengers disappear. In a final letter, the viceroy Francisco de Toledo calls upon the Inca to receive his ambassador and to heed with the greatest attention the proposals that will be put before him in the name of his majesty the king of Spain.

Few volunteers step forward to transmit the ultimatum. Known for his wisdom and for having accompanied the two monks in 1568, Atilano de Anaya, who speaks the Inca's language fluently, sets off with thirty loads of presents for him, accompanied by several servants, including a black man. He goes provided with letters from the king, the viceroy, and the pope.

Chapas and Caminahuas, the Inca's spies, warn him of the approach of a messenger from Cuzco. He sends two of his captains, Poripaucar Huanca and Cusi Paucar, to meet the Spaniard. They await Atilano de Anaya at the Chuquichaca bridge, which he must cross alone, dismissing his escort. The black servant, apprehensive, watches him sitting on a rock until nightfall.

At daybreak there is not an Indian in sight. Muffled noises kept the black servant awake. He daringly crosses the liana bridge and finds the body of his master lying at the bottom of a ravine; he has been stabbed.

When word of this crime reaches Cuzco, Lima, and Spain, it is called "high treason."

The fantastic saga of the Incas is drawing inexorably to a close.

---

[6] Father Calancha's detailed report in the *Crónica moralizada*, dated 1639, preserved in the great convent of the order of St. Augustine in Lima, was stolen at some point and remained unpublished until this century. It was anonymously put up for sale in Bordeaux in 1905.

CHAPTER SEVEN

The Vilcabamba Guerrilla

> *Along with the Inca, by my order and mandate, all the Indians and captains were taken (dead, alive, or embalmed), as well as the idols; all were brought back to the capital, Cuzco, by the captain Loyola and the head officer Juan Alvarez de Maldonado . . .*
> —Francisco de Toledo, 1572

Since Manco Inca's rebellion in 1535, the Andes of Vilcabamba have served as the refuge of the Incan forces, the cult of the sun, and the four last "Sun Kings" of South America. To rout them would be a venture comparable, Bingham writes, to how "it was for Hannibal and Napoleon . . . to bring their armies . . . through the comparatively low passes of the Alps." And these were passes "higher than the very summit of Mont Blanc."

Although at least 30,000 Indians have signed up with the conquistadors, the soldiers of the king of Spain number only in the dozens. As for the Inca's warriors, presumably he has only 500 or 600 left.

All the pacificatory missions having failed and cost lives, the viceroy Toledo, upon his arrival in Peru, views with great disfavor "the hotbed of rebellion that has existed for over thirty-six years in the far reaches of the Andes and which feeds the hope of an Incan restoration among the Indians and mestizos."

From Lima, where the terrible Inquisition reigns, Don Francisco de Toledo, a pitiless fanatic fed up with this bloody *guerrilla*, will take up the gauntlet. On April 14, 1572, he announces a formal order that "the king of Vilcabamba"—he still thinks he is dealing with Titu Cusi

—"be arrested": "He must be found and exterminated, along with his entire family."

Although the adversary's forces must be quite diminished at this point, the viceroy is worried that the Inca will retreat ever deeper into the folds of the cordillera, or even beyond, where he could arrange an alliance with friendly tribes in the Amazonian forest who are in a position to provide him with innumerable ferocious Anti warriors.

Fresh Spanish troops are placed under the command of a veteran of the Andes, General Martín Hurtado de Arbieto, accompanied by the royal standardbearer Pedro Sarmiento de Gamboa, secretary and commentator on the "war of Vilcabamba." The expedition comprises 200 professional soldiers and 2,000 Indian auxiliaries. It is one of the largest expeditions ever organized to subjugate the Incas. They depart during the month of May, by the usual route from Ollantaytambo to the Chuquichaca bridge.

Hurtado does not have to find his way. At this time the province of Vilcabamba is neither "lost" nor "unlocatable," as Bingham will believe and write. Moreover, the expeditionists are guided by Alonso Xuarez, one of the emissaries of the viceroy Marqués de Cañete, who, several years earlier, came here to take Sayri Tupac back to Lima. Thus, he knows exactly where its dangerous passages are, and he can describe in advance the forts and other defenses along this well-traveled road; undoubtedly, they have since been further consolidated by the Incas.

The hero of this war will be a Spanish captain with a particularly illustrious name: Martín Garcia de Oñaz de Loyola (nephew of the famous Jesuit), who is married to the sister of Tupac Amaru, the very man he is implacably pursuing. Daring, cynicism, guile, and greed make this knight of the order of Calatrava a prototype of the cloak-and-dagger adventurer. In his written, sworn "testimony," we read that the viceroy Toledo "offered a reward of 1,000 Indian pesos a year for two lifetimes to whoever captured the Inca." Garcia de Loyola was therefore among the first to sign up for the campaign, "as a captain ready to depart for said war with his company of high-placed personages; there he would fight alongside his soldiers, even fighting hand to hand, and would cause the deaths of many Indians and Inca captains."

From skirmishes to ambushes, nothing would impede or

halt the intrepid conquistador on a rout strewn with "many difficult parts, many mountains and swamps."

Arriving at the Chuquichaca bridge, the Spanish troop spots the camp set up by Tupac Amaru on the opposite bank. "We had our first encounter with the Inca and his men, even though the river separated us," Ocampo notes.

Why was Tupac Amaru so imprudent as to rush to meet the enemy, as far away as the "golden bridge"? Did he intend to fortify this key post of the sacred region of Vilcabamba, which sealed off the entrance to the province? And did he not have time? This historic bridge, which played a principal role in these crucial years, was all the more famous because the Incas once came here to worship one of the great idols of ancient Peru, the *huaca* Cancha Viracocha, erected alongside the river. When the *curaca* Chuquillasca, chieftain of a hostile tribe, tried to block Manco Inca's passage during his flight to Viticos, the Inca had the traitor's head cut off and threw it from this bridge into the torrent, near the confluence of the Urubamba and Vilcabamba rios.

"With four rounds of small artillery and the soldiers' harquebuses," writes Ocampo, "our forces defeated them and forced the Inca to withdraw, thereby gaining this bridge, which was no small matter for the royal camp, because these barbarians forgot to burn or destroy it." With their spirits so imbued with magical beliefs, the Incan warriors never could, in fact, get accustomed to the infernal roar of the cannon and of European firearms, which reverberated like an immense organ in the thousand echoes of the cordilleras. To their ears this noise sounded too much like the thundering voice of Illapa, the god of thunder greatly feared and venerated by the Indians— even to this day. Panicking, Tupac Amaru's warriors hastily retreated to the closest forts.

Garcia de Loyola waits for nightfall before sending his advanced guard across the bridge and 2 leagues into the Inca's territory. His men find the route so terrifying that, when the first rays of dawn illumine the landscape, many hesitate to set forth as their companions did in the dark. Enormous mountains loom before them, flanking a constricted, hilly gorge traversed by stone-bedded torrents which sweep along at a steep angle. Terrible avalanches of mud and rocks crash down during heavy rains.

Garcia de Loyola sends several men on a reconnaissance mission, dressed in clothing taken from Indians "so that, thus disguised, they would not be recognized and could discover what lay ahead."

Estéban de Rivera relates that the Inca's warriors have retrenched in the fortified pass of Chuquillasca, whence they are attacking on three sides. Slingstones rain from on high; quick, silent arrows emanate from below; lancers guard the entrances. The Indians fight spiritedly, and Garcia de Loyola is forced to deal with a prolonged resistance before he manages to make the enemy withdraw.

IN THE VALLEY OF THE FORTS

A furious chase ensues. Heading his company, Garcia de Loyola advances—despite a thousand difficulties—along a narrow ledge suspended over an abyss. Hidden behind a rock, an Indian warrior named Huallpa jumps on him, grabs him, and tries to push him over the edge, before the conquistador has a chance to unsheathe his sword. Garcia de Loyola owes his life solely to the presence of mind of a native of Yucay, Corello, who serves him faithfully and, managing to pull the weapon from its scabbard, cuts off the leg of his racial brother. Henceforth this place will bear the evocative name of "Loyola's Leap."

Foiling the plans of Tupac Amaru's spies, the Spaniards slip through several ambushes, taking prisoners. However, they are trounced on Mount Coyaochaca. The first to arrive, General Hurtado de Arbieto, stands up to the assailants, but his thirty soldiers are decimated in a narrow pass hemmed in by fortified slopes for over a kilometer.

A servant of the viceroy Toledo who participated in the Vilcabamba campaign, Antonio Capata, informs his fellow adventurers that a little farther along they will come across Pampaconas, "the Inca's livestock and foodstuff reserves."

Located at an altitude of over 3,000 meters, this city comprises some 300 houses lashed by a glacial wind. The Spanish soldiers, most of them sick, reach it at last.

The royal camp will recuperate in Pampaconas, Titu Cusi's old military base, for thirteen days. Indecision prevails among the leaders of the punitive expedition. What route should they take to get to Vilcabamba la Vieja? That already followed by the guide Alonso Xuarez, when he escorted Sayri Tupac, or, rather, a circuitous route that would avoid the redoubtable "Valley of the Forts" (a veritable Maginot line), designed by the Incas to prevent access to the ancient sacred refuge?

Garcia de Loyola always used problems to his advantage. Thus, he enlists the allegiance of Puma Inca, an Indian chieftain so far allied with Tupac Amaru; Puma Inca leaves the ranks of his own kind to join those of the conquistadors. Not only does he betray his fellow Indians, he draws a sketch of the fortified slopes, the most important of which (it is in fact impregnable, he says) is outlined in the distance. A dizzying mountain, "no wider than the blade of a sword" and at least 200 paces long, topped by watchtowers and walls pierced with lookouts, stands between them and the Huayna Pukara, the "Young Fortress." After their defeat at Chuquillasca, the greatly diminished Incan forces have placed their last hope in this strategic point, which has been reinforced over the past dozen years and is as well equipped for defense as it is for attack. A multitude of *lanceros*, *flecheros*, and *honderos*, skillfully wielding lances, bows, and slings, and warriors armed with heavy, star-shaped stone clubs are firmly entrenched there. There is no way to get through to Vilcabamba! Puma Inca thinks of another way to seize the forts: from the heights. But Garcia de Loyola must first consent to leave the horses at Pampaconas. Doubling their precautions, he leads his troops on foot, with ten days' provisions, into the gorge where no doubt the enemy intends to crush them.

Enormous reserves of slingstones and sections of rock are piled up on the slopes, ready to be hurled down onto the royal camp, which must follow the course of the torrent. Hurtado de Arbieto marches beneath this primitive but deadly grapeshot, arriving "within harquebus shot" of the fortress, where he runs up against a dense barrier made of stakes and bamboo pikes imbued with poisonous herbs.

The masterwork of the Incas is perched on an extremely high sierra; its most obvious advantage is its steep, jagged slopes. From afar, Garcia de Loyola can discern the entrance to the fortress, "barely wide enough for one man to pass through." At first sight, Huayna Pukara seems so well defended by nature as to be impregnable—were it not for the subterfuge suggested by the Indian traitor.

While Hurtado de Arbieto distracts the Incan forces at the bottom of the gorge, Garcia de Loyola climbs up to the heights by way of the unused, debris-strewn slope. Puma Inca was right: The enemy has not bothered to guard this side. Still, the maneuver is an act of heroism on the part of the Spaniards weighed down with helmets and armor, encumbered by heavy harquebuses and pieces of artillery, at an altitude which, with its cold, rarefied air, makes every effort painful.

Garcia de Loyola relies on his familiarity with the enemy's mistakes. He knows that if the attack does not take place exactly as the Incan forces have calculated, the element of surprise will work in his favor and disconcert them.

According to Puma Inca, the Young Fortress is being defended by Tupac Amaru in person; his best strategist, Quispetitu (Titu Cusi's son); and the most valiant of his military chieftains, Gualpa Yupanqui, who is greatly admired by the Indian hordes.

But is Tupac Amaru actually still there? Those who took part in the battle disagree on this point in the history of the "war of Vilcabamba." Hurtado de Arbieto claims that, thinking themselves done for, Tupac Amaru and Quispetitu had abandoned Huayna Pukara the previous evening, and went to await the Christians at Vilcabamba, leaving the defense to General Colla Topa and captains Caspina and Sutti, who resisted furiously before deserting. If we accept this version, we must assume that, since this fortress has been fortified over a ten-year period, something unexpected must happen that prompts Tupac Amaru to give up defending it himself. Perhaps Puma Inca's treason demoralizes him; he knows that his old confidant will reveal to the Spaniards the secrets of the planned line of retreat. But let us listen, instead, to Garcia de Loyola, the astute leader. According to his testimony,[1] presented to the viceroy Francisco de Toledo, the Inca was indeed at Huayna Pukara,

---

[1] One of the most important of the *Informaciones, provisiones reales, testimonios, memoriales, y juramentos auténticos* drawn up starting in 1572 by the conquistadors of Vilcabamba

"lying in wait for the advance of the royal camp on the opposite slope of the mountain, ready to give the signal for attack to several hundred Indians who were only awaiting his word to go into action." But the sudden outbreak of the Spanish mercenaries, who literally "jumped them from behind," startled and confused the defenders of the fort, who fled pell-mell. Tupac Amaru, Quispetitu, and Gualpa managed to get away and hide in the mountains, thanks to the devotion of the Incan captains who sacrificed themselves to delay the attackers.

For Tupac Amaru and the last of his followers, the fall of the principal fortress represented an irreparable loss which rapidly led to their downfall.

THE STORMING OF VILCABAMBA LA VIEJA

A few secondary defenses still remain: to Machu Pukara, Hatun Pukara, Marcanay. When the Spaniards reach the *estrechura* of Vilcabamba, the most hemmed-in place in the valley, men are replaced by women, who fight fiercely. For four days, they pour down tons of rocks and stones from the peaks where they are firmly entrenched above the royal camp. Before resuming their march, Hurtado de Arbieto and Garcia de Loyola must wait until the enemy has exhausted the supply of ammunition. Then their path is clear all the way to the forbidden city.

"It is thus," Garcia de Loyola proudly asserts, "that my company and I (50 harquebusiers, 25 *rodeleros* armed with *rondaches*, 500 Cañari Indians and other natives), with the greatest possible effort and danger, scaled and captured the aforesaid fortress and the province and the place of Vilcabamba."

In a letter dated April 15, 1581, claiming a reward which he still has not received nine years later, Pedro Sarmiento de Gamboa standardbearer for the royal camp, "who took part in the war of Vilcabamba, from the beginning to the end," informs Philip II that he *"entered Vilcabamba la*

---

and accompanied by "demands for rewards" for the capture of Tupac Amaru: these documents constituted a 400-page volume recounting the capture of the "capital of the Inca."

Vieja and claimed it in the name of His Majesty on Tuesday, June 24, 1572, the feast day of St. John the Baptist, at ten o'clock in the morning."[2]

Finally, the viceroy Toledo lifts his pen to write a letter "on the subject of the victory gained at Vilcabamba over the Indians, and the prison of the Incas, the execution of Tupac Amaru, and the discovery of the Punchao idol," in which he stipulates that *"the province of Vilcabamba was conquered,* leaving not an Inca dead or alive, nor descendants of them, nor captains, nor idols that fell into our hands, in this land where all is asperity and where it seemed incredible to think that one could rout out enemies so well fortified and entrenched."

Like all the other conquistadors, Garcia de Loyola and Sarmiento de Gamboa probably hoped to claim for their own the fabulous treasures stored, according to popular tradition, in the mysterious "University of Idolatry" which Father Calancha described—without ever having seen it. Now, regardless of what Toledo writes about their victory, how profoundly disappointed they must be! There is no sign of all the sorcerers and magi, or the chaste Virgins of the Sun so lusted after; the ancient sanctuary is totally deserted. A stirring silence reigns in the solar temple, where a few imperial mummies rise up like ghosts, their faces veiled by a fine net of gold, under the mute surveillance of Manco Inca, who seems to defy the stupefied hidalgos one last time.

The Spaniards will find nearby, hiding in the jungle that surrounds the forbidden city, old people, women, and children whom the Inca left there, because he could not burden himself with them or perhaps because he doubted their loyalty. Monumental palaces, pyramidal *huacas,* temples, and the 400 stone houses of the city are in flames—set on fire by the fugitives, or by the Spanish advance guard? Father Calancha reports, "The first soldiers who penetrated Vilcabamba left neither silver nor gold, slitting the throats of thousands of Indians in order to steal from them, and set the place on fire."

---

[2] The words that I have emphasized are those *omitted* by Bingham, which accounts for his repeated erroneous assertions to the effect that Vilcabamba was never found by the Spaniards. The testimonies quoted, which can easily be checked, formally refute this assertion.

THE INCA FLEES THROUGH THE JUNGLE

But were the fabulous treasures really pillaged? They are still being sought unflaggingly, to this day.

From the military standpoint, General Hurtado's disappointment is no less great. The Inca has once again escaped with his best chieftains and eighty Indians. They are fleeing toward Zapacati, where the Inca took the precaution of sending reserves of provisions and clothes a few days earlier.

Meanwhile, Gaspar de Sotelo, Toledo's messenger, arrives in Vilcabamba bearing a letter in which the viceroy expresses his fears: If the Inca succeeds in taking refuge among the "savages" lurking amid the forests that carpet the horizon, and especially among his fierce allies, the terrible Manaries warriors, he will surely return to the fray before long and renew hostilities. This would greatly displease the king of Spain, for, as long as the province of Vilcabamba is not cleared of all the Incas and "principal leaders," his majesty's possessions—as well as the city that the general wishes to establish there, to be populated with Spaniards—will not be safe. It is advisable to overtake the fugitive Inca at all costs.

Who will take off on the heels of Tupac Amaru? This time it is no longer a question of storming giant mountains but of plunging into the damp, unknown depths of the "Green Hell," a province so poorly thought of that is was considered uninhabitable for anyone but the Mitimaes, a type of dedicated settler whom the Inca sent "to guard his idols, *huacas,* and special objects."

What does it matter to Garcia de Loyola that his men are emaciated, ragged, trembling with swamp fever? Bewitched by the mirage of royal rewards promised to whoever catches Tupac Amaru, he again volunteers for the final act of this insane drama.

A war council is hastily called, which assigns him the mission of pursuing the Inca, capturing him, and recovering the most famous golden idol of the Sun, the Punchao, as great a symbol of the Indian resistance as the Inca himself, and its magnet. Fifty soldiers chosen from among the least exhausted will accompany Garcia de Loyola, under the command of captains Francisco de Camayo, Alonso de Carvajal, Francisco de Valenzuela, Meneses, and Sarmiento de Gamboa. All—each in his own fashion—will emphasize in their written reports the unprecedented dangers of the enterprise and the indomitable energy of their leader.

Garcia uses the tactic that has served him so well so far: He questions the natives of Vilcabamba. Whether out of fear or in order to find favor with the victors or to take revenge on the Inca, some of them give him correct information.

Thus, the Spaniards set out "amid an unhealthy terrain, harsh and mountainous, where it is difficult to make progress because of the great heat, inundated by rains." They flounder in the swamps for three days before reaching the indigenous village of Panqui, where, unfortunately, part of the Inca's retinue has lingered—"two of his brothers, one of his daughters, four nephews, several Mamacunas, a few Virgins of the Sun, and many of his Chosen Women." The conquistadors seize them, along with the gold ornaments and insignia of Tupac Amaru. Quispetitu and his family are also captured.

An Indian from Tanqui betrays the Inca, revealing to Garcia de Loyola the secret place, on a nearby promontory, where the famous "very crucial" captain Cusi Paucar must be hiding. He has been in charge of the Indian militia during the entire Vilcabamba campaign; capturing him is of the utmost importance.

Tupac Amaru has left forty-eight hours earlier, with the last of his followers, who have sworn on the *huacas* to follow him to their deaths. Given the impossibility of penetrating any farther into the dense jungle, Garcia de Loyola, encumbered with numerous prisoners and heavy booty, hastily returns to Vilcabamba with his take and then sets out again without stopping to catch his breath.

Taking advantage of this brief respite, Gualpa Yupanqui organizes Tupac Amaru's retreat: The Inca will head for the province of the Manaries, rich in fertile land and vast prairies. Having long been vassals and friends of the empire of the Tahuantinsuyo, these warriors, who are considered invincible, inhabit vast expanses in the Amazon Basin. These are "well-formed, light-skinned Indians, whose very pretty women are beautifully clothed."

The Manaries have at their disposal a flotilla of light canoes, which Tupac Amaru and his men quickly board. But Garcia de Loyola and his rabid soldiery tail the Inca.

At Huambos they catch up with the imperial rear guard, which is attempting to embark in turn. A few Indians manage to vanish into the thick forest, but eight others, captured, indicate that Tupac Amaru is headed toward the tropical valley of Momori, by way of a very uneven terrain.

Fearing that those who fled will warn the Inca of the imminent danger, Garcia de Loyola has his men assemble five large rafts, and they set out on the torrential river, amid gigantic whirlpools caused by submerged rocks which threaten to tear apart the balsa logs tied together with lianas.

A few leagues farther downriver the proud cacique Ispaca, chieftain of the Manaries, appears beside the rio, surrounded by hundreds of *flecheros*, their bows arched, ready to let fly at the Spaniards. Garcia de Loyola relates the outcome of the encounter in a letter addressed to Philip II, upon the expedition's return: "Thanks to the greatest, most skillful cunning in my possession," he writes, "I made friends with them, and with clever words and a few presents I pressed them into the service of his majesty."

Ispaca agrees to supply the conquistadors with the products of his warm land: guavas, *paltas* (avocado pears), cloves of *pacae*, coconuts. And he helps them out of a trap set by Opaca, *curaca* of the Pilcozon Indians. Moreover, he has a solid balsa raft built for them, aboard which Francisco de Camayo and a few brave men will ride the wild current of the Rio Pilcozones to try to take Gualpa Yupanqui, guardian of the marvelous golden Punchao, by surprise. Held up by the weight of the idol (which symbolizes Father Sun in all his light), the Inca general—along with the bearers overwhelmed by fatigue—camps, come evening, on a slope so precipitous that, unaware of Ispaca's treason, he thinks himself safe. Francisco de Camayo descends on him in his sleep.

It's all over for the Incas! The solid-gold Sun, haloed by golden rays, that has illumined their triumphant course for centuries is extinguished forever.

With the tenacity of a hound dog, Garcia de Loyola tracks down Tupac Amaru, who, because his wife is about to give birth, has had to give up the perilous navigation of the rapids. He withdraws *tierra adentro*, through luxuriant underbrush, trying to reach the fortified bastions of the province of the Manaries. The horrible pursuit drags on for two more days. Barefoot and in rags, the Spaniards cover 20 leagues in the most tangled of torrid forests, without food, sustained by greed.

At last they perceive, huddled beneath a tree, Tupac Amaru, tenderly protecting his exhausted young wife. He surrenders without a fight.

TOWARD THE MARVELOUS PAITITI

Few historiographers thus far have been concerned with locating, with any degree of precision, the place where the last of the Incas was captured. Sarmiento de Gamboa is content to confirm that he "personally overtook the Inca, with the greatest of efforts, costs, and risks to his person and life." But according to the testimony given by Diego Barrantes Perez, the epilogue of Tupac Amaru's tragic odyssey took place "three leagues from the Picha landing, on the Rio Taupa, in the land of the Manaries"—a rio that figures on the current maps of modern Peru.

Other mysteries, both well known and obscure, remain.

Did Titu Cusi indeed die near Viticos, as the Spaniards were led to believe? Nothing proves it definitely. In fact, there is nothing to indicate it with any degree of certainty. The only eyewitnesses, Father Diego Ortiz and the mestizo Pando, were executed, and the monk Marcos Garcia drowned while trying to flee.

Did the Incas perhaps invent the versions of the possible "poisoning" of the Inca a few years later, to serve their hidden interests? This is only a hypothesis. But in view of their long, unusual, and incomprehensible silence concerning Titu Cusi's disappearance, might one not suppose that, fearing a final disaster, he decided to leave to Tupac Amaru—now of an age to reign—the place he had usurped? And that he withdrew in time, with the majority of the beautiful Virgins of the Sun (who disappeared just as mysteriously), to a secret, hidden city *such as Machu Picchu?* This could explain the absolute and very unusual silence of the chroniclers, who were kept in ignorance concerning the "Lost City" on the Old Peak of the valley of the Rio of the Sun for this very reason.

Finally, was Tupac Amaru really captured with his entire family, as Toledo believed and boasted to the king of Spain? After reading documents from archives that

most Americanists have overlooked, I came away with
doubts. Did some brother or close relative of the Inca
succeed in escaping to the Amazonian jungle, with the
famous "treasures," which have never been found? Perhaps
much farther than Machu Picchu or Vilcabamba la Vieja,
in the inviolate labyrinth of the undiscoverable, marvelous
Paititi[3]—there where several expeditions that set out in
search of them had gotten lost, ever since the sixteenth
century and even quite recently.

But this is yet another intriguing mystery.

[3] See *La Rivière du maïs* by Bernard Lelong (Jean-Claude
Lattes, Editeur).

CHAPTER EIGHT

The Fall of Tupac Amaru and of the Golden Punchao

> *When we told you that we spoke with the Sun and that it dictated to us what we must do, it was a lie, for a piece of gold cannot speak! . . . My brother Titu Cusi tells me that what I should have worshipped was what was inside the Punchao, the Golden Sun, made from the hearts of the Incas, our ancestors.*
>
> —Tupac Amaru, 1572

THE CURSE AND THE MYTH OF INCARI

No one can read the accounts of the chroniclers of the late sixteenth century without being moved. In unison, all describe—with an emotion they cannot hide—Tupac Amaru's lugubrious march back to Cuzco and to his death.

Richly adorned in red velvet, a shirt, and a woolen mantle, and shod in multicolored sandals, the Inca, always proud, wears across his brow the *mascapaicha*, which he refuses to take off, even when Garcia de Loyola subjects him to threats and blows. Followed by the imperial escort, he enters Cuzco, "laden with gold chains, one of which, encircling his neck, connects him to Garcia, who leads him like a dog on a leash." He is locked up in the colossal palace of Colcampata. By a strange coincidence—or perhaps the better to mark the irremediable fall of the Incan Empire—this palace, which was built in the eleventh or twelfth century by Ayar Manco Capac, the first of the line of the founders of the now moribund dynasty, will be the final abode of the Incas. Tupac Amaru will leave only "mounted on a mule caparisoned for high mourning," for the grim parade through the narrow paved lanes of the ancient holy city and capital of the Tahuantinsuyo.

Tupac Amaru has donned a white wool tunic. Crucifix in hand, he advances slowly, majestic and dignified, accompanied by the Jesuit Alonso de Barrana and Father Cristobal de Molina, preacher to the Indians. Four hundred Cañaris, lances at the ready, surround the cortege.

The Inca is condemned to decapitation. (How many heads—conquistadors' as well as Incas'—have rolled since 1532!) What bitter thoughts run through Tupac Amaru's mind as he passes, for the last time, through the city, the "golden navel" and "center of the world" of his omnipotent ancestors? Does he even recognize it? For on the monolithic foundation of superb edifices that have been dismantled there now rise the pastel-painted walls of the rich *casonas* occupied by noble hidalgos. Gaps rend the cyclopean walls made of dark cubes of polished granite. Windows and grills with arabesques of forged iron have been installed, as well as heavy wooden doors studded with copper and silver. On the enormous lintels of the ancient *portadas*, where Amarus (sacred serpents of the Quechua Olympus) coil in relief, blazons adorned with maned lions and portraits of bearded conquistadors have been sculpted. The austere inner courtyards of the pre-Columbian palaces have been transformed into cheerful, flower-filled patios in the Andalusian style, surrounded by shaded galleries. A jet of water rises from a central fountain, and horses hitched to shiny carriages prance beneath the porches.

The Inca has difficulty concealing his surprise when he discovers, on one side of the monumental Aucaypata—the imperial plaza where his forebears once sat in state on golden thrones, covered by canopies of iridescent feathers —the gleaming cathedral whose Churrigueresque facade and baroque colonnades emphasize the striking contrast between two very opposite worlds.

Thousands of weeping Indians crowd the plaza and its environs. Catching sight of the Cañari executioner sharpening the blade of his ax, Tupac Amaru remains serene. Nonetheless, what hatred must fester in his heart at the sight of this Indian, whose implacable race is finally triumphing over that of the Sons of the Sun!

When the Inca arrives at the execution site, the crowd lets out a cry so rending, so despairing, that some of the most hardened Spaniards among those who worked toward his death cannot hold back their tears. Abruptly, when Tupac Amaru holds up his hand, there is a silence, even more poignant. He is about to deliver one of the most astonishing speeches in the entire history of dethroned kings: "I deserve this death," he says in a firm tone of voice, "because as a young child, *I disobeyed and annoyed my mother, who then cursed me*. She predicted that I would die decapitated. And the prediction is coming true today. O my people, never curse your children!"

This strange public avowal leaves the Quechuas speechless, and the conquistadors as well, but for quite different reasons: for the populace, because it is something unexpected, revealing a secret hitherto guarded; for the Spaniards, because there is something ridiculous about this "confession." Taken aback for a moment, the Catholic priests quickly recover and wax indignant, guessing the Inca's strategy. Why, when about to die, does Tupac Amaru reveal the maternal curse? To deprive his justiciaries of the opportunity to immolate an idolator for the glory of an intruder god. It is a subtle and extraordinary maneuver designed to convince the Indian people that the Inca will die not according to the wishes of the foreigners, who have assassinated his cosmic lineage, but through his own fault, and that of his mother!

Of course, the clergy present at this unimaginable scene will protest that Tupac Amaru died "according to God's will." Nevertheless, many Christians cannot help but admire the noble ideal of the condemned man. They turn out by the hundreds to march—led by the bishop of Cuzco and several Spanish priests—and accompany the Indian crowd, which intends to appeal to the viceroy's clemency and request that he pardon the Inca and send him in exile to Spain, so that he may there be judged impartially.

The emotion is so intense that the hardened Toledo appears moved. Will he yield to this plea for one last chance? As at Cajamarca, at the time of Atahualpa's summary execution, it certainly seems that a "production" has been orchestrated. His reins pulled up short, a knight scatters the crowd with his club, and his mount tramples the Indians who fall. It is Juan de Soto, who violently calls for the Inca's head, which Toledo grants him without further ado.

Tupac Amaru says "goodbye to his Father the Sun, good-bye to his beloved people." Already the bells of the cathedrals and those of countless monasteries, convents, and Colonial-style churches are sounding the death knell. And it is in the dust of earth once brought from the four *suyos* of the monumental Empire of the Incas to cover the sacred plaza of Cuzco that the head of the last of them rolls.

The Indians pick up this head, which nature had never favored during the Inca's life, as if it were a precious treasure. According to popular tradition, once it was impaled on a lance, it began "to grow so beautiful" that every hour the crowd of Quechuas contemplating it and adoring it grew denser.

For two days and two nights, 12,000 to 15,000 nobles and great chieftains loyal to the Inca call to their dead ruler unremittingly, prostrated before the "miraculous" head. The Spaniards go crazy listening to this fantastic lamentation, which keeps growing louder. Since no threat or punishment succeeds in putting a stop to the lugubrious din, and the human tide threatens to overwhelm the Spanish military forces, the viceroy orders that Tupac Amaru's head be buried with his body, which was laid to rest in a crypt in the cathedral, "and that masses, with organ music, be said for the repose of the soul of the Inca, who was a great lord."

The shouting finally dies down. But, in silence, the Indians begin to await—to hope for—the resurrection of the Son of the Sun, which the remarkable legend of Incari (the Inca king) predicts to this day, throughout the heart of the Andes.[1] And on the majestic peaks of the cordilleras, hidden from the eyes—and greed—of the whites and visible only to the Sun Inti, the "lost cities" of Viticos, Vilcabamba la Vieja, Paititi, Machu Picchu, and many others

---

[1] The Peruvian folklorist José Maria Arguedas has recorded one of the most popular versions of the myth of Incari: "It was long ago that the Inca [the native race] was routed by the State-King [Spanish domination] and his body was cut into small pieces, which were scattered and buried throughout Peru. But underground, his body lives on, and it is gradually reuniting, to be reborn in all its vigor. When this happens, he will go to find the head buried beneath the governor's palace, and he will drive the invader away."

will guard for four centuries (and some of them perhaps forever) the unfathomable secrets and unlocatable treasures of the Incas.

THE MYSTERY OF THE PUNCHAO

But what became of the famous gleaming gold idol of the Sun, the confiscation of which the Spaniards considered as important as the Inca's person, to the extent that it made the Vilcabamba campaign not only a military struggle, but a sort of holy war? Yet another mystery.

No chronicler, swooning with admiration in describing it, had any idea how to sketch it so that we could reconstruct its true likeness. However, whether they were men of war or men of letters, all who carried out and commented upon the Conquest of the land of the Incas understood the essential place that the extremely opulent Punchao occupied in the cosmogony and stately solar religion of the Tahuantinsuyo.

Garcilaso de la Vega, a mestizo who grew up in Cuzco (he was the same age as Sayri Tupac, whose playmate he was), speaks of "the face of the Sun, shaped in a plate of gold, twice as thick as all those which adorned the walls of the House of the Sun . . . with a round face haloed by rays and flames—all in one piece, neither greater nor smaller than painters depict it"—painters from Spain, that is.

Father Blas Valera, of Indian descent, describes "a gold idol painted like the Sun, with its rays," in a niche in the wall at the Coricancha, the marvelous Temple of Gold. For Gutierrez de Santa Clara, the effigy of the Sun amounts to the representation "of a man the size of a good *rondache*, one digit thick, with no relief, but well polished and arranged in such a way that when it is struck by the rays of the real sun, rising, the false sun shoots forth great flashes of light."

For the author of the *Crónica anónima*, written around 1600, the Punchao represented not only the Sun but the "Lord of the Day: creator of Light, *of the Sun*, the Stars, and all other things." It was made of extremely pure solid gold, with "earlobes like those of the Orejones, pierced by thick plugs of chased gold."

A few complementary, but equally cursory, descriptions show the Punchao surrounded by rays abundantly inlaid with emeralds and other precious gems, "made in the shape of the Inca seated on a gold *tiana*." A fringe of red wool, "in the style of the kings of Cuzco," bound the idol's brow, "as do the *llautas* [woolen turbans worn by the Quechuas], but without the fringe, the royal insignia."

The gold rays stemmed from the shoulders and back. But something even more extraordinary accounts for the great value of this statue, "which dictated the laws of the cult and of the solar religion in the entire realm," as Francisco de Toledo wrote Garcia de Loyola, to emphasize for him its important role and to order him to see to its all-important seizure. From the gold bench on which the Punchao was seated there rose, "like a sugarloaf," a protuberance composed of the pulverized hearts of dead emperors, covered and preserved by a fine layer of gold, whose point was embedded in the idol's entrails. "The Incas wished to express thus the idea that Apu Punchao carried the emperors to heaven, in the most intimate recesses of his soul and body," writes the anonymous chronicler.

Titu Cusi's advice to his young half-brother Tupac Amaru shows the great symbolic value of the "contents" of this sort of Holy Grail: it is not the "silent" gold that should be worshipped, he tells him, but "what is inside."

Toledo, writing to Cardinal de S——, says that "when the sun struck the Punchao, it made it shine so brilliantly that one could never look at the idol itself but only see its brilliance." In a letter to the king of Spain, he specifies, "The disks of solid gold that surrounded it were removed by Spanish soldiers when they claimed their share of the booty." Nonetheless, he adds, "this demon, whose force was recognized by the inhabitants of the territory of Vilca-bamba and who had wreaked so much havoc since the reign of the seventh Inca," seemed to him still to be—even with its rays removed—"a replica worthy of being sent to his holiness the pope." Did the viceroy send the idol to Spain? Did it arrive? Was it offered to the pope, or was it, rather, stolen and melted down? Is it still preserved in some forgotten corner of the Vatican? Or hidden away in a private collection? No one knows.

MANY GOLDEN SUNS

Does anyone have any better idea where the famous idol was kept during the glorious age of Tahuantinsuyo? And who had it made? It seems that the Apu Punchao was fashioned right in Cuzco, by the skilled master goldsmiths of the Inca Pachacutec, "in the shape of a statue of a naked child," as it appeared to him in a dream. Apparently a golden Sun constantly illuminated the interior of the imperial residence dedicated to Father Sun of the Incas, the Coricancha. But was this the Punchao? According to several chroniclers, the image was so large that it covered the entire front of the Temple of Gold, "from one wall to the other"—that is, a diameter of *18 meters!* Is it possible to imagine that Manco Inca could have succeeded in hiding so monumental an effigy under the Spaniards' very noses? Who could have transported it for days on end, over paths scarcely wide enough for the passage of one Indian, and over ice-covered peaks 4,000 meters high? Would it have been possible for Tupac Amaru, thus encumbered, to penetrate the tangled underbrush of the Amazonian forest and to embark on fragile balsa rafts spinning amid the whirlpools and rapids? It's unlikely—for us, with our modern outlook. But was anything impossible for the Incas, who were capable of hoisting and transporting monoliths weighing 100 metric tons and more?

I think, however, that numerous golden Suns must have illuminated the sacred route of the kings of Cuzco, throughout the ages and the various reigns. Undoubtedly—as it was their custom to do for all the divine representations of the planetary gods forming a swarming Andean cosmogony, for the alter egos of the kings, and for the venerated mummies—they moved all these golden Suns and Apu Punchaos around, in turn, from temples to liturgical way stations, from *huacas* to sanctuaries, in accordance with the dates of the feasts in their ritual calendar, to "display" them in their domains and offer them sacrifices (often children and pretty young women) to the sound of dances and chants accompanied by "human drums."[2] However,

[2] The conquistador Alonso de Mesa reports, "The Incas would kill the enemy captains and *curacas* who offer resistance or whom they suspect of wishing to rebel, leave their heads and

Father Calancha stipulates that the Punchao was usually kept in the Casa del Sol de Chuquipalpa, near Viticos. This would explain why the two Augustinian monks were so intent on burning the "house of the Inca Devil"—becoming, for this very reason, so odious to Titu Cusi. It would also explain the anger they aroused among the high priests of the most famous idol of the empire.

But it is fitting to note that, since Ortiz and Garcia do not boast of having found and destroyed the solar idol, it is because they did not find it there. Should one assume that Titu Cusi, wary of the monks' "apostolic fever," moved it in time, in order to hide it in the "University of Idolatry" so carefully guarded from the monks' sight? And that Tupac Amaru hoped to carry it into the heart of the jungle, as far as the inviolable Paititi?

The fall of the Punchao marked not only the end of the esoteric religion of Father Sun but, in addition to the death of the Incas, the end of one of the most prodigious civilizations that the world had ever known or will ever know.

---

arms intact, debone them, and fill them with ashes. And from the belly they make drums." Mesa adds that when the wind stirred the arms of these tom-tom men, "they would beat themselves."

CHAPTER NINE

In Search of Viticos and Vilcabamba

> *There are other ruins on the road to Vilca-*
> *bamba, the Sacred Pampa . . . Hidden at*
> *the bottom of these mysterious valleys, far-*
> *ther than Viticos, there must one find the*
> *hidden sanctuaries where sleep, amid the*
> *dark night of time, the gods who one day*
> *will leave Machu Picchu, surrounded by the*
> *mummies of their ancestors, by the soul of*
> *their race, and by the treasures that the faith*
> *of mankind has bequeathed them.*
> —Jorge Cornejo Bouroncle, 1958

OVER THREE CENTURIES OF OBLIVION

Atahualpa strangled at Cajamarca . . . Manco Inca stabbed at Viticos . . . poison for Sayri Tupac and Titu Cusi . . . Tupac Amaru decapitated at Cuzco . . . The Pizarros and the Almagros . . . all victims of violent death! After thirty-six years of a *guerrilla* bathed in blood, as in the ancient tragedies, the curtain of oblivion falls on the finale of the Empire of the Incas and their fabulous "lost cities."

However, despite the desperate uprisings of their descendants Santos Atahualpa Apu Inca and Condorcanqui Tupac Amaru II in the eighteenth century, despite the indigenist liberation movement led by Simón Bolívar in Cuzco a century later, 7 or 8 million Indians of the Andes, isolated from the rest of the world by the grandiose checkerboard of the sierra, have been prolonging the epilogue for 400 years. They continue to live "the Inca way," to speak Runa Simi, the language of the Quechuas; they have kept nearly intact the multimillenary beliefs, rites, and customs. Currently there exist in Peru some 5,000 agrarian communities, or *ayllus*, of the pre-Columbian type (each comprising an average of 200 or 300 individuals), duly recognized by the Peruvian republic, but abandoned to their own fate, in view of their natural isolation.

It happens that these *ayllus* have retained their original names. But if a town enclosed in a fold of the Andes has changed names, the work of investigators becomes that much more difficult, and sometimes the rebus is impossible to decipher. This is the case with many of the historical sites of the Sacred Valley of the Urubamba and the gorges of the Vilcabamba. From 1572 to 1911, this entire region, very closely tied to the Inca saga, underwent a profound lethargy. Then suddenly, with Hiram Bingham, a secret panel is revealed.

Nevertheless, even though he categorizes it as "the Lost City of the Incas," Bingham leaves the mysterious city that he has just discovered, because he has a feeling that, despite the splendor of the ruins (located on a summit overlooking the Urubamba Valley, and not the valley of the Rio Vilcabamba, as so many chroniclers indicated), this must not be —cannot be—Viticos, his original objective, which must be sought much farther north.

No sooner has Bingham stumbled upon Machu Picchu than he sets off again, haphazardly! He first goes off in search of the famous "great white rock over a spring of fresh water" (the Yurac Rumi described by Father Calancha), "the principal center of Sun worship" close by Viticos.

THE INCA CHAPEL OF YURAC RUMI

Hiram Bingham hopes that, beyond the Chuquichaca bridge, near Chaullay, the Indians and *hacenderos* will speak to him of Viticos. But, on the contrary, no one seems to know this name, which they swear they have never heard of; nor, moreover, have they heard the names of other places where the Indo-Spanish *guerrilla* took place during the Conquest.

Fortune continues to smile on the leader of the Yale

Peruvian Expedition. A tortuous path has just been opened in the granitic precipice beside the Rio Vilcabamba. Small tunnels have been dynamited into the rock. The scenery seems to him to correspond to the jungles and to the very deep gorge described by Ocampo. Atop a sawtoothed mountain (the sierra), at an altitude of 2,500 meters, he reaches San Juan de Lucma—finally, one of the names mentioned by the conquistadors; José de Oricain places it "a half-league north of Viticos."

Mogrevejo, the governor of the province, shows Bingham one of the fortresses from which Yurac Rumi was chased, and points out to him, on the horizon, a truncated mountain, surrounded by a jumble of rocks. Important ruins, he says, lie on the summit, behind a barrier of snow-covered peaks. The Indians of the region know them by their modern name, Rosaspata.

In these ruins dismantled by treasure-seekers, Bingham visits "a residence fit for a royal Inca," which has no windows but is illumined by thirty impressive *portadas*, fifteen on each side. A dozen large rooms are connected by three long corridors.

A partly enclosed compound crowns the hill. It consists of thirteen or fourteen square buildings with a central patio and inner courtyards. Despite the destruction caused by the pillagers, the buildings' perfect symmetry suggests to Bingham the "familiar Inca sense" of architecture. In his view, the ruins of Rosaspata match the chroniclers' descriptions perfectly. He is convinced that this time he has indeed found Viticos, or Vitcos!

The expeditionists follow the trail through thick woods, strewn with carved boulders—one in the shape of a "saddle," another in the form of an Intihuatana, or "sundial nubbin." Suddenly they arrive at an open place called Nusta Ispanna.

Beneath the trees there still remain the ruins of an Incan temple, and, close by, a gigantic granite boulder, one end of which overhangs a small pool of running water, which for this reason appears "black." Now, Father Calancha, in describing Yurac Rumi, notes that "close by Vitcos in a village called Chuquipalpa, is a Casa del Sol and in it a white stone over a spring of water, worshipped as something divine." It was, the chronicler specifies, "the principal *mochadero*[2] of those mountains, where the Devil appeared visibly to the idolators who worshipped him."[3]

Continuing his account, Calancha further writes that this "cruel Devil, leader of a *caterva* [group of minions], was present in this House of the Sun and responded to the idolatrous Indians, for whom he showed a great affection. But he killed or wounded those who ceased to worship him. Thus, he was feared by all; they offered him gifts and sacrifices, and they flocked from great distances and the most remote villages."

It is on August 9, 1911, that Bingham discovers this famous sanctuary, devoured by the jungle and absolutely silent: "an ideal place," he notes, "for practicing the mystic ceremonies of an ancient cult . . . In the days of Titu Cusi, the Inca priests faced the east, greeted the rising sun . . ."[4]

The excavations carried out at Rosaspata by the Yale Peruvian Expedition brought to light "a mass of rough

---

[2] Place where the Indians go to worship an idol, extending their hands toward it, then throwing kisses at it. It is, Calancha explains, "a ceremony of the most profound resignation and reverence."

[3] Calancha is mistaken. The Incas never worshipped the devil. And those who thought they saw him at Yurac Rumi were certainly not the Quechuas but the Spanish monks, zealous "extirpators of idolatry."

[4] This is also the opinion of Victor Angles Vargas, organizer of two Peruvian expeditions in 1968 and 1971, which traced the Incan paths on foot; the first expedition went from Cuzco to Machu Picchu, the second from the Chuquichaca bridge to Vilcabamba (now called Espiritu Pampa). Two kilometers from Pucyura, Angles Vargas in fact passed through Choquepalta and ended up, like Bingham, at Nusta Ispanna. Located at an altitude of 3,000 meters, an enormous boulder, magnificently sculpted into platforms, benches, horizontal moldings, and prismatic peaks, corresponds on every point to Calancha's description. It measures 22 meters long, 16 wide, and 8 high. A great slab of an immaculate whiteness, carved with nine cavities in a row, parallel to four liturgical baths, must be the origin of the ancient name "Yurac Rumi," the "White Stone." As for the name "Nusta Ispanna," it must derive from a curious canalization which stems from a throne carved in the top of the rock and leads to the liturgical baths, which gave the Indians the idea that it must have been the "bidet" or "toilet" of the Inca princess.

potsherds, a few Inca whirl-bobs and bronze shawl-pins, and also a number of iron articles of *European origin*, heavily rusted horseshoe nails, a buckle, *a pair of scissors*." Now, Rodriguez de Figueroa mentions that he offered "two pairs" to Titu Cusi.

Having—in theory—identified Viticos, Manco Inca's political and military capital, what will Bingham look for next? The intriguing traditional and religious center Vilcabamba la Vieja—elusive, like a mirage.

To explain the incredible "disappearance" of this site (which must be hidden, presumably, "at three days' journey"), Bingham becomes increasingly convinced that there "was a period of nearly three hundred years when no one [other than] the ordinary Indian shepherd lived anywhere near Puquiura or Lucma, [which were] extremely difficult of access," until Señor Pancorvo opened his new road.

"Nine generations," Bingham calculates, "lived and died in the province of Vilcabamba between the death of . . . Tupac Amaru and the arrival of the first modern explorers." In conclusion, Bingham states, "It was not until the renaissance of historical and geographical curiosity in the nineteenth century, that it occurred to any one to look for Manco's capital." It would be necessary to specify further that the idea did not occur to *the official scholars*, for countless were the treasure-seekers in the valley who excavated all these ruins, as the geographer Cosme Bueno remarked as early as 1768.

FROM PAMPACONAS TO ESPIRITU PAMPA

Hiram Bingham begins by visiting San Francisco de la Victoria de Vilcabamba, a small mining town which Baltazar de Ocampo founded on October 4, 1571, 3 or 4 leagues from Pucyura, in the Hoyara Valley, at the site of the Incan mines of Ongoy. This city he finds easily. He is even able to enter the old church built by the friars of Nuestra Señora de la Merced, where mass is still said—very rarely, it is true—amid the ruins.

Located at an altitude of 3,600 meters, the colonial village is surrounded by bleak plateaus where, replacing the thousands of llamas and alpacas of the Incas, herds of cattle, sheep, and horses graze. Ocampo notes that "sixty miners" had houses here, constructed near a vein of quartz.

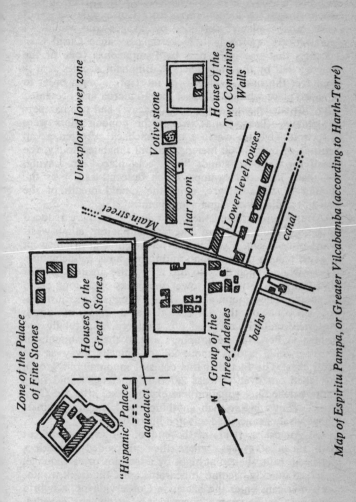

Map of Espíritu Pampa, or Greater Vilcabamba (according to Harth-Terré)

As Bingham learns from the Indian Cuspi Cusi, "Ruins of an Incan town were discovered ten years earlier, toward the northwest, by a *caoutchero* from Conservidayoc"—but in "a terrible place," defended by savages who would not let strangers approach it. Nevertheless, since Cuspi Cusi specifies that one must pass by Pampaconas (one of the places cited by the chroniclers!), Bingham decides that— whatever the risks involved—he must press on in order to find the place where Titu Cusi met Figueroa and presented him with a *guacamayo* parakeet (macaw) and two hampers of peanuts—Pampaconas, where the conquistadors were forced to give up warfare on horseback! Erected at an altitude of over 3,000 meters and still inhabited today, the small town indeed stands "in a cold place." In leaving, Bingham finds the swamps which descend as far as the hamlet of Vista Alegre, amid the humid breath of the forest, teeming with jaguars and pumas.

After having crossed the Rio Vilcabamba, here reduced to a tiny brook, Bingham and his companions climb west- ward once again. Reaching a very high and wind-swept peak, Bingham turns around and thinks he is hallucinating. There where, according to the maps, the gigantic gap of the Apurimac should be, tower the peaks of "a long chain of snow-capped mountains"! Hiram Bingham has just dis- covered one of the largest glaciated areas of South America, neither described nor explored, and totally un- known to Peruvian geographers and to the inhabitants of Cuzco, which is only about 200 kilometers away as the crow flies! The fact that this colossal mountainous group, stretched out over at least 2,000 kilometers, "could have so long defied investigation and exploration" after the Con- quest, "shows better than anything else," Bingham thinks, "how wisely Manco had selected his refuge."

On August 9, 1911, at the end of a horrible path cut with Incan stairways, where they proceeded beneath a persistent rain, shaken at night by a temblor or earthquake, in a heat quickly become unbearable amid the thick woods, the Americans enter the hacienda Conservidayoc, a hybrid Quechua-Castilian name, given to it by its owner, Saavedra, "because its isolation," he says, "has enabled him to lead a free life." In a terrain rich in humus grow coffee, bananas, tobacco, peanuts, and sweet potatoes. The neighboring sugar-cane plantation gives Saavedra "more than he can grind." And he boils the juice in enormous, authentic Incan jars that were found nearby, beneath the forest. Each holds 6 gallons, but because of their typical shape—known as the aryballus type, having a pointed base and handles midway up—the Indians can easily carry them on their backs, using a rope.

Bingham examines some pre-Columbian tombs, carved in the shape of a "bottle," with walls lined in stone and entrances covered with a flat slab or even a sheet of silver. These sepulchers contain stone implements, bronze axes, and other objects that "eloquently [proved], beyond the peradventure of a doubt, that Incas had once lived down here in this damp jungle."

As for the ruins promised by the Indian at Pampaconas, they are still a half-hour's walk away, near the village of Espiritu Pampa,[5] at the foot of the promontory that supports the house of the hacienda. An ancient stone stairway leads to an irregular group of some twenty circular houses, possibly once inhabited by the fierce Antis whom Rodriguez de Figueroa saw living near the Inca.

In a *rancho* an Indian woman is cooking over a small fire "in two black ollas of Inca origin, hundreds of years old."

Guided by three sturdy savages armed with bows and long arrows, wearing tunics and bamboo fillets, Hiram Bingham arrives—amid a terrible storm, after a half-hour's march through the jungle, along the banks of a little tributary of the Rio Pampaconas—at the artificial terraces of Eromboni Pampa. A typical Indian fountain with three spouts flanks a large rectangular building, which was never completed, the American explorer believes, and is of a more recent type, a kind that did not take long to build.

All the next day, Saavedra's sons, aided by the "savages," clear away the tangled growth. They thus uncover two very well-preserved Inca buildings, of superior construction, fitted with stone pegs and niches, symmetrically arranged; the buildings stand on a terrace where, the day before, they had noticed nothing! Nothing gives a better idea of the

---

[5] These ruins were actually discovered in 1892 by three inhabitants of Cuzco: Manuel Ugarte, Manuel Lopez Torres, and Juan Cancio Saavedra. More recently, the topographer Christian Bues had visited them.

density of the jungle than this fortuitous find made by the natives, who had often been within 5 feet of these buildings without being aware of their existence. These are, notes Bingham, "the best Inca ruins found in the valley." However, when questioned by Bingham, the Indians answer that they know of no other ruins nearby. The scholar from Yale deduces that "the ruins here are those of one of the favorite residences of Titu Cusi. It may have been the place from which he journeyed to meet Rodriguez in 1565."

Could this be Vilcabamba la Vieja, the "University of Idolatry" that the friars Marcos Garcia and Diego Ortiz were unable to reach? Bingham is tempted to believe it is. For him there is no doubt that Eromboni Pampa and the Pampaconas Valley meet the requirements of the place which Captain Garcia's companions referred to as Vilcabamba; they spoke of it as the town and valley to which Tupac Amaru escaped, it is said, after his forces had lost "the young fortress of Viticos."[6]

This statement of Bingham's assumes a great significance, since it proves that he indeed places, in 1911, the site explored *at the very entrance to Vilcabamba la Vieja*, at the bottom of the valley of the same name. Then he resumes—more proof—the pursuit of Tupac Amaru "to the country of the Manaries Indians, a warlike tribe," which he locates, correctly, "farther into the woods . . . inland toward the valley of Simaponte . . . where *balsas* and canoes were posted to save him and enable him to escape."

Bingham even adds that the distance from Espiritu Pampa to where one could navigate canoes would have been but a short journey, and that evidently the Inca's friends were "canoemen."

However, he concludes: "We still had not identified . . . the 'principal city' of Manco and his sons." Why this apparent contradiction? Because, after arguments intended to "explain" Machu Picchu, his great discovery, Bingham will have to "adapt the facts as one moves chess pieces to win the game," as Juvenal Lara accuses him of doing. And he will "ingenuously" pair Vilcabamba and the "Lost City" of

---

[6] Another error on Bingham's part: the "young fortress," or Huayna Pukara, was located not at Viticos but at the entrance to Vilcabamba, as all the written declarations of the Spaniards prove.

the Incas, even though the latter is located—as he must know—in the opposite direction!

Nevertheless, the fact that he divulged to the entire world the most astonishing of the wonders of antiquity earns the American explorer a place of honor among the great historians of the early twentieth century. After all, did they not write world history by often adapting it, like Bingham, as much to their own convenience as to the tastes of current readers?

At the time, therefore, it is of utmost importance to the young scholar from Yale that Vilcabamba remain, in the naive eyes of his contemporaries, a "lost" city in the true sense of the word, which—this condition is essential, to give it a transcendent value—no Spaniard ever succeeded in penetrating! This, as we have seen, was not the case with Vilcabamba la Vieja, which was violated, pillaged, burned, and occupied by Garcia's conquistadors—but it was, on the other hand, true of Machu Picchu.

TOO MANY UNKNOWN RUINS

During the six decades since the renaissance of Machu Picchu, historical research has evolved considerably. The hypotheses heretofore principally based on intuition or hearsay have been confirmed or dismissed in the light of archaeological findings.

In reexamining Bingham's inconsistent theories, there are many reputable investigators today (apart from a few "timid" pontiffs) who claim they disagree with him. But one uncertainty persists: Did Hiram Bingham guess the true nature of Espiritu Pampa, the "Pampa of Ghosts"? Several recent explorations which should have answered this question have only complicated it by bringing to light too many unexpected ruins!

Near the gold mines of Maria Isabel de Pampaconas, in the Choquesafra Cordillera, Antonio Santander Cascelli, an old explorer from Cuzco, came upon a "lost city" with tiered terraces 3 kilometers long. In addition to walls pierced with great imperial *portadas*, paved roads and boulders carved with curious bas-reliefs adorn these ruins, which the Indians in the vicinity designate by the name "Hatun Vilcabamba," or "the high city of Vilcabamba." Cascelli learned that pillagers of the Incan tombs had disinterred several mummies wrapped in extraordinary woolen mantles, woven on a weft of gold threads and embroidered with multicolored macaw feathers. He photographed intriguing ideograms reproduced on the rocks staking out commercial routes or sacred roads, which could be a form of pictographic writing. However, the unique entrance to these mysterious ruins, a half-moon perforated in a granite block, may suggest, he says, "a late Hispanic influence . . ."

In the same region, Juan Pablo Mocoso, another pioneer, has pointed out, about 30 kilometers from Lucma, other very extensive ruins, at Choquetacarpu, where innumerable Incan buildings have been ravaged by treasure-seekers.

In 1963, four parachutists from the National Geographic Society dropped onto the Vilcabamba Cordillera, in a virgin area, blank on all the Peruvian maps. The place seemed to them to have been abandoned for centuries. Unexplored, the chain (located 400 kilometers south of Lima, as the crow flies) must have covered over 4,000 square kilometers. The American parachutists wandered about for three months, in a perpetual fog which saturated the air with humidity and made a wood fire impossible. Isolated from the rest of the world, and advancing (with difficulty) a few kilometers a day, at altitudes of 4,000 meters, they crossed "lunar, glaciated" deserts pocked with lagoons, showing no trace of a "lost city" but "a very beautiful panorama of desolation and emptiness."

Several military and civilian expeditions went similarly unrewarded, impeded by nature and the presence of fierce Indians. Major José Carreon, assigned to make a topographical survey of the Vilcabamba Cordillera in 1955, was unable to penetrate to any great depth, because hostile tribes guarded the borders of the territory contained between the Urubamba, Ene, Tambo, and Apurimac rios. He heard curious rumors, according to which these natives, the Paucapacuris, were the "descendants of the Incas and [had been] the guardians of Vilcabamba la Vieja since the fall of the empire. They were apparently preserving the treasures of the Incas in a lagoon . . ."

I once had in my hands a parchment that may have dated from the seventeenth century. Traced in a dotted line, as if by a clumsy or hesitant hand, a path, circling a lagoon, ended in a cross drawn in ink, under which was written: *"Here, the city of the Inca."* Was this map authentic? Who in Cuzco and the Convención Valley is without a copy! There is, however, no precise indication of the orientation. Nevertheless, an infinite number of "lost" ruins are surely found to be there, as the *cuzqueño* archaeologist Cornejo Bouroncle confirms, speaking of the "cities that are being reborn in the provinces of the Antis and Tampus, toward the eastern jungles where remains of sanctuaries and pilgrimage sites have already been found, all 'connected' by impeccably traced paths."

GENE SAVOY'S EXPEDITION

Much better prepared was the great expedition which another American explorer, Gene Savoy (founder of the Andean Explorers Club in Lima), organized to search for elements that would permit a study of the original population of South America.

Savoy is one of the rare investigators daring enough to dream that it might be possible to discover important archaeological remains in the heart of the immense, nearly unexplored Amazonian jungles which extend to the east of the cordillera—a hypothesis rejected by the majority of the conventional scholars of North and South America, who see it as "fantastic and farfetched." One of these, Gary Vescelius, at least went so far as to predict that if Savoy succeeded in bringing to light pre-Columbian ruins in the Amazon Basin, he would revolutionize Peruvian archaeology.[7]

An admirer of the Incas (like Bingham), Savoy deduced from their known history that, if the Empire of the Andes was called the Tahuantinsuyo because it consisted of four vast *suyos*, or geographical areas, the part called Antisuyo, or the Land of the Antis, logically was part of the whole. In all probability, he should find there—as elsewhere in the vast territory conquered by the Incas—just as many ruins of fortified cities, sanctuaries, necropolises, paved roads,

---

[7] Gene Savoy discovered in the jungles of Chachapoyas the ruins of the Gran Pajaten, which are magnificent (though not as spectacular as Machu Picchu) and decorated with strange bas-reliefs recalling the Mayan frescoes of the Yucatan. See my book *Mystérieux mondes incas perdus et retrouvés* (Editions S.C.E.M.I.).

and other masterworks, now engulfed by the vegetal ocean of the jungles of eastern Peru.

In sum, Gene Savoy thought it nearly certain that the forests of the Amazon Basin were the cradle of brilliant civilizations that have disappeared, as were the cordilleras and coastal deserts of the Pacific—civilizations like those which arose in the jungles of the Yucatan, of Mexico, Guatemala, and Honduras and died out without an echo.

Long before Gene Savoy, Julis César Tello, the "father" of Peruvian archaeology, suggested with equal audacity— and arousing comparable incredulity among his colleagues —that "the farther one goes toward the east, the more ancient the pre-Columbian cultures appear to be."

Starting with his initial explorations, Savoy quickly came to the conclusion that, just as he had thought, the Antisuyo had been flourishing under the Incan rule when the unexpected incursion of the Spanish conquistadors occurred.

Interrogated by the order of the viceroy Toledo, the *quipucamayocs* revealed that the Inca Pachacutec Yupanqui "undertook to conquer the land to extend the domination of the Sons of the Sun" over the other peoples. With his brother, Captain Inca Roca, he traveled along the banks of the Urubamba ("a region rich in veins of copper"), subdued the *sinchis* of Ollantaytambo, and had all the inhabitants executed. Then he headed toward the Vilcabamba Valley, where he knew he would find gold and silver in abundance. By his order, bridges were thrown across torrents, including that of Chuquichaca. His successes were so significant that two months of festivities followed his return to Cuzco, to celebrate his victories and the discovery of mines so rich that henceforth they would supply all the metalworkers in the capital.

Gene Savoy discovered the old roads that connected the two great population centers of the Andes with the shores of the Pacific and the Amazon Basin. Hiram Bingham, he thought, was on the verge of reaching the goal when he decided not to press any farther into the forest to find the legendary hideaway of the last Incas. Descendants of the fierce Antis, the Machiguengas, who provided him with information, denied the existence of other cities buried beneath the jungle, because, being extremely superstitious, they still believed the magic ghosts of the Sacred Pampa (hence the modern name "Espiritu Pampa") were inclined to wreak revenge on those who betray the secret. A similar misfortune befell the Peruvian explorer José Pancorvo in 1964: The Machiguengas insisted that there were no Incan ruins beyond Rosaspata-Viticos, because they feared that their crops would be afflicted by a "curse." They themselves are very careful to "appease" the ghosts with offerings and praise when they empty the tombs of precious objects because, as they are very poor, hunger forces them to do so.

WHERE THE "SACRED SPIRITS" ROAM

Having prepared for the expedition for three years, Gene Savoy, guided by Santander Cascelli and Victor Ardiles, governor of the province of Vilcabamba, and escorted by policemen, soldiers, and some sixty Peruvian porters, set out in 1964 for a period of about four months.

Beyond the Chaullay bridge, the difficulties began. Poisonous insects bit Savoy and Cascelli, forcing them to return to the base camp for treatment; Cascelli had to abandon the project. The altitude, the constant rain, the impassibility of the *cañon*, and the jagged peaks greatly impeded progress. Nine "taboo" lagoons required interminable detours; then they ran up against the liquid barrier of one of the largest waterfalls in the world.[8] Gene Savoy calculates its height at over 300 meters. The water falls with an astonishing din on four successive platforms, from a summit 3,000 meters high, which outlines a human profile, in which the Machiguengas see the specter of the coronated Manco Inca. Surrounded by "nests" of jaguars, Savoy was able to reach only the virgin—and therefore all the more "taboo"—peak of Orpococha, on which there stands a magnificent chapel.

To retrace the road the Incas used to penetrate the Antisuyo, Savoy had to enlist the help of the Peruvian aviation company Fawcett. Infrared aerial views, taken with specially designed equipment over lush jungles that extend as far as the eye can see, revealed vast archaeological

---

[8] The highest waterfalls now known are in Venezuela: the Salto Angel, which falls over 1,000 meters vertically, and Cuquenan (600 meters). Next is the Sutherland waterfall (580 meters) in New Zealand.

"beds," in the cyclopean mode, which were totally invisible to the naked eye. Some fifteen groups of quadrangular platforms, staggered between 1,000 and 3,500 meters altitude and measuring about 100 meters long by 5 meters wide, were discovered thus. They support approximately 150 circular structures (some are oval), which are very rare in South America and are, according to Savoy, always located in rain forests where Caribbean peoples survive. The whole is in fact located in the Conservidayoc Valley and on the "Pampa of Ghosts," along the Rio Chontapampa, which Hiram Bingham failed to reach.

The Lima-based architect Emilio Harth-Terré, who carried out a detailed study of these ruins, explains that "the climatic leveling" so intelligently conceived and practiced by the Incas—from the humid sauna of the lowland forests to the bracing cold of the heights—enabled them to diversify their economic activities by matching the crops to the environment. "Moreover," he remarks, "the Vilcabamba complex, unlike the restricted surface of the ancient cities crowning the high peaks, was planned by the Inca architects in such a way that the groups—located in a forest so voracious that, in the centuries to come, it would engulf them much as Vesuvius' lava did Pompeii and Herculaneum—were spaced out so as to 'aerate' them."

Harth-Terré assumes that the archaeological complex discovered by Savoy, which covers a surface four times as large as that of Machu Picchu, was an immense "city of agricultural colonists," protected by crude fortified walls made of stone and by *atalayas*, or watchtowers, overlooking the valleys and rivers. According to the Indians, the platforms were connected to one another by secret tunnels, the entrances to which could be concealed beneath a large quadrangular block, 1.5 meters on each side, which was part of the wall.

Everything exhumed from the virgin forest by the Andean Explorers Club bears the mark of the classical style of the Incas of Cuzco—and their road builders (*clavas*, or fitted stones, and stone rings identical to those found at Machu Picchu), as well as their ceramists (aryballus jars and funerary pottery) and metallurgists (spoon-shaped copper *tupus* with great carved heads, which the Indian women used to pin their woolen shawls).

Savoy did not discover any gold objects. But he revealed that the Machiguengas had in their possession idols and ears of corn made of solid gold, which they would sell to collectors in nearby villages. I myself was able to photograph a splendid gold condor.

About 700 meters from Espiritu Pampa, at the place called Eromboni Pampa, Savoy made some startling discoveries, which supported the possibility of a Hispanic occupation and reinforced the idea that this was indeed Vilcabamba la Vieja: first of all, scattered about at ground level, Inca remnants and tools made of copper, and a large horseshoe in an obsolete style, which the conquistadors used for their mounts; and, above all, hundreds of tiles (which were unknown in South America before the Conquest), covered with a layer of dirt 5 meters thick, thus buried and hidden in the patio of a vast monument comprising thirteen rooms, which the explorers soon baptized the "Palace of the Tiles." These are crudely made tiles, but what is even more surprising, in this out-of-the-way place, is the fact that they are coated with the glaze characteristic of pre-Columbian ceramics and decorated with typically Inca motifs, such as Amaru serpents and birds of the virgin forest, painted in bright colors. They were perhaps fashioned by potters who, though native, were already familiar with the European technique of the new masters, or perhaps by Spanish "slaves" of Manco Inca, whom he forced to teach their techniques to his artisans. These are the two hypotheses posited thus far concerning these exceptional tiles, for no other find of this sort has yet been made in the Incan region.

Now—and this is a detail of the utmost importance, which argues even more convincingly in favor of this place's being Vilcabamba la Vieja—in his chronical regarding the capture of Tupac Amaru, Friar Martín de Morua, describing "the city of Vilcabamba, which was one-half league wide, with houses and huts covered with sturdy thatch," informs us that "the house of the Inca, comprising an upper and lower part, was covered with tiles, and the entire palace, with exceedingly perfumed cedar doors, was adorned with paintings of various sorts, as was their custom, and this was indeed a sight worth seeing."

IS THIS THE FAMOUS "LOST CAPITAL"?

Gene Savoy had to organize two successive expeditions in order to clear the immense archaeological complex, submerged in a jungle that was, he notes, "terrifying." Rescued from the forest, large buildings, lined up opposite one another, reappeared along an axial route that opens onto a great ceremonial plaza. The most impressive building measures 65 meters long by 7 meters wide. Its shape recalls the spacious *galpones* (long covered halls) where the people of Cuzco would gather to celebrate reunions and festivals when it was raining, as Garcilaso de la Vega informs us. Twelve giant trapezoidal *portadas* pierce each facade. One notes, inside, a monolithic altar, and, behind the "Palace of the Two Enclosing Walls," a *mochadero* underscored by a low wall, consisting of an enormous votive stone, present in all the sanctuaries dedicated to the solar cult.

Savoy has described with ecstasy the "Palace of Fine Stones," with mathematically mounted corners and a surface polished like glass—an extreme refinement of a form of architecture that points to the imperial apogee of the Tahuantinsuyo. Many of the princely residences still retain —this is another valid argument, for it echoes the statements of Friar Martín de Morua—traces of an interior facing of red stucco (which appears varnished), richly illuminating the walls.

Here and there, cruder constructions alternate with the splendid buildings made of polyhedrons or rectangles of light-colored granite, similar in every way—as Hermann Buse notes—to those found in the beautiful cities lost and rediscovered in the Sacred Valley of the Urubamba. These are probably the dwellings the Manco Inca caused to be hastily built around the ancient temples and palaces. Another similarity with Machu Picchu: Thermal baths are distributed throughout the city, fed by a network of canals and gutters which collect the waters of the lagoon of Pisca Cocha and conduct them into large reservoirs, then distribute them through the twenty distinct districts of Espiritu Pampa. Perfect monolithic gargoyles still emerge from certain walls.

Everywhere, and generally grouped in threes, *andenes* supported by high walls are tiered at graduated levels.

Stripped of the ocean of chlorophyll, of the vegetal curtain of tangled lianas, of the shroud of trees over 60 meters high, which had covered it for centuries, the city that Savoy discovered (but which was pointed out to him by Peruvians) is three days' journey from the nearest town. It covers some 30 hectares. A study of its stratigraphy and technology would require several years' work. Viewed from afar, it outlines a colossal squared pyramid; its various courses are connected by stone stairways and overlook two Intihuatanas for the observation of solar movements. However, it cannot be compared with Machu Picchu, which is unique in the world by virtue of its majestic position atop the Picchus of the Sacred Valley.

In Gene Savoy's view, the Espiritu Pampa complex can only be the seat of the expansion of the culture of the Incas toward the borders of the Amazonian forests—from Cuzco, Madre de Dios, Ayacucho (formerly Huamanga), as far as the borders of Brazil and Bolivia. This shows, he concludes, "the conquering and civilizing spirit of the Incan dynasty, which transformed the most terrifying jungle there is into a bustling hive."

Recalling that, according to Titu Cusi, who grew up there, Manco Inca (his father) made Vilcabamba "his customary residence because of the warm climate," and observing that Espiritu Pampa is close by the torrential rivers on which Garcia de Loyola and his officers embarked in pursuit of Tupac Amaru and the golden idol of the Punchao, one tends to agree with Savoy that he has undoubtedly identified the famous "lost capital" of the last Incas.

What do the Peruvian archaeologists think? When questioned, Luis E. Valcarcel, one of the most famous of these and one known for the prudence of his opinions, declared: "It is very likely that this is Vilcabamba la Grande [Greater Vilcabamba], which was founded on the site of Vilcabamba la Chica [Lesser Vilcabamba], where Manco Inca took refuge in 1537. Judging from the Incan and Spanish elements, this indeed seems to be the capital called 'Vilcabamba le Vieja' which was established a few years after the contact between the two cultures."

Another archaeologist to declare himself in favor of Gene Savoy's theory is Father Avencio Villarejo, who has reconstructed the history of the Augustinian monks in Peru; they were the first to have penetrated this rebellious Incan province. "All the sites, the routes, the length of the voyage, the geographical features coincide," says the priest, "with the conquistadors' descriptions."

This opinion is not shared, however, by Gustavo Alencastre Montufar, regional inspector of the archaeological monuments in a region measuring nearly 400 square kilometers, which he visited in 1965. Alencastre even accused Savoy of having carried out "clandestine excavations" and of having "betrayed the public trust"—an accusation against which the American explorer defended himself vehemently, pointing to the presence of the Peruvian military escort. His adversary maintains that Vilcabamba la Vieja "is much farther still, and still lost," although he claims to have uncovered the secret route, bordered with stone constructions, which once were "relay stations for shelter and rest" for travelers during the time of the Incas.

Will the future decide which of the opposing camps is correct?

PART THREE

The True History of Machu Picchu

A thousand questions . . . Not a single certain answer!

—Vincente Achala

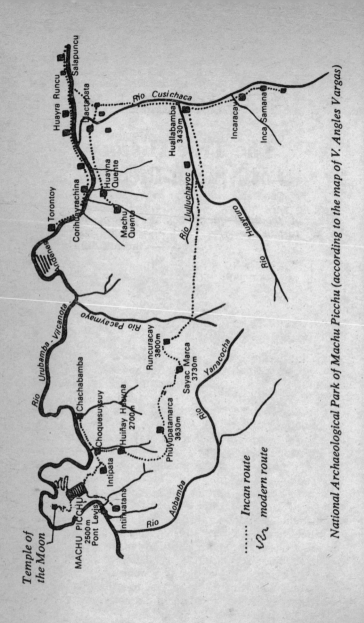

National Archaeological Park of Machu Picchu (according to the map of V. Angles Vargas)

CHAPTER TEN

The "Dignity of Silence"

> *Those familiar with these remote, solitary places were the survivors of the Conquest in the sixteenth century: the Inca's court and the Inca himself, the controllers of traffic between Cuzco and Machu Picchu, the chasquis and the farmers of the three peaks, the builders, and, finally, the Mamacunas and the Chosen Women.*
>
> —José Uriel Garcia, 1961

MACHU PICCHU IS NOT VILCABAMBA LA VIEJA

As the first definite statement to emerge from my extensive work reconstructing the facts, it appears that Machu Picchu—which is located *southeast* of the key point of Chuquichaca (instead of northwest, as is indicated by the numerous geographical references in documents signed by conquistadors on oath, all of whom participated in the Vilcabamba *guerrilla*)—can in no way be confused with Vilcabamba la Vieja.

To clear up (as much as is possible today) the intriguing question of the "Lost City" of the Incas, it is thus necessary to review all the data—which is what the history professor José Uriel Garcia did, some time before me, when a knee injury immobilized him in Cuzco, by the most fortunate of coincidences, in a very ancient *notaría* cluttered with dusty files from previous centuries. He made an absolutely miraculous find: a notarial record dating from 1782, referring to Machu Picchu—the only document concerning the famous "Lost City" now known to exist. Even more important, it reveals what Bingham did not know: the real name of the ruins on the Old Peak.

121

Moreover, this notarial record—which, incomprehensibly, was never mentioned by the majority of Peruvian historians—answers a question often posed: Is it possible to believe that no one had ever heard of the existence of this enchanting city, forgotten for so long? And who, then, visited it?

Analyzing the surprising silence that clung to Machu Picchu for four centuries, Uriel Garcia broke it down into several sequences, which he designated as "absolute ignorance," "knowledge through hearsay," "knowledge obvious from the secrecy," and "written but unpublished reference."

"Absolute ignorance" brings us up to the end of the sixteenth century, right after the dramatic twilight of the Inca gods.

It is quite possible that Manco gave the formal order to conceal—under pain of death—the existence of the sanctuary of the sacred mountain, and that the secret was respected as much out of dignity as from fear of punishment. Or else, using an extreme measure connected with the Inca law frequently observed by his forefathers (a law that could even affect his brothers and closest relatives), Manco Inca saw to the execution, at the very gates of the city, of all those who shared the secret and might be tempted or forced to reveal it—in particular, Indian bearers and servants who did not belong to the nobility by descent or privilege, or to the sacerdotal caste. For the fall of Cuzco, crushed by Pizarro, would inevitably lead to the loss of all the fortified cities (fortified against archaic weapons and not against gunfire) on the peaks of the Valley of the Sun. This certainly justified the most drastic measures.

At least, Manco and those who followed him into exile had completed their journey and by 1536 were settled in the tropical forests of Vilcabamba. There is a possible explanation for this: the insufficient quantity of vital resources in the formidably steep area of Machu Picchu, which was unsuited for food crops and for the fodder indispensable to the large herds of llamas that followed the Inca, which were used both as beasts of burden and for cult sacrifices, as well as to feed several thousand people.

Or there are all kinds of other reasons, among them the fact that, as Bingham would suggest, the "most sublime sanctuary in the empire" had become, at this crucial epoch, the exclusive hiding place of the beautiful Acllas of the Sun, saved from disaster but doomed to a slow, lonely death; the last of the Virgins, Uriel Garcia imagines, "took to her grave the secret that would endow with eternal dignity all those who, while alive, knew how to remain forever silent."

"Knowledge through hearsay" lasts probably into the seventeenth century. Some people were able to acquire this knowledge either through their contact with agricultural settlers in the valley or through the jumbled rumors coming from Cuzco, "exchanged over a glass of *chicha* by caravaneers returning from the huge rural haciendas, with loads of fruits and other products from the tropical regions. But these rather vague suggestions aroused only a feeble interest, which never went beyond the bounds of the capital of the Andes: their echo died within the taverns' depths."

Uriel Garcia is surprised that, by virtue of this "dignity of silence" practiced by the Quechuas, Machu Picchu remained unknown—as Incan ruins—to the catechists and to the fanatic pack of "extirpators of idolatry," who, during and after the tortures and burnings at the stake carried out during the Inquisition, inflicted furious repressions on the Indians. Under their exacerbated influence, Spanish "instructors" roamed the Andes, doggedly tearing down hidden idols and breaking votive stones. Hoping thus to uproot the natives' ancient magico-religious beliefs, these vandals dismantled superb pre-Columbian monuments.

It appears, thus, that apart from the *huaqueros*—"professional" defilers and pillagers of Peruvian antiquities, upon whom silence was implicitly imposed if they wished to avoid prosecution by law—ignorance of the archaeological treasures of Machu Picchu can be considered probable.

Moreover, other circumstances could have contributed to the "secret" of Machu Picchu. Deprived of their rich ancestral lands and reduced to an inhuman slavery under the Hispanic regime, Indians died by tens of thousands in the exploitation of the gold, silver, and copper mines located at high altitudes, as well as in agricultural cultivation. Finally, the violent rebellions and native uprisings that led to the era of the emancipation and liberation of Latin America set off waves of persecution and prohibitions against anything that might recall the age-old traditions— requiring, in counterpart, this astonishing "silence."

Uriel Garcia was pleased, moreover, that the "secret" survived the destructive, murderous earthquake of 1650, which caused the flow of great masses of natives of the Sacred Valley to Cuzco, where they were employed in the reconstruction of houses or religious edifices that had been shaken or destroyed by the earthquake. Undoubtedly, the difficulties of extracting and transporting the monoliths of the famous "Lost City" over the distance that separates these ruins from the Andean capital, as well as the geographic apocalypse of the *cañon* that defends them, contributed toward prolonging "the secret of the jewels petrified beneath a savage wood."

It was not until the beginning of the nineteenth century that the social ambiance of the Indians reflected the changes of modern times. After Simón Bolívar's visit to Cuzco in 1825, tolerance sprang up in the shade of a growing sympathy toward the ancient autochthonous cultures. The "Liberator of Latin America" outlined democratic measures to benefit the Inca's heirs. He visited the archaeological centers of Sacsahuaman, Ollantaytambo, and many other sites in the Sacred Valley, without ever suspecting—even he—that he was just missing the most exceptional site of them all.

Parallel to the evolution of ideas, rich *cuzqueños* were then growing interested in Incan antiquities. As a result, legions of Indian and mestizo *huaqueros* set out across mountains and through forests in order to supply the collectors. It is still a miracle that none among them betrayed the extraordinary silence, thanks to the ordinances that threatened those who committed sacrilege with severe punishments. But this apparently fortuitous silence persists despite all; it is agonizing today, when archaeologists are unable to figure out the exact origin of the admirable specimens that we contemplate in small and large museums (which are as officious as they are official).

The unforgettable, Aladdinesque fate of Francisco Pizarro, growing richer daily from the treasures that

Atahualpa collected in order to pay a pointless ransom, continued to fire people's imaginations. The secret of Machu Picchu, Uriel Garcia remarks, "dribbled out in gold drops into the greedy hands of the farmers and *peones* of the Sacred Valley who lived at the foot of the Picchus. The perilous climb did not discourage them from going to dig in the funerary caves and the tunnels that must exist beneath the famous 'Lost City.' " How else can one explain the fact that Bingham found the tombs defiled —except for one intact sepulcher located in the most astonishing of the cemeteries? Neither gold nor silver in the royal sepulchers of the most beautiful Inca city in ruins? This is what is so strange and seems so unlikely to most Peruvians! But is it true? It is necessary to digress at this point.

BINGHAM DENOUNCED

A few years ago a Peruvian writer, Enrique Portugal, published in the Buenos Aires press a series of articles on Bingham and Machu Picchu which created an uproar in Argentina. In it the American scholar was depicted as a "pirate, adventurer, and mere mountain climber." Portugal accused him of having "unqualifiably pillaged, sacked, and stripped Machu Picchu, carrying off an extremely rich cargo of gold objects and works of art."

Actually, Portugal was merely reviving the denunciation voiced by a famous Argentinian intellectual, Ana de Cabrera, and published as early as 1938 by the newspaper *La Nación*: "Disgracefully," she writes, "the Bingham expedition removed from Peru a great number of crates containing a chapter of the ancient history of the American people. When the shipment of so rich a booty arrived at Mollendo [a Peruvian port on the Pacific], the people of the city, aroused, wished to prevent its departure by violent means . . ."

Portugal says that during his childhood, spent in Arequipa (the second-largest city in Peru), he was aware that "crates presumably filled with Incan potsherds and mummies were constantly being sent to the U.S.A., which finally aroused the suspicions of a customs officer at the Bolivian border, by which the fradulent shipments were surreptitiously leaving, to be shipped, finally, to the Chilean port of Arica." Everything at Machu Picchu, Portugal claims, "was taken away by the daring explorer, by moonlight."

It is all the more difficult to decide whether to side with Bingham's detractors or his supporters, since he did not publish a list of what he discovered during the expeditions of 1912 and 1913, which were much more significant than that of 1911. But one fact is undeniable: No Peruvian museum—not even that of Machu Picchu—is able to exhibit the slightest Incan objet d'art found in the "Lost City" by the American explorers. Finally, taking a stand, Luis E. Valcarcel does not hesitate to declare that "while the Spaniards did not succeed in dismantling Machu Picchu, the North Americans accomplished the task for them. I've seen at Yale," he states, "everything that Hiram Bingham took back from his digs . . . The Tampus, along with their bones, emigrated as far as the museums of 'Yankee Land,' for Bingham did not miss a single cranium!"[1]

MACHU PICCHU SOLD IN 1776!

"Knowledge obvious from the secrecy" of the marvelous cities still "lost" or officially rediscovered on the peaks of the Sacred Valley of the Incas aroused, during the eighteenth century, the interest of great voyagers such as Charles Wiener, who was responsible for the detailed account and *the map published in 1875* which launched Hiram Bingham onto the historic trail of the last Incas.

A new mystery: Was Wiener himself perhaps let in on the secret by a man who was known at the time as "the king of the Santa Ana Valley"? I discovered that this man, Don Martín de Concha, was then the owner of Machu Picchu! He had inherited it from his father-in-law, a very rich *latifundista* from the valley of the Rio of the Sun, Major Marcos Antonio de la Camara y Escudero, who had

[1] Professor Oswaldo Baca of Cuzco assured me that as a young boy he had seen stored at his father's house in Ollantaytambo, where Bingham rented a room, *two hundred boxes* containing objects dug up at Machu Picchu by the Yale Peruvian Expedition.

married an authentic marquesa of Cuzco. Now, this noble personage, who was Charles Wiener's informant, in fact plays a primary role in the "secret" unraveled by José Uriel Garcia. Indeed, the handwritten scriptures of the records of the notary Ambrosio de Lira in Cuzco, on sheet 20 of the protocol of the year 1782, shows him buying the entire mountain of Machu Picchu—along with other neighboring peaks. The names of the sites are clearly specified in the document, which is entitled "Sale of Lands." It reads:

> To whom It May Concern: I, Don Ambrosio Landivisnay y Valdes, licensed notary and presbyter domiciled in the archbishopric of Cuzco, do state that through my arrangement and intervention, Doña Manuela Almiron y Villegas, widow of Don Federico Mendo y Valdes, sold to Don Pedro and Don Antonio Ochoa, brothers (my nephews), certain lands (without tools, chattel, or houses) known as Quenti, Masacucho, Pacaymayu, Carmenga, Yanacaca, Masacaca, *Picchu, Machu Picchu, and Huayna Picchu*, and other names, located downriver, toward the confluence of the great Amaybamba and Vilcamayo rios; that the aforementioned lands are located three leagues lower than the city of Vilcabamba, province of Calca, Lares, and Vilcabamba . . . whose titles and the provisions concerning them are free of charge, pawn, mortgage, or any other specific or general alienations, for the price and quantity of *350 pesos*, free of tax, which was paid by the seller, according to the receipt issued by the royal customs officer, Colonel Lucas Garay, on August 8, 1776, and which is incorporated in this document, etc. The sale that the aforementioned licensed notary is making this year, 1782, is to Major *Marcos Antonio de la Camara y Escudero*, for the price of 450 pesos.

This notarial act thus proves that a century before Wiener heard these names pronounced, and inscribed them on a map (not as simple names of mountains, but as the "pedestal of ancient cities" corresponding to a group of

Bronze knife with a fisherboy,
found by Hiram Bingham at Machu Picchu

Inca-style monuments), *the ruins on the Old and Young peaks were already known as Machu Picchu and Huayna Picchu.*[2]

Once this primordial mystery has been cleared up, another question arises: Did the widow Almiron y Villegas, who was selling the lands of the Machu Picchu, Huayna Picchu, and other high peaks, know them by sight? We can reasonably doubt that she did, and assume that, on the contrary, she never visited them, since, according to the terms of the notarial document, she believed them to be —and sold them as being—"without houses." Their low price seems to indicate, moreover, that these lands were never rentable from an agricultural point of view. The fact (which has already been noted) that no passable road linked the Urubamba Cañon with Cuzco explains, moreover, the probable reason that the successive owners decided not to visit them in person in order to arrange for their cultivation.

As for the notary, the public scribe, and priest, and other witnesses cited, were they any better acquainted with the lands involved in the transaction than were the sellers

[2] This mountain, Uriel Garcia notes, would be called simply "Picchu" were it not for the two extreme peaks to the southwest and northeast—the Machu Picchu (at 3,140 meters altitude) and the Huayna Picchu (at 2,760). The part named "Picchu," properly speaking, extends between the two peaks; average and even, it is the place where the city was built. *Machu* and *huayna* are comparative Quechua terms ("the old," "the young") which are currently used to distinguish, visually, the heights of Andean peaks.

and buyers? Did the buyers imagine that they were coming into possession of one of the most fabulous ancient cities in the world? If they had been aware of these ruins, Uriel Garcia believes, the clergyman as well as the soldier and the *hacendados* would have denounced them to the prelate or to the corregidor in Cuzco so that they might order their implacable destruction! For at the time, following the revolutionary movement led by Tupac Amaru II, which placed the privileged ruling classes in grave danger, the persecution of all evidence of the grandeur of the natives' past doubled in intensity—to the extent that the sadistic execution of this famous popular Peruvian hero (a descendant of the Inca Atahualpa), who fell into the bloody hands of the inspector Areche (whom the Indians called Supaypahuahuan, or "Satan's Henchman"), was followed by a second rebellion, in precisely the year 1782, organized by his cousin Diego Cristobal Tupac Amaru.

A conclusion extremely important in terms of the unknown history of Machu Picchu: The notarial record found by Uriel Garcia puts an end to the mystery that Bingham created surrounding the real name of the "Lost City" of the Incas, which he designated "the ruins of Machu Picchu," because, he said, "no one knew what else to call them." For a long time this ambiguous phrase blinded the Americanists most familiar with the subject. All of them thought, in fact, that the Quechuas of the Picchus had forgotten the authentic name, whereas it was necessary merely to realize that, since this name had never been erased from their memories, there was no reason for them to call the ruins anything else!

CHAPTER ELEVEN

To Be Filed
in the
Historical Dossier

Peruvian prehistory is like a blank puzzle.
✵ *One has no idea what image must be* ✵
reconstructed.

—Olivier Pecquet, 1966

THE SECRET OF ACLLA GUALCA

Now that one of the major mysteries of Machu Picchu had been cleared up, was it not possible to find other documents—even if less legal—that could be filed in the historical dossier of the "Lost City" of the Incas? I undertook the task of finding them and thus came across the interesting chronicle of Don Antonio Altamirano, a conquistador who took part in the defense of Cuzco when it was being besieged by Manco, and who later managed a rural hacienda in the vicinity of the capital of the Andes, where he died in 1555.

Altamirano relates that he befriended the soldier Miguel Rufino, a native of Burgos who had fled Spain after being compromised in a bloody duel that took place in Toledo. Together they embarked for Peru, in the service of Francisco Pizarro. But Rufino could not accept the many iniquities committed against the Indians by the Spanish mercenaries, who, inflamed by lust for gold, engaged in the most scandalous immoral acts. The injustices, committed "in the name of the king and the divine religion of Christ," so repulsed Rufino that he decided to "withdraw to some place where the echoes of such infamies would not venture to reach his ears."

Let us note, however, that love had more than a little to

do with this concern for solitude and voluntary exile. For
Miguel Rufino was—according to Altamirano—the hero
of a skirmish that would lead him beyond his wildest
dreams.

The chronicler relates that one day Father Valverde
(an unpleasant memory: he was directly involved in
Atahualpa's execution, going against Pizarro's word)
authorized the soldiery to pillage the Acllahuasi, the house
of the Chosen Women of the Inca and of the Sun. While
the monks "were driving out the pagan gods by exorcising
the Incan convent with barrels of incense and rivers of holy
water," the drunken soldiers were dragging the Nustas
outside, through a narrow little door that faced the palace
of Pucamarca. As Miguel Rufino was walking down the
kikllu (a very narrow Incan alley, hemmed in between
colossal megalithic walls), one of the princesses of the
blood royal, still an adolescent, who was being carried off
by a Spaniard and screaming horribly, escaped from him
and threw herself at Rufino's feet. To defend her, and to
save her from certain rape, Rufino struck the ruffian with
his sword—thereby committing a murder that would have
severe consequences if the news were to reach Pizarro's
ears, for Rufino would be accused of being a "traitor and
heretic." He hid for several days in a house in Cuzco with
the Incan princess, Aclla Gualca, who offered to guide him
to a city that no one could find, "except for the Virgins of
the Sun, because this city had been sacred since ancient
times."

The two fugitives reached the Ollantaytambo Valley,
following the course of the Urubamba for three days, at
the end of which time they threaded their way into a dense
jungle. They scaled a peaked ridge, climbing up to heights
invisible from the bottom of the *cañon*; here, Rufino
realized, "fate would be kind to him and he would be
protected from man." Rufino was greatly surprised, nonetheless (just as Bingham would be four centuries later), to
find that this city, "built as if on the cutting edge of the
blade of a sword," was inhabited! A centenarian Indian
man, with a harsh expression, barred their path. Addressing
the young Indian woman, he asked her what the two of
them had come to find. Gualca bowed to the Amauta;
then, with her head still lowered, she told him that they
were looking for "the peace that Viracocha grants." Stand-

ing aside, the ancestor pointed out the paved stairway that descended toward the unknown city. Gardens, flowering orchards, and tiered terraces bordered the path, which turned into a stairway carved into the rock. Abandoned houses, palaces, and temples—their doors and windows empty, roofs caved in—rose all around. On their right, Miguel Rufino noticed a peak that surpassed the other summits, "pointing like a gigantic finger" and darkened at the top by a temple which appeared inaccessible. How had men been able to transport to the top of so steep a mountain the stone blocks necessary for this construction worthy of the gods?

The voice of the Amauta suddenly disrupted his exhilaration. Rufino and his companion had to swear to "obey the laws of the Inti" and never to reveal this sacred place to any stranger; the conquistador and the Aclla were then authorized to set up housekeeping in a palace that was already in ruins, but in which "gold idols still shone in the trapezoidal niches."

A year passed in the huge silence of the cordilleras. Gualca, who had a child by Rufino, wove fine woolen mantles, accompanied by the song of the *checollo*, the nightingale of the Andes, under trees flecked with pink orchids and flowers resembling brightly colored butterflies.

But one evening an Indian showed up in the city, bearing a knotted cord. Deciphered, the *quipus* from Manco Inca enjoined all the men in the mountains to take up arms and join him at Ollantaytambo, where he was preparing a secret war against the whites.

Miguel Rufino left his retreat with those who had adopted him. At Ollantaytambo, where a formidable camp of warriors swarmed over the tiers of the fortress, the Amauta presented him to the Inca. Manco trusted him and kept Rufino with him so that Rufino might teach his men how to handle European firearms. But when, having regained the outlying districts of Cuzco with the Indians, Rufino saw his old comrades-in-arms falling beneath the clubs of Incan warriors, he could no longer contain himself. As he was trying to get help for one of his wounded compatriots, he was hurled into a precipice, along with the injured man.

Although Don Antonio Altamirano does not mention the name Machu Picchu, the account concurs with the

events of the period of Manco's insurrection in 1535.[1] It
appears that, as the lost city of a noble race (which was
perhaps *pre-Incan*, since it was already in ruins at the
beginning of the Spanish Conquest), Machu Picchu must
have later become the secret of the Chosen Women of the
Acllahuasi of Cuzco. This would explain why no chronicler
ever heard or spoke a word about it after the downfall of
the Incas.

THE AMAZONS OF THE SUN AND THE MOON?

A paragraph from the account of the memorable expedition led by Francisco de Orellana in search of El
Dorado and the Fountain of Youth in 1542 aroused the
curiosity of the writer Juan Larrea.

Father Gaspar de Carvajal, the chaplain and chronicler
of the adventure, in the course of which the Amazon River
was accidentally discovered, relates that upon arriving at
the confluence of the Rio Madeira with the great Rio
Marañon, the Spaniards heard talk of "certain female
warriors." The team of brigands questioned all the Indians,
thus learning that there existed, "in the mountains, a
province populated by women who lived in stone houses
and dressed in fine woolen clothing in the style of Cuzco."
The most important city contained five splendid temples.
The province was governed by a "head woman," named
Conori. All the women worshipped the Sun, the Moon,
and golden female idols. They ate from gold dishes.[2]

Even though its value is "problematical," Larrea associated this new information with Machu Picchu. Since the
chroniclers make no other mention of a population of
women in the Andes, "However improbable it may be," he
writes, "nothing prevents one from supposing that knowledge of the existence of this stone city inhabited solely by
women would have spread very quickly all the way to the
Amazon Basin by a river route. This would lead," he adds,

---

[1] Carrying out a few quick probes at Machu Picchu in 1944,
the great Peruvian archaeologist J. C. Tello unearthed "a piece
of carved Spanish alabaster," which was therefore brought there
after the Conquest.

[2] See my book *Mystérieux mondes incas perdus et retrouvés*
(Editions S.C.E.M.I.).

"to the extraordinary possibility that the name of the largest river in the world—the Amazon—may be connected to the history of the Virgins of the Sun who abandoned Cuzco at the fall of the Empire."

A DOCUMENT DATED 1562

I also found an *official document*—which had apparently escaped the Americanists' notice—directly related to Machu Picchu's past. In the enormous file of *Juicios de limites* (Judgments of boundaries) there is a "Provision of the Viceroy Count de Nieva to Doctor Cuenca, for subduing Tupac Amaru's uprising at Vilcabamba," dated 1562, which reads thus: "It has been reported to us that Tupac Amaru and Titu Cusi Yupanqui, his brother, the other captains, and the warring Indians with them, whom they have raised up against us in the valley of Biticos, left the aforementioned seat of Vilcabamba, armed, and pillaged and burned all the Indian houses of the *repartimientos* of Amaybamba and Picchu."

These were sacred sites, since Cristobal de Molina specifies that the deities Apu Tiki Viracocha and Urco Suyu Viracocha had their *huacas* there, but no doubt the Incas sacked them in order to create a vacuum before the conquistadors.

WHO WERE THE GUARDIANS OF THE PICCHUS IN 1614?

A "border dispute" broke out in 1614 between the proprietors of the lands of the Salccantay, on whose flanks the "Lost City" lies. Three centuries passed before Christian Bues, a German topographical engineer stationed in the Sacred Valley and in charge of carrying out surveys, noticed that the ruins uncovered by Hiram Bingham in 1911 belonged to the lands under litigation. Intrigued, Bues himself undertook researches which led him to publish, in the Cuzco newspaper *El Sol* in 1919, an article whose title caused a sensation at the time: "Who Were the Guardians of Machu Picchu?"

It was a question no one had ever asked! Now, the "Decision Regarding Borders," which put an end to the conflict (and which Bues found), answers that question, unequivocally, for once and for all. The lands of the Salccantay were allocated, as late as 1614, "to the *mitimaes* of the *ayllu* of the Cañari *chasqueros*, represented by their cacique Don Francisco Poma Gualpa"—that is, to a direct descendant of the clan of Ecuadorian Indians who came to Cuzco with Pizarro and were kept there in their ancient office of message-bearers, as in the time of the Empire of the Incas![3]

As we shall soon see, this document is doubly important because the presence of the Cañaris—the Incas' enemies and executioners—on the wild mountain of the Sacred Valley will be a precious clue for approaching another mystery set up by Bingham, concerning the "green stone chips" that he unearthed from the tombs at Machu Picchu.

A new question comes to mind: Did the proprietors of Machu Picchu and Huayna Picchu already mentioned know that the Ecuadorian *chasquis* had settled on the Salccantay? Everything suggests that they did know—which strengthens the impression that they never visited their property.

Bues found a second document which proves that these *chasquis* continued to occupy the sacred mountain in 1793. They then received "14 pesos a year to transport the mail from Cuzco to Arequipa," no doubt by way of the hidden route of the peaks, which passed through the "Lost City" of the Incas, climbed the high summits of the Salccantay, and redescended through the snow-covered slopes toward the Apurimac—the same route that the Vicomte de Sartiges used, grazing Machu Picchu!

[3] *Mitimaes*: a Quechua word (derived from *micmac*) designating settlers or groups of allies transferred by the Incas in order to populate an empty province or one rebelling against their influence. In the case of the Cañaris, for them to be sent to Machu Picchu was no doubt a form of reward, on the part of the conquistadors, for their faithful service; this might explain why the Indians burned the "Indian houses" of the Picchus.

Chasqueros or *chasquis*: a type of pedestrian mailman, who transported—on foot, throughout the empire, by means of a relay system—verbal or mnemonic messages, or occasional foodstuffs (such as fish from the Pacific) to the table of the ruling Inca in Cuzco.

DON LUIS BEJAR,
FIRST EXPLORER OF MACHU PICCHU

In 1894 and from then on, it is no longer possible to deny that Machu Picchu was known, at least by name, by all the *hacendados* and farmers of the Sacred Valley. At this time the ancient pre-Columbian city, abandoned but not *lost*, saw its age-old terraces bloom again, as Don Luis Bejar Ugarte, one of the earliest daring explorers of the Picchus, confirmed. He was led there by the young Agustín Lizarraga, *one of the guides Hiram Bingham would hire seventeen years later!*

Bejar Ugarte and Lizarraga discovered an Incan tunnel dug under the bed of the Rio Urubamba, but they did not reveal its exact location and they covered up the entrance. It was rediscovered only in 1930, by the engineer Oswaldo Paez Patino, and then its existence was confirmed by Senator Pancorvo, who ventured "into the subterranean passage with stone walls." This secret passage was designed, they imagined, to guarantee the safety of the Virgins of the Sun sheltered in the Picchus. How else would one explain the fact that in many places suspension bridges had connected the banks of the Rio of the Sun, whereas here, at the foot of the most remarkable sanctuary, no work of that sort had been planned by the anonymous builders!

THREE NAMES CARVED
ON A PALACE IN 1901

From this point on, there was much talk in Cuzco of the famous ruins to which Agustín Lizarraga, in 1901, led two of his friends (farmers and treasure-seekers from the region of San Miguel and the Colpani hacienda, to which Machu Picchu belonged). Together with him, these men— Don Enrique Palma and Gabino Sanchez—explored all the visible portions of Machu Picchu. They found "a rope so admirably preserved" that they used it in their work. They also carried off a mummy! Moreover, *they carved their names and the date of their visit*—July 14—on the megalithic wall of a palace, "for posterity," and, one imagines, to Hiram Bingham's profound disappointment.

MACHU PICCHU RENTED FOR $20 A YEAR

Amid the ruins the three adventurers came across the Indian Anacleto Alvarez, who, for the past eight years, had been renting the *andenes* of Machu Picchu for the modest sum of twelve soles a year. But, tired of the isolation, Anacleto was preparing to leave this place and the palace, the roof of which he had carefully restored with rushes and straw in order to shelter his family.

In 1914 the "tenant" of Machu Picchu is Melquiades Alvarez, who grows all the regional crops in the "hanging gardens" of the "Lost City." In 1906 the keeper of the bridge at San Miguel, at the foot of the ruins, talks about them at length with the muleteer Rodriguez Carpio, *another future companion of Bingham's.*

In 1911, Antonio Santander Cascelli (previously mentioned) admires the beans, *camotes,* pumpkins, and red peppers grown by Toribio Richarte, who now rents the ruins for twelve soles a year from the proprietor of the Cutija hacienda, Dr. Abull Vizcarra. In July of that same year, a few days before he sets out for the Sacred Valley, Hiram Bingham acquires from Tomas Alvistur, the great collector from Cuzco, three "Incan" specimens which Alvistur says he bought from *huaqueros* who swore they found them "on the *andenes* of Machu Picchu."

Also in 1911, the American Alberto Giesecke, accompanied by the deputy Don Braulio Polo y la Borda stops over at Mandor Pampa. A torrential rain prevents them from undertaking the planned climb up to the "Lost City" on the Old Peak. Nevertheless, Giesecke, a compatriot and good friend of Bingham's, gets from Melchor Arteaga, proprietor of the muleteers' way-station which the Yale expeditionists will soon pass by, all the details that will enable Hiram Bingham to make—without looking very hard—one of the most fantastic archaeological finds of this century!

CHAPTER TWELVE

The Last Living Witnesses

Equipped with the providential information that I gave him, Hiram Bingham reached ✖ *the extraordinary ruins of Machu Picchu* ✖ *on July 24, 1911.*

—Alberto Giesecke, 1961

INDIAN MULETEERS AND REVOLUTIONARIES

Might there still remain, among the inhabitants of Cuzco and the Sacred Valley, a few living witnesses from the Yale Peruvian Expedition, over a half-century later? I feared—correctly—that there might not be many. Many, indeed, missed their rendezvous with history.

Agustín Lizarraga, for instance, that picturesque treasure-seeker and indispensable guide for all the explorers of the Picchus well before Bingham. Agile as a vicuña, intrepid Lizarraga met with a tragic end one day when he was headed for a small corn plantation he owned on an island in the middle of the torrent. He slipped on a bridge made of branches and was carried off by the tumultuous waves of the Rio of the Sun; his body was never found.

Nevertheless, I was able to round up enough eyewitnesses to illumine—often in a very different light—Bingham's exploit and to record the names of many of his humble companions which do not appear on the honor roll of the pioneers of Machu Picchu, alongside those of the Americans—a gap that I hoped thus to fill in. These men, moreover, retained an occasionally touching memory of the young scholar from Yale. All described him to me as "cordial, friendly, fluent in Spanish—charming, in fact, with an indomitable dynamism and energy." If their statements sometimes contradict Bingham's declarations, the fact that none of the *peones* hired by the American ever read any of the books or articles that the explorer published upon his return to the United States makes their memories all the more sincere and lends them even greater value.

Luis Rodriguez Carpio, a native of Arequipa, first came to Cuzco in 1906. He traveled back and forth along the length of the Urubamba, from the capital of the Andes to Santa Ana, driving his fourteen mules loaded with sacks of coconuts for the rich *hacendado* already mentioned, Don Braulio Polo y la Borda, owner of the Echarate hacienda, one of the most famous in the lower valley, located far below Machu Picchu.

Carpio told me that the idea of visiting the "Lost City" had never occurred to him, even though he had heard talk of it every time he was forced to stop at Mandor Pampa on his journeys. It was mentioned not, as I imagined, as an admirable archaeological ruin but for a much more ordinary reason: because the unusually large *rocotos* "that grew in the Inca houses"—which were gathered by farmers who made a greater profit on them by going to sell them in the Indian market at Cuzco—were much hotter and burned his mouth more than any other red pepper from the area! Rodriguez Carpio's coppery face crumpled into amused wrinkles just imagining the surprise of the lovers of these *rocotos* had they known that these condiments were ripened on age-old terraces once reserved solely for the feasts of the Sun and its consecrated virgins.

The old muleteer of the Andes savored the memories of his youth, with no lapse of memory, even though he must have been well along in years when I met him. He pictured himself once again seated in a Cuzco *cerveceria*, drinking a glass of beer, when Don Lomellini came to him to offer him a fee of forty soles a week to guide the Yale Peruvian Expedition into the Sacred Valley. In accepting this salary (which was quite decent at the time), Caprio had no idea, he told me, that he was thereby signing up for three consecutive years. He recalled that Luis Valle, the governor of Ollantaytambo, procured four additional *peones* for them and that at San Miguel, Lizarraga and Monroy joined the expedition.

The prodigious climb to Machu Picchu took seven hours. Despite the altitude, Bingham went ahead of Carpio, waving his arms, letting out shouts, and bounding into the dense wood. But what struck the guide most of all was Bingham's attitude: He did not exhibit any of the enthusiasm or ecstasy that one would expect of someone confronted with the sight of the landscape and the splendid ruins. If he did experience such a feeling, as he notes in his book, it was not until the following year, 1912, during the second expedition. When Bingham discovered the marvelous "Lost City," forgotten for so long, Carpio heard him murmur: *"This is not what I was looking for!"*

Unlike most of the guides with the expedition, Oscar Santander Cascelli knows the date of his birth: July 3, 1899. Still lean and graying in 1964, he relates his experience haltingly. In 1911, at the age of twelve, he traversed the thick forests which conceal fabulous unexplored cities in the company of his father, who was being pursued by the constabulary for having been actively involved in the "revolution of Samanes." Hiding out in the mountains of the Sacred Valley, they became friends with Lizarraga and Toribio Richarte, whom they met at the entrance to Machu Picchu. But at that time, the young Santander, who would later become fascinated with archaeology, did not realize the significance of the ruins. What he appreciated much more were the pyramids of *andenes*, which were so well cultivated and which he described to the American scholar.

Gerardo Farfan, who participated in 1961 in a televised broadcast made by the Peruvian Channel 4 out of Lima, upon the occasion of the fiftieth anniversary of the discovery of Machu Picchu, recounted his memories publicly. He must have been about twenty-five years old when he hired himself out, along with his *recua* of forty mules, to the expeditionists. This was such a fantastic adventure for the muleteer that ever since, it has been his only topic of conversation in speaking with his neighbors and other caravaneers from the valley. For Farfan the clock stopped in July 1911, and the inexorable wheels of time went on without him.

Ricardo Charaja, another *peón* with the American expedition, was mentioned in Bingham's book; Bingham admired him and attributed to him the discovery of the "royal road of the Incas."

As chief muleteer, Charaja was responsible for both a caravan comprising 120 beasts of burden and a large team of Indian porters. Enjoying Bingham's complete confidence, he was proud of the fact that, by Bingham's order, he had also supervised the clearing of the ruins.

Marcos Arenas, from Ollantaytambo, died in 1970: he was over eighty years old. He was the eldest of the muleteers with the Yale Peruvian Expedition. Skilled from long experience, he was hired by Bingham and quickly became, he told me, Bingham's "favorite" when it came to preparing the loads—a task which requires extensive knowledge of the particular nature of each mule, for an unstable load, poorly balanced or not properly attached to the animal's flanks, can send it into the abyss.

According to popular rumor, Marcos Arenas—who had already accompanied Hiram Bingham in 1902, during his difficult trip to the ruins of Choquequirao—shared with Bingham certain "secrets" concerning other "lost cities" of great beauty, which they discovered together before and after Machu Picchu. But the American made him promise, I was told, never to reveal these secrets, and the muleteer kept his word till the day he died.

THE GENDARME AND THE *CHIUCHE*

Tomas Cobinas, a gendarme, took part in the second expedition, along with ten strong, heavy-set Indians recruited to erect a bridge across the Urubamba. Under his direction, they felled trees whose trunks measured 120 feet long, using as a support a rock implanted in the midst of the raging current. But the first red cedar trunk that they used got away from them, nearly carrying them along with it, and disappeared "from their sight like a wisp of straw in less time than it takes to say so."

Cobinas, who expressed himself in the highly imaged, poetic style of the Quechuas, called the torrent *"el señor Rio"* ("the Lord River") and spoke of it with great respect, saying that it "swept him away" with its violent fury.

It was this picturesque gendarme who, with his machete, first cleared—for Melchor Arteaga and the American engineer Heald—a narrow path "along the edge of the

Silver earpick,
representing a parakeet (Ara militaris)

precipice" to the top of the Huayna Picchu, where they arrived "skinned alive" by mesquite thorns.

These six men—with their etched features, tempered by the wind, the cold, and the Andean sun—viewed with narrowed eyes the unforgettable vision of a "lost city" which no one would ever again see as they were able to, still "virgin," untrod by Bingham. These are the last witnesses whose real-life memories I could collect. But perhaps there remain others, who recall—with the "dignity of silence" established by their ancestors—the fantastic saga of the *cañon* floor and the summit of the Picchus. Will their voices die out—if they have not already done so—without leaving an echo? Like that of the mysterious Quechua child who took Bingham by the hand and showed him the fabulous ruins?

The testimony of Mamani, the *chiuche* (foremost on the list of the guides of the Yale Peruvian Expedition), will no doubt always be lacking. Whatever became of the Indian boy who disappeared at the top of a temple like an "Indian sprite"? This mystery, added on to so many mysteries and long considered secondary, suddenly intensified in 1961 when the assemblyman Oscar Guzman Marquina grew indignant at the thought that, while the fiftieth anniversary of the discovery of Machu Picchu was being celebrated, no one could come up with one of Peru's "national heroes"! A bit later, however, the Peruvian parliament finally shook off its torpor. Forgetting red tape, they envisaged the creation of an "investigatory committee to identify him and reward him." But the project must now be gathering dust in some drawer.

Who, then, was this *chiuche*, a sort of Quechua gamin, who—at the instant Bingham, discouraged, was about to give up the search—was the instrument of fate and, by the same token, the source of the American scholar's discovery? Did he even exist?

A spirited controversy created two opposing camps. Without even bothering to reread Bingham's work, some denied the Indian child's assistance; others defended him. Together they engaged in pointless hostilities and sowed a doubt that still lingers.

In a detailed speech which he made—again, on the occasion of the fiftieth anniversary of the discovery of the "Lost City"—Alberto Giesecke recounted the very phrase in Quechua that the *chiuche* used to overcome Bingham's hesitancy: "Sir, Come . . . I know where there are Incan houses, over there . . . I know the way." Giesecke concluded that if Bingham finally discovered the famous "Lost City," it was "thanks to the providential insistence and help of a mysterious Indian boy, about whom nothing more was ever learned." This witness—*the most important of all*—thought the anonymous *muchacho* must have been the son of one of the Indian families that were then cultivating the "hanging gardens" of Machu Picchu for Melchor Arteaga.

According to another informant, the boy was called Mamani—the most common name in the Sacred Valley. And the mystery has not yet been cleared up.

THE AMENDATION OF THE DELEGATE COSIO

Two witnesses remain to be quoted, whom I have kept for last—one because he came later, and the other because he provides one of the most important "conclusions" in my entire inquiry.

Don José Gabriel Cosio accompanied the second Yale Peruvian Expedition in 1912, as a delegate of the Peruvian government and the Geography Society of Lima. This expedition, funded by Yale University and the National Geographic Society ($10,000 each), comprised, in addition to Bingham, ten American technicians[1] and the Peruvian engineer Carlos A. Duque.

When the National Geographic Society published Bingham's reports on the first Yale Peruvian Expedition, under the title "In the Wonderland of Peru," containing the detailed story of the sensational discovery of the "Lost City of the Incas,"[2] the impact on the scientific world was tremendous.

Publicized in all the American papers, the news aroused equal admiration among the general public. But in Peru? Even though it marked a red-letter day in the history of the archaeological investigation of the country's nebulous pre-Columbian past, Cosio claims that the Americans simply did not make the results of their scientific work known. "We only knew," he declares, "that Dr. Hiram Bingham came to Cuzco certain that he would find vestiges

---

[1] Professor E. Gregory Herbert, geologist; Dr. George F. Eaton, osteologist, ethnologist; Dr. Luther T. Nelson, surgeon; Albert H. Bumstead, topographer; Kenneth C. Heald, mining engineer; Robert Stephenson, assistant topographer; Ellwood C. Erdis, archaeological engineer; Paul Bertos, secretary; Osgood Hardy and Joseph Prescott Little, assistants.

[2] The special issue of *National Geographic* contains 180 pages illustrated with over 250 photographs. Printed in an edition of 1,000 copies, each costing $50, it is now extremely rare.

of the ancient Peruvian civilization which extended as far
as the region of the tropical forests, where it had one of
its principal seats."

José Gabriel Cosio was informed of Bingham's extraordinary find only in the month of October, in a letter from
the rector of the University of Cuzco, whom sickness had
kept at Lima and who was none other than Bingham's
"informant," Alberto Giesecke.

This delay, which is also inexplicable, was not, one
imagines, to the *cuzqueño*'s taste. A certain indignation
was evidenced, echoes of which persist to this day. Consider, for example, this personal memo from the delegate
Cosio to the Peruvian Minister of Public Education:
"During his second trip to Peru, Dr. H. Bingham reached
the peak of Machu Picchu, where he found the city of the
same name, which he claims—illegitimately—to have discovered . . ." Chivalrous despite all, Cosio did not quibble
with the American over who deserved credit for having
been the first to give Machu Picchu "the seal of fame and
archaeological interest." And he drew up a laudatory
account of the results obtained by the Americans, among
which he emphasized the osteological studies carried out by
Eaton in the legendary region of Pacaritampu. Numerous
fossil remains were unearthed, which reveal an extremely
varied fauna, totally extinct for millennia: fragments of
elephant tusk, the bones of a megatherium, and the
mandible of a primitive horse, practically at ground level
in the Ayusbamba hacienda, which was founded on the old
bed of a dried-up lake countless centuries ago.[3]

Other fossilized bones from the *quebrada* Aya Huaco
(the "Ravine of Cadavers") led Bingham to believe that
"the history of Cuzco is longer and that it began thousands
of years before that of other sites in America."

Geographical studies would seem to indicate that these
remains of vertebrate animals were carried along by alluvia

---

[3] At least ten thousand years ago a pre-Columbian horse was
contemporaneous with Amerindian peoples who came by way
of the Bering Strait, which at that time was frozen over. I've
described in my book *Tiahuanaco* the cave paintings depicting
men on horseback recently discovered at an altitude of 4,500
feet in the caves of Mazo Cruz and Kelkatani, near Lake
Titicaca.

before being covered with a layer of glacial clay 30–80 meters thick, "30,000 or 40,000 years ago." The pelvic bone of a gigantic beast from the Tertiary Epoch, eight times larger than the corresponding bone on a modern horse, which the osteologist Eaton found in the Huancaco *quebrada*, could, in his view, "date back 70,000 years." The most disturbing thing is that these bones of bisons, wolves, and a guanaco *are mixed in with the remains of human occupation.*

GIESECKE'S EXTRAORDINARY UNPUBLISHED REVELATION

Because of the primary role that he played in the unknown history of the Machu Picchu, Alberto A. Giesecke overpowers the less forceful witnesses previously interviewed. Long before them, it was he—the possessor, through hearsay, of the most precise "secret" concerning the "Lost City"—who communicated it to his compatriot. Why did Bingham never cite him in any of his writings? When, at the end of the preface of his book, he "very sincerely" thanks all those who helped him (fourteen names follow), why do we not find—in the place of honor —that of his friend Giesecke? Why did Giesecke reveal the truth publicly only in 1961, during a conference held at the Peruvian-American cultural center, causing general amazement among those present at the time? He would not tell me.

He revealed only that in late June 1911 it was he who organized the official reception for Bingham. The explorer would visit his home every night. "We spoke mainly of the Urubamba Valley and the possible sites for ruins," he said. "Finding the exotic Viticos, the refuge of the last Incas fleeing before the Spaniards, had become an obsession, an *idée fixe* of Bingham's . . . At the invitation of the assembly-man Braulio y la Borda, I undertook the trip on muleback as far as the great Echarate hacienda. For seven days he told me about all the traditions, ways, and customs of the day-to-day life of the territory we covered, and with his hand pointed out to me the peaks where, according to the accounts of Indians who had gone off in pursuit of stray livestock, ancient ruins were hidden beneath the dense foliage. *One of the sites indicated by Don Polo was, in fact, Machu Picchu.*"

Was this trip (taken a few weeks before Hiram Bingham's arrival in Cuzco), which brought Giesecke to the very foot of the Picchus (which he would have visited had the rains not prevented him), a simple, lucky coincidence— or did it constitute a preliminary reconnaissance of the area for the sake of the young scholar from Yale? Alberto Giesecke would not answer this question, any more than he would the previous one. But he knew enough about it, he admits, so that Bingham, equipped with this "providential information," was able to discover the famous "Lost City" of the Incas.

CHAPTER THIRTEEN

From Mystical Nan Cuna to Railroad

All the roads remain . . . silent, disarticulated "living dead" who have forgotten the footfall of man; like giant serpents, they sleep through the night of neglect.
—Hermann Buse, 1961

THE "HIRAM BINGHAM ROAD"

Thirty-three years and two world wars pass before Hiram Bingham returns, in 1948, to Machu Picchu, at the invitation of the Peruvian government, to cut the blue ribbon that symbolically obstructs the brand-new steel bridge spanning the waters of the Rio of the Sun. This simple gesture precedes the inauguration of the narrow road that ever since has borne the name "Hiram Bingham Road."

With a width of 5 meters, constantly encroached upon by the luxuriant jungle that borders it, this modern road climbs a dizzying height of 500 meters in less than 8 kilometers, right up to the entrance to the ruins, by way of lightning zigzags cut into the Salccantay's steep flank.

On this day Hiram Bingham is no longer the eager young Yankee from the memorable Yale Peruvian Expeditions, but a sixty-three-year-old man with white hair. His blue eyes, scarcely dimmed and still as fascinating, are filled with emotion over this reunion with the enchanted city that he rescued from oblivion and offered up for the admiration of the world at the beginning of the century. Does he perhaps have a premonition that this trip will be the last time he sees Machu Picchu?

Erected in 1961, a bronze plaque engraved with the portrait and name of Hiram Bingham, "scientific discoverer of Machu Picchu," will henceforth greet some 15,000 tourists a year, who come from everywhere, braving the altitude and the vicissitudes of the journey in order to gaze —intoxicated by a cosmic ecstasy, in a site unique in the world, at an altitude of over 2,500 meters—upon the most famous "lost city," now reclaimed from a thousand and one Peruvian nights.

THE TRIP TO MACHU PICCHU: STILL AN ODYSSEY

At the time when Machu Picchu emerged from oblivion and the historical void, getting there from Lima still represented a veritable expedition. Obviously, the conditions have changed. While some miss the spirit of adventure, the simple tourist can be grateful—although there still remains, even today, enough of the unexpected for this "organized" trip to take on a touch of odyssey. Flying level with peaks which exceed 6,000 meters in altitude and suddenly give way to a churning sea of white clouds beneath the airplane's wings is enough to distress the most daring of travelers. The waves of leaden granite, crumpled and petrified, from which emerge snow-covered peaks and sparkling glaciers, evince the birth of Dantesque worlds which are still in eruption, and far from settled. Beneath the cabin shaken by air pockets, through the windows, are outlined Indian pueblos which suggest Christmas crèches. All around, the crazed forest invades constricted gorges. Everywhere, the Inca *andenes*, still cultivated, flourish as they did thousands of years ago, with ears of corn, but also with fields of barley and wheat—grains imported by the conquistadors.

Between the jagged peaks, isolated lagoons—with glaucous water the color of turquoise, emerald, or steel—fill ancient extinct craters, where half-wild horses and earthbound waders come to quench their thirst.

When the rock "heads" of the Salccantay come into profile, plastered white, the pilot of the plane begins a long descent, in order to land on the swampy Pampa de Anta, bordered by weeping willows.

Because of the altitude of the landing strip (about 3,500 meters), the stewardess warns the passangers to move and walk slowly. Nevertheless, as soon as the door is opened, it sometimes happens that one of them is suddenly knocked out by the scarcity of oxygen and falls unconscious, overcome by *soroche*, the terrible "mountain sickness."[1]

Just as in Bingham's time, when the true adventure began in Cuzco, the capital of the Andes, today it starts in the small, picturesque station of the Cuzco–Santa Ana *ferrocarril*.

The traditional history of the Incas and the conquistadors begins at the outskirts of Cuzco, on the threshold of the Sacred Valley. Bloody battles once took place on the immense Pampa de Anta, a sandy plain bronzed and oxidized like old copper, enlivened by flocks and natives in multicolored costumes. The battles first took place between the Incan legions and their hereditary enemies, the savage Chancas; then both were allied in an epic struggle against the Spanish invader. Finally the Spaniards fought among themselves, Pizarrists versus Almagrists.

Soon the immaculate *nevados* of the Urubamba and Vilcabamba are gleaming on the horizon. The railway and road, parallel for a moment, follow and repeatedly cross the ancient paved road of the Incas, long undiscovered, which, according to recent findings, ended at Huaca Puncu, the sacred entrance to Machu Picchu, which has not yet been cleared of debris and the devouring tropical jungle.

Stretching past, the "green summer garden of the Incas" of the Yucay Valley is strewn with brick *ranchos* made of reddish earth dried in the sun. They are the same color as the ground; one can distinguish them only by their straw roofs, which let off trails of smoke. Occasionally there is a bouquet of red flowers or a few ears of corn attached to a bamboo pole hanging over the door, to indicate a *chichería*.[2] All the Indian huts are sheltered behind a curtain of cacti, including thorny nopals and gigantic agaves. Here and there, tall candle cacti loom, bristling with sharp needles, bordering the railway or the road. Then the valley closes in on the railway, which now follows the sinuous course of

---

[1] See the tourist information at the end of the book.

[2] Shop that makes corn *chicha*, which is not "masticated and spit back out by women" (as certain imaginative—or imaginary—voyagers claim, confusing it with the *masato* of the Amazonian tribes), but fermented, after the grains have been boiled, in enormous ceramic jars called *chimbas*.

the river, giving way to the grandiose Urubamba Cañon, festooned with riotous vegetation. The tentacles of a dense bush, characteristic of equatorial jungles, shoot up toward the sheer flanks of the granitic peak. The trees drip with a permanent humidity which hangs long reddish beards and pendants on branches tangled with lianas and delicate orchids. Waterfalls trickle over the train, which slips into a series of tunnels bored into the very rock. When it emerges, a profusion of colors and shapes fill a terrifyingly wild natural setting, swarming with closed squadrons of *puma-waqachis*, tiny mosquitoes which bite until they draw blood. How did the Quechuas succeed in penetrating such a terrain and mastering so chaotic a place? One never ceases to be astonished!

Beyond Cedrobamba is a shabby, decrepit little town—unlike most Andean villages, which are usually brightly colored—which nonetheless bears the most resonant name in all Peru, that of Machu Picchu, subtitled "Aguas Calientes." As in the Old West, the train travels along the center of the "main street"—the only street in the rustic hamlet. This Machu Picchu is but the "port," the resting place of the mestizo caravaneers whom one finds drinking straight from bottles and playing dominoes in the *piquantería,* where they linger from the late beginning of a cloudy day until night, which falls early in the notch of the *cañon* wrapped in milk-white clouds. The Indians walk barefoot on the rails and are dislodged—with a great spurt of steam and a clanging of copper bells by the train—or else by the *autocarril*, which slips among the houses without even slowing down, and tears into "Machu Picchu Station." Hence the anxiety of the tourists, who, their hearts pounding, can nowhere find—no matter how high they look—any signs of the famous "Lost City," still invisible in the blue crevice of the sky. If forewarned, they may be able to distinguish the light spots of a few *andenes* suspended from the Old Peak and—even more incredible—the granite arrowhead of the Young Peak.

One can easily see why, after the Spanish colonization, few were the whites who sallied forth as far as this impasse at the edge of the world. And if some did venture this far, they never suspected the presence of the admirable pre-Columbian city whose occupants, fleeing society, willingly allowed it to disguise itself in the conniving forests.

THE STOP AT "PUENTE RUINAS"

It is at the other side of the "Puente Ruinas," scarcely wider than the minibuses jammed with international tourists, and a few paces from the Museo de Sitio, that there begins—with the Hiram Bingham Road—a phantasmagorical return to past eras.

An acrobatic journey, lasting about twenty minutes, replaces the assault on foot, with machete in hand, of Bingham's party, and, after that, the uncomfortable climb on muleback up a dizzying path, which took another three hours or more.

Waterfalls and huge ferns flank the modern road, which ends at the flower-covered front steps of the Hotel Machu Picchu.[3] Only a few steps beyond, a panorama to take one's breath away plunges, hundreds of meters below, to the bottom of the precipice carved out by the Rio of the Sun (which ties a silver loop around the base of the Picchus) and rises high into the clouds, where the uninhibited dance of the Andes lets loose. A hundred paces farther—even though from the hotel one cannot always guess its presence —the tourist suddenly discovers the entire famous "Lost City" of the Andes.

From the top of this abyssal slope (after having climbed, one by one, the steps of the mountainous labyrinth that leads to the entrance to the ancient sacred city), overwhelmed by "the strange sensation that here strips all human beings of their terrestrial contingencies," the poet Juan Larrea admires it, as if it were "hung from the stars." Like the Indian, he feels it makes his soul take wing, and he becomes a cosmogonic Son of the Sun. This is not the work of men, he believes, "but of beings intoxicated by a metaphysical vertigo that forced them to respond, with the best part of themselves, to a mysterious call."

THE IMPERIAL ROAD OF THE CORDILLERAS

In pre-Hispanic times, unlike today, access to Machu Picchu was not gained starting from the riverbanks and

---

[3] In 1972 the Peruvian government undertook a project to construct a large nine-story tourist hotel, designed so as not to interfere with the harmony of the landscape.

proceeding toward the peak, but, inversely, from above, redescending bit by bit. The discovery of the secret tunnel beneath the river indeed seems to prove that there was no intentional passage in this part of the *cañon*. However, a road for agricultural traffic probably linked all the riverside towns, as Angles Vargas claims, thereby setting his word against the opinion currently held by his colleagues, who are secure in the belief that before this century no route existed beyond Ollantaytambo and in the hollow of the Urubamba Valley, as the chroniclers suggest.

Guided by Ricardo Charaja, Bingham went along part of the ancient route, which, snaking along the spine of the cordillera, connected a long rosary of splendid residences and fortified sanctuaries,[4] all overlooking, from high above, the Sacred Valley of the Incas and the *cañon*. This route, which was part of the Inca Nan or Nan Cuna, the impressive imperial road, was a masterly demonstration of what the frail human hand was capable of accomplishing in the intelligent struggle with an insane topography.

The Inca Nan traversed all of the Tahuantinsuyo, "on the path of the Sun," from the central Andes of Quito, the capital of Ecuador, into Argentina and Chile. The main route was connected with a vast network of secondary roads, linking the high summits to the coastal deserts of the Pacific and even the edges of the Amazonian forests, beyond the eastern Andes. It is paved or covered with granite slabs between two stone retaining walls, equipped with stairways with steps carved or set in the rock where slopes are too steep, and raised over swamps; its straightness surprised the conquistadors all the more because the road, instead of going around peaks, transected them practically in a straight line. It has been written: "By virtue of its construction, its extent, and the daring of its builders, it seemed to them superior to the Roman routes of the time,

---

[4] Runcu Racay (altitude: 3,800 meters), Sayacmarca (or Cedrobamba, 3,730 meters), Huayna Qente (2,850 meters), Phuyupatamarca (or Coriwayrachina, 3,650 meters), Huiña Huayna (2,700 meters), Intipata (2,900 meters), and, much lower, over the Urubamba, the ruins of Chachabamba, Choquesuysuy, and Llactapata (about 2,000 meters).

to the pyramids of Egypt, and to anything that any king had ever invented, be he Alexander, Darius, or Cyrius."[5]

Four or 5 meters wide, and constantly traversed—from one end of the empire to the other—by the *chasquis* with extraordinary speed, the Nan Cuna also accommodated a military column. This flat road permitted "clear passage for one or two Spanish carts or six knights side by side without touching," the chroniclers tell us. And as early as the pre-Hispanic era, it accommodated caravans of slow, proud llamas, the only beasts of burden used in ancient Peru.[6]

Constantly cleaned, the Incan routes "were tidy, without a single pebble or weed or wisp of straw, before the Inca's litter," Cieza de León raved, adding: "How and in what way were such grand, superb roads, so large and good, made? . . . What human forces and what instruments were able to raze mountains and move boulders? I believe that, no matter how great the power of Charles V may be, if he wished to order that another road like that which goes from Quito to Cuzco, and from Cuzco to Chile, be built, it would not be enough without the great order with which the Incas commanded that it be done."

"In peacetime," wrote Zarate, his contemporary, "the Inca would set out to visit his kingdom with great majesty, seated on a rich litter of excellent wood encrusted with gold and silver, sculpted with designs of the Sun and Moon or great coiling serpents. Curtains of woven wool, hung from two high gold arcs, protected him from being seen, but they had holes in them so that he could see out."

---

[5] The Nan Cuna, or "path of time," consisted of two major, parallel networks, one running through the heights of the sierras, the other along the seacoast. Its total length, according to the chroniclers, was between 10,000 and 20,000 kilometers: 8,000 in Peru and the rest distributed among Ecuador, Chile, Bolivia, and even Argentina.

[6] The great Maya and Aztec civilizations of Central America felt the lack of the llama (common from southern Colombia into Argentina), even though its carrying capacity is poor. However, the fossilized bones of guanacos have been found in North America, proving that the species lived there, but in earlier epochs.

Zarate also describes "the king's guard, with halberdiers and archers," who marched in ranks around the litter, "followed by 5,000 men with their captains . . . *Chasquis* went ahead to announce the Inca's arrival, and the mountains were covered with people, who shouted praises as if to a god."

The bearers covered "four leagues or more a day." The Inca collected fresh supplies at the *tambos*, and mobilized all the men and children to carry the loads from one city to another.

The archaeologist Paul Fejos notes that currently "most of the Inca ruins would be practically inaccessible without the ancient roads." Many are unexplored. A number of legends hold that these roads—"the most daring in the world," according to Hermann Buse—lead to other "lost cities," full of Inca treasures. Who would not believe them?

MAGICAL ROUTES ALONG A "LINE OF COSMIC FORCE"

Other than the Inca, his legions, and his *chasquis*, the only people allowed to travel great distances were his "special envoys" (in charge of overseeing the territory, public works, statistics, and control of supplies; recruiting artisans, artists, and Chosen Women; drawing up taxes consisting of livestock, crops, wool, and cotton), provincial administrators, certain travelers engaged in commerce or barter, pilgrims and processions, and the *callawayas*, herbalists and empirical healers.

All travelers were required to display at all times "passports," or signs befitting their social station, which proved that the Inca had authorized their journey.

But knowledge of the "mystical" routes that connected the cities of the gods and the high priests of the cult was certainly forbidden to the common Indian mortals and reserved solely for the elite closely related to the Inca and for the sacerdotal class. An ignominious death was probably the penalty for the slightest infraction of the secret ritual. And the road to Machu Picchu probably was connected to the *sekes*, or "magical" routes, along which proliferated *huacas*, or liturgical stations, and which constituted a "cosmic force line," interpreted according to divine interventions, by Incan seers and magi.

Thus, one can assume that the celestial trail of the "Lost City" and of its satellites found thus far (there must remain others still masked by the jungle) was in no way a "national" or public route, and that the only people to use it—showing great respect—were the most illustrious personages in the empire: the Sapan Inca (supreme leader), his family, his gynaeceum, his court, his great captains, the members of the solar clergy, and his faithful vassals, whom the monarch invited to sumptuous ceremonial feasts. A strict supervision must have guaranteed secrecy and security. This is shown by the innumerable monolithic watchtowers that mark the summits overhanging the banks of the Rio of the Sun, erected at strategic points and enjoying an ideal panoramic view of the Sacred Valley as well as the nearby peaks. They were located in such a way that each was within another's line of sight, thereby preventing any risk of surprise, whether profane commerce or sacrilegious violation. This surveillance, entrusted to warriors whose loyalty had long been proved (the assignment constituted one of the most sought-after rewards), enabled them to discover and turn back any traveler not provided with the "sesame" conferred by the Inca himself: a strand of red wool pulled from the *mascapaicha*, or imperial headdress.

In 1912 José Gabriel Cosio discovered the branch that, opposite Ollantaytambo, stems from the ruins of Incasamana (the "Inca's Resting-Place") and leads toward Machu Picchu along extremely perilous slopes. The Indians who pointed it out to him still used it, they admitted, but secretly.

Other paved ramifications stem from Sacsahuaman, above Cuzco, and pass through Anta, Huatta, Huarocondo, Zurite, and Limatambo. Cleaving to the orography of the majestic peaks, these routes are provided with long flights of practically vertical carved steps and "flying staircases," or else tunnels fitted with interior stairways and benches. Now, *they all converge in the direction of Machu Picchu.* From the height of the Young Peak, I made out the main branches, which disappear under the green shroud of the jungle or in the faults opened up by earthquakes. This serves to show—almost to prove— that, far from being an isolated city, the "Lost City" was not "unknown" to the Incas, as certain investigators imagine, having failed to consider the facts. But this network of roads, now disjointed, was so cleverly concealed that neither the Spaniards nor the archaeologists coming from Cuzco (for example, Tello and Fejos, who in 1942 painstakingly explored the peaks of the Urubamba) ever discovered it!

The better to protect the mystery that surrounded Machu Picchu, the Nan Cuna vanished in the steepest spots. Certain passages leave room only for a foot's width and allow travelers to proceed only in Indian file. Thus, any espionage mission or mass attack was impossible, and Machu Picchu remained invulnerable by night as well as by day, "in its rank as imperial city, the most secret of them all."

A UNIQUE DISCOVERY: AN INCA DRAWBRIDGE

As if all these precautions were not enough, the inhabitants of Machu Picchu invented a system of drawbridges, the only known example of which was recently discovered by Angles Vargas. Located 2 kilometers from the entrance to the "Lost City," this ingenious device prevented anyone from approaching from the south, even though this would have been possible only by way of a terrible path, along a narrow ledge beside a harrowing ravine. Another discovery, among the most unusual ever made in Peru, is the fact that this path is itself artificial: it is, in fact, composed of the top of a narrow and very high wall which rises up from the bottom of the abyss!

"The work of Titans," swears the explorer who made this find, this path-wall supports a rustic bridge made from four tree trunks, located at the point where passage is most difficult; if raised by the guards posted on the side of the city, it would leave, gaping over the void, a space too large to jump across.

The construction of the whole—wall, path, and bridge— "conforms," Angles Vargas emphasizes, "to well-thought-out security measures. In fact, it would have been much simpler for the Incas to build another road, larger and easier to travel, in the same direction. But they needed a route that would make it easy to defend the site and that could be used at will."

AERIAL SIGNAL STATIONS

Hiram Bingham, overcome with vertigo, with two of his Indian guides hanging onto his legs, made out the ruins of several signal stations, "from which it was possible for messages to be sent and received across the mountains . . . located on top of one of the most stupendous precipices in the Andes."

Their construction, he noted, "required great skill and extraordinary courage." The American explorer calculated that "If any of the workmen . . . slipped he must have fallen three thousand feet before striking any portion of the cliff broad enough to stop his body."

Similar stations for fire and smoke signals are found at the top of the summits neighboring Machu Picchu, from which, moreover, one could discern the most distant human form and from which it was easy to alert the guardians of the sacred city so that they might turn away the undesirable visitors.

From atop the Huayna Picchu, which overlooks the "Lost City," the Incan sentries could easily keep watch on a large portion of the Sacred Valley. They could maintain without interruption—or establish in record time—contact with all the surrounding cities, by means of prearranged aerial signals visible from Machu Picchu all the way to Cuzco.

PART FOUR

Machu Picchu,
Skyscraper
of Ancient Peru

*At an altitude of 2,500 meters, Machu
Picchu was programmed for solitary man in
search of his soul.*
—Bernard Lelong, 1973

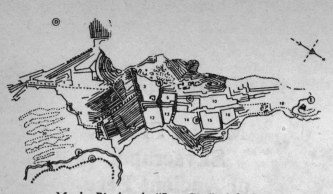

Machu Picchu, the "Lost City" of the Incas

A. Hanan, the upper city. B. Hurin, the lower city. C. Picchu, central summit. D. Machu Picchu, the Old Peak (altitude: 3,140 meters). E. Huayna Picchu, the Young Peak (altitude: 2,760 meters). F. Rio Urubamba. G. Cuzco–Santa Ana railroad.

1. Route of the Apacheta, or Inca Nan. 2. Huaca Puncu *portada*. 3. Central group, or Yachay Huasi. 4. Torréon of the Sun, or Sumtur Huasi, and Royal Mausoleum. 5. King's group, or Inca Huasi. 6. Temple of the Three Windows. 7. Principal Temple, or Carpahuasi. 8. Sacred Plaza, or Inti Cancha. 9. Pyramid of the Intihuatana. 10. Intipampa, public plaza. 11. Great Stairway of the Fountains. 12. Lower group. 13. Prisons and sacrificial condor. 14. Group of the Two *Morteros*, or Pucamarca. 15. Group of the Three Gateways, or Acllahuasi. 16. Upper group. 17. Sacred Rock, or Pachamama Huasi. 18. Path to the Huaynu Picchu. 19. Upper *andenes*. 20. Amphitheater of *andenes*. 21. Western *andenes*. 22. Great southern *andenes*. 23. Exterior Barracas. 24. Path to the inn and the ruins. 25. Eastern *andenes*. 26. Ancient tombs. 27. Aqueduct. 28. Modern inn for *turistas*. 29. Funerary rock. 30. Puente Ruinas. 31. Hiram Bingham Road.

CHAPTER FOURTEEN

An Opera in Stone

> *In the eyes of those who look upon it for the first time, Machu Picchu is a dazzling, enchanted city, invented on another planet. A miracle of thaumaturgy, it retains, in its entrails, something that surpasses the majesty of the Roman Forum and the Parthenon of Athens.*
>
> —Luis Pardo, 1961

A PETRIFIED MODEL

In 1967 the French architect André Frischander, a consultant for UNESCO, was assigned to study a project to restore the ruins of Machu Picchu. All he needed to do was examine the photographs of the "Lost City" that were submitted to him to decide that the present access to the "skyscraper" of the Incas should be modified, because it leads tourists right up to the monuments, without any transition to allow them to appreciate—from the summits, as in the day of the Incas—a truly magical view of the whole.

Less circumspect, the Peruvian technicians call the modern entrance to the ruins—by way of agricultural terraces and past the so-called "farmers' houses"—a "sacrilege."

It is quite obvious that, in order to respect the past, the sacred city should be approached by way of the ancient Nan Cuna straddling the peaks.

This imperial highway, which overlooks the entire archaeological complex, reveals, like a fascinating kaleidoscope, a panorama without equal on this planet. Frischander believes that if tourists were able to take this route, they would sense, from the moment they arrived, "the emanations that this incomparable city gives off," or—

as another romantic visitor has expressed it, even more
poetically—"the life force, the mystery of death, the round
of world, and the birth of gods which inspired its
anonymous creators."

Hiram Bingham dedicated about a hundred pages to the
history of the Incas and nearly as many to the search for
the "lost capitals" of Manco Inca. But he devoted less than
thirty to the description of Machu Picchu. It will take me
many more to examine and retrace all the mysteries and
beauties of this "opera in stone," as seen by Alberto
Hidalgo, "made from the passion, dreams, and blood of
men who gave it wings."

It is true: The sight of Machu Picchu, anchored on a
granite pedestal which floats on a billow of white clouds,
arouses—like no other place, because of the intoxicating
effect of the high-altitude air—an irresistible feeling of
ecstasy. From the first glance, Machu Picchu appears as
the admirable symbiosis of a perfect harmony between the
natural setting and human endeavor.

Bordered on three sides by bottomless precipices, surrounded by hollowed-out funerary caves, lightened by the
flight of pyramidal terraces and the green space of the great
central squares, as well as by the gradation of the ritual
baths, the framework of the resuscitated city (which covers
700 meters from north to south, along a width of 400
meters) is balanced by the fantastic network of stairway-
streets which connect all the groups in the two sectors
(that of the upper part, or Hanan, and that of the lower,
or Hurin: twelve districts all told), to which are added the
two levels corresponding to the agricultural area. In all,
there are 216 buildings, palaces, temples, dwellings, or
miradors with three or four walls, of which about forty
have an upper story.

THE APACHETA

At the edge of the crests, the Inca Nan reaches an
altitude of 3,100 meters (within sight of the sleeping city),
by way of a series of descending ramps, graded between
the parapets that prevent one from straying from the path.
The closer one gets, the more the Incan highway assumes
the characteristics of a *via sacra*, in which the visitor can
progress only from gateway to gateway, and from paved

landing to landing, counting from two to nine tiers which keep growing larger, right up to the main checkpoint, the Apacheta, which blocks the passage. It is impossible to get around this quadrangular building 16 meters long and 8 wide, with walls a good meter thick, made of monoliths which guarantee invulnerability and the safety of the esoteric mysteries of the monumental city.

Five high *portadas* (two for entering, three for leaving) and nine trapezoidal niches—like all the apertures of the typically Incan or ancient Egyptian style—adorn the building, which the road runs through. As one leaves the Apacheta—opposite the pointed cupola of Huayna Picchu, veiled in bluish mist—one can make out, in the distance, the imperial highway and the Sacred Valley.

Everywhere the buildings, harmonious despite their austerity, break down into their geometrical lines, like those of a dazzling model, thanks to the rhythm and leveling of the groups. One discerns, overlooking the city from the highest artificial pyramid, the Intihuatana, dedicated to the solar cult, preceded by the Incan "chapels"; then, on a lower level, the intriguing wall pierced with three "windows" which perhaps are symbolic. In the middle, the green esplanade of the Intipampa, a vast rectangular plaza with several levels, separates the high western sector from the low eastern district surrounded by gigantic walls.

On the upper slopes extends the district of the royalty and nobility; lower down are those of the artisans and the enclosure of the Chosen Women; on the lower slope are the disturbing "prisons." Here and there are rocks that are deified, votive, or intended for sacrifices. And alongside the precipices, outlining a "Cyclops' ladder" from the piedmont up to the peaks, are the "hanging gardens," suspended hundreds of meters over the *cañon* and the Sacred Rio.

Thus revealed, the "Lost City" looms as if magically rooted in the mountain, which supports it and hoists it onto its back, level with the sky. Looking out over the panorama gives one a sense of bottomlessness. Still, this did not faze the daring funambulists of the pre-Columbian Andes who—defying at each step the powerful attraction of the void, vertigo, and the death wish—here took (more so than any other architects and builders in antiquity) unimaginable risks.

"Whosoever sees you from here—o eternal, nearly intact monument to the glory of Peru!—believes in your people and will never forget you," exclaims Hermann Buse, one of the few Peruvian archaeologists to have studied Machu Picchu, stone by stone, in its entirety.

Fascinated by this indescribable sight, one stops, before proceeding any farther, to ponder for a moment what deserves the most praise amid this flawless city built of light-colored granite, posed like a diadem on the Old Peak. The site, simultaneously Dantesque and Edenic? The megalithic complex? Or the dark apocalypse of the sierras? Or perhaps the omnipotence of the jungle which embellishes the paradise of the Quechuas, embroidering it with flowers?

And one wonders, like Luis Velasco Aragon, whether actually "Machu Picchu was not built by the winged men represented on the Door of the Sun at Tiahuanaco."

THE FORTIFICATIONS

Defended from the base of the Picchus by the vertical *cañon* and the torrential Urubamba, Machu Picchu was defended from above as well; there the access slope (on the Huayna Picchu side), which was impassable because of its narrowness and the feeling of vertigo, was such that a few men could easily have headed off an army, however intrepid. To the north, east, and west, the vertical slopes over the abyss are equally inaccessible. Moreover, warriors posted on the promontories could easily have tipped tons of rocks onto potential attackers—"a favorite method of Inca soldiers," notes Bingham correctly.

To the south was "a veritable Thermopylae," he adds: "No one could reach the sacred precincts unless the Inca so decreed"—without running the risk of being crushed by projectiles. But wherever the abyss did not naturally provide an invulnerable defense, stone-lined ditches, at least 3 meters deep, or walls made out of polygonal blocks, reaching twice that height and 2 meters thick along the base, protected the city, which—as we have already seen—was cut off by a sort of rustic drawbridge. Finally, interior ramparts enclosing each group completed the system of fortifications. Thus, it seems that Machu Picchu must have been a fortified city, in the real sense of the word, not just to prevent the profanation of the sanctuary but also for military purposes.

Past the Apacheta, a monolithic stairway unfurls like a fan, in nine steps, bordered on one side by a *mirador* in the form of a balcony perched over a dizzying fault in the *cañon*, at the bottom of which coils the Urubamba, so far down that one can scarcely hear its rumbling. Then the path inclines gradually down twenty steps, to the Tambo located below.

TAMBO AND TOMBS

A second guardpost, which once again blocks the passage, the Tambo must also be traversed in order to follow the path, and one imagines that vigils were kept there day and night.

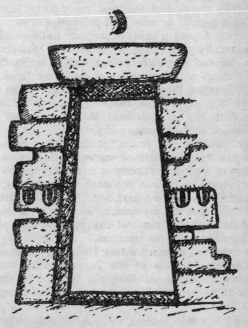

*Portada of the central group,
with "locking" mechanism, Machu Picchu*

We know that thousands of *tambos* were built all along the Nan Cuna, spaced one *jornada*[1] apart. Square or rectangular, this type of waystation was divided into compartments with facing doorways. According to the chroniclers, certain *tambos* along the royal roads could shelter hundreds of warriors posted in the adjacent fortresses. To the permanent garrison were added stores of military material for traveling armies, food, clothing, weapons, and the necessities of each profession, as well as provincial tributes. The state officials and other authorized travelers found, in the Incan *tambos*, a resting place and protection from the cold and the freezing rains. A llama park and small enclosures for guinea pigs were also present.

From the "scale-model" Tambo at Machu Picchu, the paved way descends to a white rock, carved along several geometrical planes, which give it the appearance of a pyramid in progress, as is shown by the granite blocks piled up by the side of the road, ready to be fit into the monolithic puzzle, or only half-polished.

Passersby deposited ritual offerings on this divinized rock before actually penetrating the sacred city. Another rock, with a pointed shape, decorated with a scalar "box of bricks," stands a little lower; it is called the "rock of the tombs," because Bingham exhumed bodies at its foot— "Chosen Women," he said, beautiful Acllas of the Sun who belonged to the elite devoted to the cult and to the maintenance of the sanctuary-city.

Near these "Virgins' tombs," in the shadow of the *cerro* Wairuru, a third votive rock, carved with steps, assumed the shape of a recumbent body or a funerary bed on which, the archaeologists believe, the dead were laid out so that they might be rendered a final, supreme homage. However, others think that the presence of an *argolla* on the north side of the rock indicates that the rock was used not only for funerals but also for sacrifices.

The extensive researches that I carried out concerning the elaborate worship of the Peruvian mummies have taught me that, in ancient Peru, the "afterlife" of the Incas and pre-Incas paralleled the daily life of the living. That

---

[1] Length of a day's journey, which varied with the terrain. A *jornada* was generally 5 or 6 colonial leagues (each of these covered about 8 kilometers).

the cult was so exacting explains why, upon their arrival, visitors to the "Lost City" were required, before greeting the living, to traverse, with unction, the residential district of the mummies and to converse with their immortal souls.

Strange monticules, paved with pebbles from the sacred river, rise from a polygonal platform in this upper "cemetery." These "tomb signs" suggest coffins. Before they were defiled and pillaged, did these tombs contain the remains of a clan that was privileged but did not belong to the aristocratic elite whose mummies were installed in beautiful mausoleums distributed outside the city itself?

From the angle of the platform, one can still see the stone hut of the Ayacamayoc, the gatekeeper and guardian of the dead.

A magnificent amphitheater composed of *andenes* tiered above the site could have been reserved for particularly careful cultivation of edible plants destined to feed the otherworldly hunger of the departed.

On the upper terrace another *tambo*, a long building with eight *portadas* opening onto an *anden* that served as a street, no doubt lodged a great number of servants or sentries.

THE "HANGING GARDENS" OF MACHU PICCHU

The "Lost City" springs from and is detached from the mountain by way of a cascade of "hanging gardens," which descend in degrees from the summit to the very edge of the abyss. To the east and west, the agricultural terraces recall —though they are even more daring—the famous gardens of Semiramis, in Babylon, ranked among the Seven Wonders of the World.

How lovely the sight of these "hanging gardens" must once have been, when they harbored plants with multi-colored blooms and were not merely carpeted with weeds!

Emilio Romero, one of the greatest Peruvian geographers, considers the *anden* "the most surprising creation in the superhuman work carried out by the men of the cordillera." This challenge hurled in the face of the Andean terrain—its domination in every sense—is, he declares, "the very foundation of the extraordinary agricultural and artistic civilization of ancient Peru."

Throughout the Sacred Valley, as at Machu Picchu, it is not unusual to see *a hundred tiers* of artificial terraces clinging to the perpendicular flanks of the mountains, which are outlined against and blend into a colossal landscape. The praises of these veritable "gardens of paradise" are sung by all the Quechua poets, lovers of the imposing natural setting that rules their fate.

The length of an *anden* varies with the orography. Some measure about 20 meters long (rectilinear or curved), 7 or 8 meters wide, and about a third as high. Others are as much as—or over—100 meters long.

Though all the *andenes* in the Sacred Valley are admirable in their ingenuity, the perspective offered by those at Machu Picchu is of a rare symmetrical perfection. Upon discovering, in the planimetric alignments and the superimposition of long rectangular areas, the arrangement of the bastion ramparts of military constructions, Hermann Buse wonders "what Vauban would have thought of them."

A short platform with 90-degree angles completes each terrace. The access to the enclosure, through an extremely narrow doorway, poses a question: For whom—or what—was it designed?

Two notched cyclopean walls flank the *andenes* of Machu Picchu; each is approximately 50 meters long and follows the inclined slope.

Many *andenes* certainly date back to distant pre-Incan epochs.[2] But we know that the great Inca Pachacutec, the

---

[2] The subject of the agricultural terraces of the ancient Peruvians leads to the question—still widely debated—of the introduction of agriculture in the New World. Frédéric Engel, a French investigator who has settled in Peru, is a specialist in the field. Nevertheless, and despite radiocarbon dating, he finds it difficult to distinguish between mere gatherers of woodland plants and the first primitive farmers.

Engel emphasizes the fact that in South America animal breeding was not contemporaneous with the beginnings of agriculture (as it was in the Near East, where the grains of barley and wheat and the bones of domestic animals have been found mixed together). The botanists, he notes, list the follow-

"Restorer" of the empire, distributed the arable lands of Cuzco among lords of the area and *curacas* allied with the state. As the surfaces proved insufficient, he ordered that all the slopes of the surrounding valleys be provided with well-constructed *andenes*. This mammoth enterprise, which must have taken five years, was so carefully carried out that the terraces are still used today by the farmers of the region, over a length of more than 150 kilometers! The surface thus gained must represent 7,500 hectares. Luis E. Valcarcel has calculated that with the carved stones from the containing walls of the *andenes*, one could circle the globe with a wall 2 meters high!

The earth for the tiers was carried up in baskets on men's backs, often to altitudes of over 4,000 meters, then spread over a porous bed of gravel and sand, which allows the copious rainwater to run off. This was yet another task for Titans, but also that of consummate mathematicians, for the inclination of the platforms demonstrates a precise calculation of the drainage of water by means of a system of canals and stone-lined gutters tunneled from one *anden* to the next, distributing the water to all levels before emptying the excess into a long sink.

At Machu Picchu a deep canal descends from the triumphal gateway to the city, in a straight line along the sharp decline, and ends just below the districts. A sink, as

---

ing under cultivated American plants: cotton, peanuts, corn, red peppers, beans, and—among the fruits—guava, *lucuma*, *palta* (avocado), and *chirimoya*, which have been found in ancient beds dating back 5,000–6,000 years on the Pacific coast and 3,500 years in the Andes. The gourd—which appeared much earlier (30,000 years ago)—in an object of controversy. Nothing so far has enabled the botanists to decide whether it should be classified with the potato, *camote* (sweet potato), *yuca* (manioc), and *olluca* and *jiquima* (which are exclusive to the high Andes); with the number of wild species; or with the vegetables that man already knew how to grow. Perhaps, Engel remarked, "gourds were propagated in such a way that, in view of their great usefulness cut in two (as bowls), man watered them, tending them without, however, knowing how to seed plants . . ."

straight as if it had been traced with a cord, and following an adequate slope, collects the excess water, preventing seepage and saturation, which would have undermined the terraces.

Hiram Bingham commented on the surprising irrigation of the Andes, effected by melting snow from the high peaks, which was collected and routed in gutters that follow the contours of the valleys along endless distances. "Inca engineers must have had good eyes and a fine sense of grading," he states, "since they had none of the instruments on which our engineers depend to lay out similar projects."

Cook, the botanist with the Yale Peruvian Expedition, a specialist in tropical agriculture, claims that "the Incas and their predecessors domesticated more kinds of food and medicinal plants than any other people in the world." They thus discovered an edible plant—the *papa* (which the conquistadors called the "potato")—which grows at altitudes of up to 4,500 meters, on the top of the Andes; over the millennia, they would develop a great number of varieties. Today, in the province of Cuzco, twenty-seven varities of *papás* are still being cultivated. All of them have great nutritional value; one bears the name "the royal root of the Incas." Certain *papas* harvested at a hacienda in Pumasillo, at the top of the Sacred Valley, weigh over 1.5 kilos—as big as a pumpkin.

However, it took almost three centuries after the Spanish Conquest of Peru before this irreplaceable tuber—the basis, along with corn, of the Incan economy—was introduced into the Old World, famine-stricken at that time.

As for corn (*Zea mays* or *zara* in Quechua), its origin remains one of the major mysteries confronting Americanists. According to MacNeish, the primitive plant originated in Mexico, where fossilized ears have been found which date back 4,000 years. Others contend that it appeared in Guatemala, where *teosinte*, a similar vegetable, grows—or else in Peru, where forerunners of corn (then unknown) produced, through hybridization with *Tripsacum, Zea mays*. We know one thing for certain: corn was cultivated in 1400 B.C., according to Kauffmann Doig, and 3500 B.C., according to Frédéric Engel, bringing about, he says, "the creation of skilled societies, as the first ceramists planted it in the central Andes, thereby modifying, for 3,000 years, the alimentary customs."

COCA, THE "GREEN GOLD OF THE ANDES"

The majority of the *andenes* in Machu Picchu provided alimentary plants for a population that must have totaled, presumably, some 1,000 individuals. But what else was grown on these extraordinary "hanging gardens"? A hundred species of orchids and other rare, sacred flowers, such as the red *kantuta* (*Cantua buxifolia*) and datura, with its heavy bells, snow-white and very heavily perfumed; also, medicinal plants, such as *pacae* (for its pods and leaves) and *huayruro* (for its talismanic grains, shaped like beans, half red and half black). But it is especially coca, the most magical herb and divinized leaf of all, that Eugenio Alarco thinks of when he looks at the *andenes* of the "Lost City": they emphasize, he says, the "central nature" of its cult.

Not only did the "green gold of the Andes" once stimulate the energy of the living (suppressing fatigue, thirst, and hunger, and anesthetizing pain from wounds or operations), it was "pleasing" to the mummies, as well as to the sun. Its shiny leaves were among the first order of sacrificial offerings for honoring idols, *huacas*, deities, mountains, springs, and *apachetas* (pyramidal rock piles which the Indians erected in mountain passes). Burned, they constituted the "incense" of the sun. Magi and master sorcerers used it in the divinatory art "to fly, by casting off earthly weight."

The name *coca*, which is not Quechua but Aymara, signifies "supreme plant." Its divine origin is explained by a widespread myth that has it being born in the body of a very pretty "savage" woman of the Antisuyo, whom the other women of the tribe immolated, jealous of the evil use to which she put her charms. The immoral woman was cut in half, and her remains nourished the first shrub known as Mama Coca. Because of the taboo, men were allowed to chew its magical leaves only after having performed the carnal act.[3]

[3] However, as Elizabeth della Santa (professor of Inca history at the University of Arequipa) notes, "In the time of the Incas, many *pallas* and women of royal blood were given the name Mama Coca, denoting 'the spirit of the plants' " and a woman of pleasure.

Long a rare drug,[4] coca was at first the monopoly of the
Inca; the green leaves were harvested from the imperial
plantations exclusively for his use. The Inca presented it
to the solar cult and offered his loyal allies little *chuspas*
(pouches made of beautifully woven wool or sometimes
llama hide), each containing a few leaves from the shrub.

Known for many centuries before the Incas, coca must
have been appreciated by them starting with Inca Roca,
following his conquest of the tropical forests. The historian
Cossio del Pomar relates that this domineering Inca sent
his son Yawar Huacac, "he who cries blood," to lead the
imperial legions. But the prince suffered terribly from the
atmosphere of the lower regions, which was too rich in
oxygen, and from the humidity. An Indian from the
Yungas, the Amazonian plains, who had with him a bag of
mysterious leaves, assured the young Inca captain that they
possessed magical properties. He taught him the way to
chacchar the bitter wad of coca with *llipta*,[5] in order to

---

[4] The leaves of *Erythroxylon novogratense* (*kkoka*) were
first brought back to Germany in 1857 by Karl von Scherzer.
The chemists Friedrich Wohler and Albert Niemann analyzed
it and isolated cocaine, which was thenceforth used in medi-
cine as a local anesthetic. Slightly rounder and smaller than the
leaf of the laurel, coca leaves, shiny and bright green, cover
thick bushes, about 3 meters high, which grow in sheltered
valleys, at altitudes of up to 3,000 meters, and are harvested
four times a year. At the beginning of the Spanish Conquest, the
viceroy Toledo, who considered it to be a vice among the
Indians, forbade cultivation: in Bolivia, the native miners of
Potosí were consuming 95,000 baskets a year! The yield
diminished so greatly, after the ordinance, that the civil authorities had to have it quickly annulled. Today coca is sold—as a
monopoly of the state—in all the markets in the cordillera,
where it serves as currency. The Indians practice *chaccheo*
from childhood (beginning at the age of five or six). A great
problem in Andean Peru, the annual consumption of coca now
amounts to tens of millions of kilos—enough to provide the
entire world with cocaine for at least twenty-five years.

[5] *Llipta* is a paste made of carbonate of lime and the ashes
of *quinoa* twigs, which doubles the dose of cocaine extracted
from the quid, or *acullico*. The Indian of the Andes consumes,
on the average, 60 grams of green coca leaves a day, from
which he distills—with the help of *llipta*—250 micrograms of
cocaine. Now, according to Dr. Kuczinski Godard, the human
body cannot tolerate more than 30 micrograms!

absorb only the juice, which would increase his forces
tenfold. The masticated drug indeed renewed Yawar
Huacac's vigor, and he ordered it to be distributed among
his weakened warriors.

The Indian told the Inca that his fellow Yungas worshipped the plant as a deity. From this time forward, "the
Inca was never seen without a pouch hung from his waist,
embroidered with gold and silver thread, and full of
precious leaves."

With the proliferation of the nobility and sacerdotal
castes empowered to use it, the demand for coca grew ever
greater. Now, as Eugenio Alarco remarks, it was precisely
at the time when the Incas were extending their dominion
toward the jungles of Vilcabamba that the use of the
"magical leaf" intensified throughout the empire, which
leads this author to believe that, given the fertility of the
cocales of this region, the splendid constructions of the
Urubamba Valley may have been "conceived for great
personages who lived near the plantations of sacred
bushes."

For his part, Uriel Garcia states that "the sorcerers of
Machu Picchu chewed coca during ritual preparations for
the union of the Virgins and the Inca, who represented the
Sun on Earth." Moreover, making a connection between
this hypothesis and the term *picchu* (translated as "peak"
or "mountainous protuberance"), he explains that this
Quechua word derives from the infinitive *picchay*, "to
masticate coca," whence the word *picchu*, used to describe
the quid that distorts the coppery cheek of the Indian
coquero. The wad of salivated leaves forms, in fact, a
distinct cone, which one often sees depicted, swelling the
faces of ancient wooden or gold idols, or those of the
ceramic "portrait vases" from the northern coast of the
Peruvian Pacific.

In this way the Quechua, endowed with an ingrained
sense of humor (interpreting, in its most subtle nuances,
his poetic idiom), would have made a metaphysical com-
parison between "the colossal granitic protuberance of
Machu Picchu, formed by nature on the face of the Andes,
and that which permanently distends his own face." As
supporting evidence, Uriel Garcia notes that the nearly
conical mountain that rises to the east of Cuzco is also

called Picchu and that the sun sets behind it—"which gives the word itself a concrete meaning."

Also, what is the exact meaning of *machu,* generally translated as "old"? In the Sacred Valley, where sorcery plays the most prominent role from the medical standpoint (for the Indian, sickness is "magical"), *machu* also designates, I was told, *an evil deity.* Should we not therefore translate Machu Picchu as "the Peak of the Sorcerer"— he who knew the magic capable of killing? Or, on the contrary, he who knew how to vanquish the god of evil?

As for the identity of the coca cultivators, one fact is obvious: They were Cañari Indians, whom we have already encountered so often near the Incas! Carlos Troll, a famous geographer, assumed that the Antis conquered by the legions from Cuzco (including the Cañaris) became "forced laborers," or *cocamayocs,* on the imperial plantations. He notes, in fact, that the sacred bush is found only in areas farther in the direction of the Amazon Basin. "Where the tropical valley is no longer cultivable," he notes, "there are no more fortified cities like Machu Picchu."

In conclusion: Were the *andenes* of the "Lost City" perhaps the famous "imperial coca fields" mentioned (without further details) by the chroniclers? According to a chanting legend, related by the folklorist Alfonsina Barrionuevo, "Achankaray, the prettiest of the Virgins of the Sun, grew between her warm palms the *akulli* which gave strength and vigor to the builders of the chapel-city . . ."

THE OUTER BARRACAS

The rural area of Machu Picchu is separated into residential or ceremonial districts by a wall which cleaves to the slope and the features of the terrain, delimiting the area and ensuring respect for the necessary social norms. Did this means that the clan of farmers were forbidden access to the interior of the magnificent city? One hesitates to think so, given the presence of "flying stairways" formed by five *sarutas* set into a wall, which lead to an entryway near the Torreón of the Sun. Thus, direct communication between the profane sector and the private groups seems to have been provided for—under certain circumstances or at certain times. Perhaps a sort of curfew existed at Machu

Picchu, which required that the Chosen Women (whom men were forbidden to look upon) return to the Acllahuasi, located on the other side of the city, in the low Hurin district, so that men could circulate there, in order to attend to their jobs or take their turn on guard duty.

It is through this area that the present-day "tourist" path—which starts from the Hotel Machu Picchu and leads to the groups known as the Barracas—enters the famous "Lost City." These buildings, more rustic, are located at the foot of the first pyramid of hanging terraces, alongside a second series which is just as monumental. The houses, tiered on six separate platforms, follow the rapid slope and end in one of the long "stairway-streets" of the archaeological complex.

Quadrangular, these buildings, constructed of wedged quarry stones, by means of *pachillas* (small irregular stones) which fill the interstices, housed—according to the most widely accepted theory—the *yanaconas* and *mitayos* of the groups of farmers, whose utilitarian pottery and broken *chicha* jars Hiram Bingham would discover. However, Bingham was not convinced that these were farmers! Perhaps, he said, these buildings were used, rather, as "barracks" for the soldiers who protected the city on the one side where it was relatively vulnerable.

Open on the north (that is, in the direction of the aristocratic sectors), *huaironas*—a kind of facade-less belvedere-gallery, roofed with lime—afforded a view of all comings and goings, whether nearby or distant. All this clearly suggests a careful watch.

THE HUACA PUNCU, SACRED GATEWAY

The Nan Cuna led the visitor to the highest point of the urban sector, to the very entrance to the city, where stands the Huaca Puncu, or Sacred Gateway (also known as the Cuzco Gateway), amid the monolithic surrounding wall. Was it possible to close off this *portada*, large and trapezoidal, made of granite polyhedrons of varying dimensions? And if so, how? No gateway—in the sense in which we use the word—has ever been found in any other pre-Columbian city in the Urubamba Valley that could objectively clear up this question. Nevertheless, most archaeologists, like Bingham, think that the door for these openings consisted of a frame of tree trunks, tied together by ropes made of braided agave fibers, which eventually disintegrated over time because of the humidity.

The enormous parallelepipedical lintel of the Huaca Puncu is surmounted, in the center, by a large ring stone. This "eye-bonder" must have served to secure the wooden panel by means of a vertical bar, fastened with a second bar which was placed horizontally, after its ends had been inserted on each side in cavities designed for this purpose. Victor Angles has found, in the hollows, a cylindrical piece of stone arranged vertically, around which the ropes that were part of the closing mechanisms rolled.

The screen closing the *portada* may have been made of llama hide stretched over a wooden frame. Other investigators picture a simple woolen curtain attached to the granite ring, or else strands of wool, whose color, thickness, and length constituted a "secret code." Only those who knew the "sesame" of the message could read in it whether, for example, pilgrims were allowed to enter, at what time, and under what conditions. Luis Pardo is of the opinion that the lateral orifices, carved in the body of the triumphal gateway, held the chains of "pumas or jaguars, felines symbolizing energy and courage."[6]

In addition, to reinforce the security system, the *portada* was topped—hastily, it seems, and in a later period, judging from the different style (quarry stones and clay mortar)—with a platform, from the top of which the defenders could easily repulse or wipe out attackers.

A romantic Hiram Bingham paused for a moment on the threshold of Huaca Puncu to recall—according to Alberto Giesecke—"its history of past splendors," imagining "the great personages of the empire, the supreme officiants of the cult, the regional kings allied with Cuzco, the lofty members of the nobility, and the famous men who enjoyed the Inca's esteem and crossed this threshold."

[6] A hypothesis based on a precedent: The access gateways of the Island of the Sun, on Lake Titicaca, were guarded thus. Moreover, the Cuzco plain had the shape of a feline, and Chavez Ballon, who believes that Machu Picchu was "a miniature Cuzco," wonders whether the "Lost City" was not also conceived so as to reproduce the outline of a puma or jaguar, the totemic animals of the Incas.

Who, today, preparing to enter the "Lost City," would not—however down-to-earth he might be—sense, indefinably, the invisible presence of the Incas? What tourists, Bernard Lelong wonders, however jaded they might be after an organized tour around the world, would not discover Machu Picchu as if they were "entering into religion"? Everyone expects that the surroundings will come to life and that the magic spectacle will begin anew; that the palaces will awaken and the wind will rustle the gold and silver leaves hung from the trees made of the same precious metals; that a perfumed Virgin of the Sun will invite us to follow the hieratic procession of the high priests going up to "tie" Father Sun to the liturgical rock; and that the Inca, covered with feathers and bedecked with gold, will offer us bitter *chicha* from the *kero* of lacquered wood encrusted with turquoises.

Intoxicated by the profound silence of the ruins, we shall have a hard time giving up the idea of reviving this mysterious world, the indelible memory of which arouses our curiosity and fires our imagination.

ONE HUNDRED STAIRWAYS
AND 3,000 STEPS

Before losing track, the members of the Yale Peruvian Expedition counted over 3,000 steps at Machu Picchu. Added to these now are numerous steps since brought to light; and an infinite number of other steps are still covered by the tropical bush. No one could fail to be transported by the nimble scales and acrobatic arpeggios of the stairways distributed throughout the city—or to think, along with Bingham, that "it must have taken somebody a long, long while and a good deal of effort to carve these steps out of the living rock. At any rate, the stone-cutter had the satisfaction of knowing that his work would achieve something as near immortality as anything made by the hands of man."

These 3,000 steps add up to over a hundred stairways, from very long ones to very short ones, which furrow—in every direction and on various levels—the worried brow of the "Lost City." They shape it with a rhythm rich with motion and life, and impart a sort of "transparency" to its perspective.

The lower steps spring from the hollows of the *cañon* and rise up to lose themselves in the clouds that hover over the city day and night. Hence, the pedestrian is obliged to mount and descend them unceasingly, in air that, at this altitude, is already rarefied. By turns low (as if designed for dwarfs) and large (on the scale of giants), these stone steps sometimes allow one to proceed only by squeezing between two walls, if the stairway is functional; or else, if it is ceremonial, they widen to the point where impressive processions could take place. Some fan out, slip among interior gardens, flare before a palace, or hurl themselves at a temple. The longer stairways are broken up into landings, where fortunately one can catch one's breath. They connect all the vital points, whether noble or common, from Hanan (the upper city, aristocratic and sacred) to Hurin (the lower city, urban and artisan), in a system that copies that of Cuzco and applies to all Incan cities.

MAIN STAIRWAYS OF MACHU PICCHU

ACCORDING TO H. BUSE

	No. of steps
Stairway of the thermal baths	239
Stairway of the Barracas	148
Stairway of the sink	152
Central stairway	79
Stairway to the top of the Old Peak	77
Stairway to the Intihuatana	70
Stairway to the Apacheta	31
Stairway to the Huayna Picchu	600

Nothing escapes their petrified weft, which embroiders the miracle city, giving it its architectural tonality. Moreover, this magnified scalar symbol "realizes the divine union of Heaven and Earth, the supreme cosmic couple," as the ethnologist Federico Costa y Laurent notes; he places Machu Picchu "between two poles, depth and altitude . . . military and monastic, both decorative and as naked as eternal man . . . and navigating on the rio of time."

This fantastic symbol of the union between the various groups of the "Lost City" surpass all that is now known in the way of stairway-streets in the modern as well as the prehistoric cities of the Old and New Worlds.

Sculpted into the granite itself or set into the rock, these 3,000 steps indeed justify the nickname of "stairway city" often given to Machu Picchu ever since it was discovered.

AMANAHUASIS: PUBLIC OR LITURGICAL BATHS?

The majority of the archaeological complexes of the Sacred Valley include what the Quechuas today call an "Inca's bath" or "Nusta's bath," similar to the one at Ollantaytambo described earlier. All the investigators are astounded by the knowledge of hydraulics required for the installation of these intriguing amanahuasis, under conditions that would challenge the understanding of modern engineers. At an altitude where every effort multiplies one's fatigue, finely worked stones were laid out along entire mountains—a patient undertaking which required, beforehand, an exhaustive study of the orography of the terrain, of its composition, of the slopes, of the very variable output of the sources, and of one hundred other extremely complex matters, which were perfectly resolved by pre-Columbian topographers and technicians, who had no form of writing, nor any precision instruments.

Today the hydraulic science of the ancient Peruvians and their mathematical victory over an indomitable terrain seem inconceivable. Nothing was improvised or left to chance, as is shown by the amanahuasis of the "Lost City," which were, without a doubt, foreseen, thought-out, calculated before it was even built—whence the necessity for a preliminary model, in order to locate the construction of the monolithic "vats" at suitable sites (that is, close to the palaces and other buildings of the aristocratic sector), as well as the ingress and egress of water in each one, to avoid any risk of loss, flooding, or drying up.

But what should they be called? No one knows any more! According to the scholar M. E. Rivero, amanahuasi can be translated as "bathhouse"—a rather vague designation which may or may not correspond to the sixteen-odd vats, sinks, and tanks tiered in a spectacular

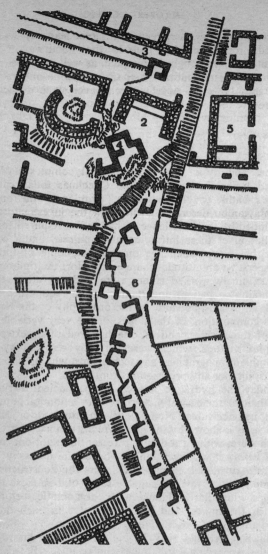

Amanahuasis: the sixteen baths
1. Torreón. 2. Huairona. 3. Aqueduct.
4. Inca's bath. 5. Inca's Palace. 6. Successive
baths.

descending series, parallel to the great stairway which is called, for this very reason, the "Stairway of the Fountains." One might be tempted, as well, to translate the term as "thermal baths," "baths," or even "fountains"; one hesitates, however, since we do not know the exact way they were used. As a simple yet ingenious way of distributing running water for domestic use throughout the orographic "leveling" of the city? As ritual baths, in view of the care with which they are distributed and their geometric elegance? As liturgical fountains for the high priests and those governing? Do they suggest a "water cult,"[7] which is known to have existed? Father Morua described the five fountains of Cuzco, in which the pure water of the Andean torrents arrived at the Coricancha, the Temple of Gold, by way of pipes and basins lined with gold or silver. One of the engraved gold disks of the Sun— won, then lost by the conquistador Leguizama in a game —was actually the "cover" for the Bath of the Sun, a clepsydra that was filled with *chicha* for some ceremonial feasts.

Were these public baths? Some investigators have thought that the lustral water of the first "bath" was reserved for the Inca. Then his entire family and court would— successively and in hieratic order—rinse themselves in this water, which in touching him had become (so to speak) "holy."

Moreover, at the hottest time of day, when the atmosphere of the Old Peak, saturated with tropical humidity, would become insufferable under the scarlet sun, the cascading glacier water must have been a delightful sight for the inhabitants of the "Lost City"—like the fountains at Versailles or the Alhambra.

Bingham discovered many of the *puquios* that provided the city with water—"within a mile of the heart of the city," he notes. He traced the irrigation conduit that climbs

[7] The Sun, Viracocha, Manco Capac, and Mama Ocllo, founders of the Incan dynasty, mysteriously emerged from Lake Titicaca (at an altitude of 4,000 meters); the Chancas, another great Andean people, were said to have been born from the Choclococha, the Lake of Corn; in Colombia, the Chibchas were an aquatic civilization which worshipped all lagoons, daughters of the moon, etc.

the mountain's slope to guide the water. The conduit is partially caved in and covered with rubble, but it runs alongside one of the principal agricultural terraces, crosses the dry moat of the fortification by way of a stone aqueduct, passes under the surrounding wall through a narrow groove, and ends in the first "bath."

The most abundant source came from the south and ran toward the Apacheta. Diverted at present, after erosion and earthquakes, the water cascades into the abyss. But during the period when Machu Picchu was bustling with activity, the precious liquid, ingeniously captured, descended the slope, checked by the curves which braked its course and avoided spillovers.

The distribution system for the water—the subterranean channel of which crosses again and again under the main stairway—was designed in such a way that the liquid falls from a height of 1 meter, as if from a gargoyle carved in the upper part of the monolith, into the bottom of a vat which can hold a few liters. Once it had completed its course, having irrigated, one after another, the sixteen "thermal baths" located on various levels (no one bath was independent from the whole), the water flowed out into a ditch.

Quadrangular, of various dimensions, the vats are composed of a sealed assemblage of granite blocks, magnificently smooth and perfectly fitted, without mortar. The water streamed down the wall and then was drawn into the little basin at the bottom, or else it gushed with considerable force from the rectangular channel above and fell directly into the mouth of a ceramic jar.

The beauty of the cyclopean style of these "baths" is augmented by the niches that adorn the interior, halfway up. What was kept there? "A cup," Bingham answers prosaically, "or possibly the stoppers of the bottles, made of fiber or twisted bunches of grass" that the women and children came to fill at the fountain. Laughing and chatting, their bare feet slipping on the damp steps, they would leave the pitchers poised on their brown heads, to prepare food or *chicha*, or to water flowers and orchards.

Stoppers or plugs made of twisted straw, wood, or stone must also have been kept there to plug up, at will, the opening located in the bottom of the vats or to allow them to be emptied. On the other hand, no system of closure was installed to block the narrow passage permitting access to the setup—hence, the obvious impossibility of taking a "bath" in one, in the true sense of the word, or to collect rainwater. However, by crouching, one could take a light shower.

Actually, Bingham and the majority of the investigators did not believe that these vats were ever used as public "bathtubs," given the narrowness of the stone ducts that draw the water into them. They think that this detail seems to indicate, on the contrary, the wish to conserve the rare liquid as much as possible. "The reason for the sixteen basins was not only in order to permit many jars to be filled at once," says Bingham, "but to keep the all too precious liquid from escaping."

For most of the Americanists, the presence of these "fountains" suggests, rather, the ritual ablutions—indeed, veritable liturgical "baptisms"—practiced by many other ancient religions, the water having been imbued with exemplary virtue after having successively washed the men of the highest rank. Thus, the ornamental cavities no doubt must have held small idols made of gold, silver, or fine ceramic, related to the aquatic deities. But why, then, is the principal "bath"—the one reserved for the Inca—not the first of the sixteen but the second, and far from the most spacious or well made?

Near this remarkable work there rises not only the most beautiful monument of Machu Picchu (the Torreón, or Temple of the Sun), but also a strange building, open like a belvedere, which overhangs it. A long, enormous stone couch, wide enough for four people to sit on it side by side, and two high niches seem to evoke the presence of the high priests of the cult, celebrating spectacular liturgical ceremonies or directing the ritual of the lustral bath of the famous Acllas, virgins consecrated to Father Sun. The closeness of the Torreón is certainly not coincidental, especially since this beautiful *amanahuasi* is located right beneath the strange scalar "Window of the Serpents," the most unusual window in the entire "Lost City"; its significance has never ceased to intrigue researchers.

Uriel Garcia speaks, moreover, "of families in charge of cleaning the canals and fountains," as was being done in Cuzco when the conquistadors arrived. These clans, he says, who lived near the hydraulic installations, saw to it that there was never a dearth of small shellfish, "which were thought to keep the sources alive, and made it impossible for them to dry up."

But was it solely the pure, clear water of the glaciers of the Salccantay that ran into the thermal baths of Machu Picchu? The Quechuas of the Sacred Valley have sowed some doubt, by telling all who will listen that these vats were used for washing gold! They were neither baths nor liturgical fountains but *lavaderos de oro*.[8] Others hold that it was the *chicha* of divine libations that cascaded from sink to sink, or else the warm blood from sacrifices that streamed all the way to the bottom of the *cañon*, to restore the powers of the waters of the Sacred Rio.

And finally there is one last hypothesis (the most unexpected!): Uriel Garcia claims that the basins of the "Lost City" were used to dye and rinse the wool of guanacos, a raw material sent from Cuzco, which was woven, all day long and with great skill, by the Chosen Women cloistered in this unimaginable 'condor's nest.' "

---

[8] One disturbing fact: Located not far from Machu Picchu, the ruins of Corihuayrana, whose name indicates that they were associated with the working of gold nuggets, contain similar "baths." However, there is nothing that indicates that their name is authentic. It may date from modern times.

CHAPTER FIFTEEN

Hanan,
the Upper City

Tell me whether the taciturn Amautas *lived* ✸
✸ *atop the emerald pyramid, weaving the*
golden hair of the Sun on their quipus . . .
—Efrain Morote Best

YACHAY HUASI, OR THE CENTRAL GROUP

It is already in a "state of grace" that, in the footsteps of the noble visitors who once trod the stones of the ceremonial stairway, and in Bingham's wake, we cross the yawning threshold of Huaca Puncu and enter Hanan, the high western sector of temples and palaces said to be royal, to admire with Morote Best "this poem of time engraved on the mountain" or with Juan Larrea "the swan song of the Inca soul."

From the moment we first glimpse the heart of the city, the central group is set apart by the famous Torreón of the Sun, jutting out over an enormous boulder. But to reach it we must first cross, descending, five of the six tiered platforms of this ensemble, which outlines a gigantic trapezoid of light-colored granite, bordered on the north by the "Stairway of the Fountains" and on the south by the deep fortified dry moat, often thought to be a sink.

The long corridor of the upper group curves toward the labyrinth of the lower rows, of a flawless symmetry. Vast rectangular buildings, some of which probably had an additional story since destroyed, alternate with passages, small groups of steps, and interior patios which open onto "bedrooms," or even "classrooms" or "workshops."

The granitic puzzle of the walls abounds, everywhere adorned with magnificent trapezoidal niches and impressive

185

framed *portadas* equipped with cavities set up for security purposes. This detail indicates that the sector was reserved for a prominent group. The facades of the "royal houses," remarkably aligned, face an *anden*-street, while their bases, adjoining the preceding platform, in fact constitute a long unbroken wall.

The fourth row also introduces a rebus: The *portada* is so low that one has to double over to get through it! All the apertures are on this same reduced scale. Have we entered the domain of the Inca Tom Thumb? Or perhaps it is, rather, a district of dwarfs, the jesters of the great lord of Machu Picchu, like those which are represented surrounding the Coya and the Inca on the *keros* illustrated with

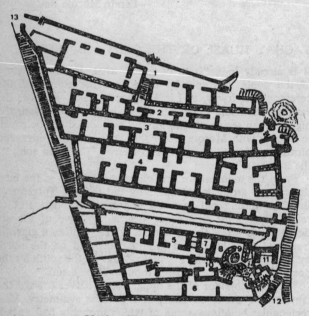

Yachay Huasi: central group
*1–6. The rows. 7. Nusta's Palace.
8. Torreón of the Sun. 9. The calva.
10. Royal Mausoleum. 11. Huairona. 12. Stairway
of the Fountains. 13. Huaca Puncu.*

scenes from imperial life (a splendid example of which decorates the Museum of the Ruins).

Then the path descends toward a corridor bordered by a cyclopean wall 3 meters high, made of granite blocks arranged in horizontal rows, joined by means of a technique so precise that their "solder" is practically indiscernible. A large *portada* 2.3 meters high yawns at the end of the impasse. One has only to close it off and one could live in this building free from any outside interference. According to Hermann Buse, the absolute isolation proclaims "the esoteric nature of the cult that was celebrated in the Torreón and its strange cave in the basement." Alas! "The silence of the stones imbued with a monastic austerity" conceals from us the story of the secret rites that took place here.

SUMTUR HUASI, OR THE TORREÓN OF THE SUN

By way of seven steps and a passage hemmed in by two rectilinear walls, we reach the mysterious group of the Torreón, one of the masterpieces of the "Lost City" of the Incas. Unique in the entire pre-Columbian area thus far explored[1] (with the exception of the monolithic foundation of the Coricancha at Cuzco, in the shape of a cyclopean "half-drum"), this monument was simultaneously erected on, adapted to, and literally set into the "magical" rock that serves as its pedestal; crowning it, the Torreón cleaves to its slightest irregularity. Bingham observed that the Torreón "winds around it like one's arm around one's loved one."

In this arrangement of cubes tightly assembled with neither mortar nor tenons, not a single element has budged over the centuries. It is so well arranged that, according to a stereotyped image, one cannot slip the thinnest steel blade between the monoliths—and one's hand cannot resist the urge to stroke such "precious" stones.

[1] This does not mean that the round shape was unknown to the pre-Columbian architects. The circular structure even predominates in the more ancient of the nearby villages. At Paracas in southern Peru, for example, Frédéric Engel has uncovered numerous rounded substructures which by radiocarbon dating are about 9,000 years old.

But who built it? Uriel Garcia pictures a constellation of master *pircacs* (architects), *lucrics* (quarriers), and *checocs* (stonecutters), sent from Cuzco by the supreme Inca (which?) to initiate the work enthusiastically and to tackle, with the same fervor, the imposing boulder implanted there since the birth of the Andean gods—without working against the monstrous stone, which would have constituted an obstacle for any other people. The Inca builders, on the contrary, revered this topographical flaw and—without patently changing its profile or modifying it any more than was necessary—turned it into a jewel, adorning the deified rock with a diadem of satiny granite which remains the most beautiful monument of the Tahuantinsuyo.

By means of slow, patient rubbing with wet sand, they polished its monoliths until they resembled angel's skin, and, with prodigious skill, set up its flat surfaces so accurately that the Torreón looks as if it had been expelled, in a single thrust, from the womb of the Mother Earth.

The extraordinary creation of Indian genius, each course of the incomplete tower differs in size from the preceding or following row. The carved monoliths decrease in size as they get higher, following an inclination which recedes toward the top. It is a slope so elegantly designed that it lightens a massive architecture to the point where one forgets the building's weight.

Foreseeing that the blocks would tend to separate in time, the artists who conceived the idea of this wall curved like a horseshoe avoided possible breaks in the places likely to be subject to the greatest strain by alternating a polyhedron with another, rectangular stone equipped with—according to Bingham—a "hookstone . . . making a series of keys." This "permanent object of beauty" is reflected in the intimate union of the Torreón with the neighboring building by way of a raised terrace patio which bonds the two monuments by the quarry-stone wall that also connects them along the bottom of the atrium.

After having cleared the Torreón of the exuberant vegetation carpeting it, Bingham discovered that "the most experienced mason of his time had here constructed the most beautiful wall in America."

The curvilinear wall of the Torreón is decorated with interior niches, arranged in a straight line and surmounted by great "stone pegs" of intercalary stones, which project from it.

The axis, mark, and symbol of the "Lost City," the Torreón is also one of its profound mysteries, because of its three trapezoidal openings, which foster theories, all of them daring to some degree.

Did these "windows"—which look out over the majestic Inca's group, the chain of "baths," the outline of the great temple, and, farther in the distance, the pyramid of the Intihuatana—fulfill a function other than that of displaying the panorama? Were they pierced in order to illumine and aerate the half-tower—assuming that the latter was ever covered? As for the four protuberances outside each window (near the corners of these mysterious openings), are they purely ornamental? It would certainly be naive to claim they were "emergency exits" for a building wide open on every side and some 12 meters above ground level!

No less curious is José Uriel Garcia's theory, according to which "a supreme window-city, given the sloping topography, Machu Picchu was governed from the Torreón, by way of these openings, intended not as simple elements that were functional, decorative, or designed for ventilation, much less for use in ceremonies linked to the sacerdotal practices of magic or sorcery, as one might think, but for long-distance communication."

They acted, he thinks, as "loudspeakers" and made it possible, depending on the circumstances, "to give orders or to summon the inhabitants of the lower city to their daily chores." They may even have been used for communicating over greater distances, as far as the Andean piedmont and perhaps the Sacred Valley. But how was it possible to amplify the human voice so that it could carry so far? "This system, favored by the diaphanous atmosphere of the Picchus, having a great power, amplifiable through the abysses of the cañon, was completed by a metallic megaphone made of gold or silver, set in the opening of the windows so as to obtain a stronger vibration from the shouted word." Hence the presence of the four protuberances framing each of the two windows located facing east and south, "to hold up the acoustic system."

Moreover—still according to Uriel Garcia—"Braids of various colors were hung from the two other stone protuberances, located on the right, a short distance from the openings, to attract—by the very sight of them—the attention of the occupants of the most distant regions and to request those from such-and-such a district (depending on the colors) to listen, a few minutes later, to the call of the Indian 'muezzin' from this 'Inca minaret.' "

This method of communication, by "bans," was used at that time in Cuzco, the investigator affirms, during the pre-Hispanic epoch, and later, during the colonial and then republican eras, in all the towns of native origin, in order to broadcast higher orders. By day the open bays of the "Lost City" must have served as phonic windows, for the proclamation, over great distances, of public ordinances to the matrons directing the Acllas and to the artisans' guilds; by night they must have been used to spread through the dwellings the melodious sounds of the *quenas*, sobbing or spirited Indian flutes, which entoned ardent *huaynos* or desperate *harawis* (love songs), moving appeals to life on the part of the young virgins of the Acllahuasi, captives of the lonely Picchus, "whose only connection with the world was the magic of poetry and music."[2]

In truth, José Uriel Garcia's hypotheses are not echoed by any of his Peruvian colleagues, who, for the most part, see the stone "teats" of the Torreón as a means of attaching a solar disk, "as large as a cartwheel." Perhaps this is the case with one of the bays, but the second? Why not picture there the silver image of the Moon, wife of the Sun?

Hiram Bingham was the first to write that these unusual protuberances might constitute supports to which were attached the gold ornaments connected with the Temple of the Sun—if this was indeed a Temple of the Sun! This is a question that Americanists have asked themselves for half a century and which they answer, as a rule, in the affirmative. For all, the sight of the curved building evokes "a chapel dedicated to a basic cult," a "holy place if ever there was one," an "oratory of the solar religion," copied from the famous Coricancha at Cuzco.

Bingham believes that the round foundation at Cuzco was built "in memory of Machu Picchu," although the

---

[2] It is said in Peru that, for lack of a form of writing, the flute of the Andes expresses, in an ever-impassioned musical and literary style, the joys and sorrows of the Indian soul.

reverse is probably true. The Torreón would recall the principal sanctuary, where one could officiate in the same way as in the abandoned capital.

For some, the Torreón was a "military bastion," or a "watchtower" ensuring the city's immunity.

Uriel Garcia contests the Torreón's very name. He proposes the older, more fitting name of Sumtur Huasi, or "House of Government," where audiences were held and justice was meted out. This is the correct name, he maintains, accompanying his assertion with a legendary event, illustrated by an oil painting made after the Conquest, the work of a conquistador: the miraculous *Descent of the Virgin* over Cuzco, which long graced the back choir of the cathedral.[8] This takes us back to 1535 once again:

Pizarro's troops find themselves being barbarously besieged by the thousands of Indian warriors under orders from Manco Inca. Holding the heights that surround the village, they intend to set it on fire by sending down a rain of flaming arrows onto the straw roofs.

Suffocated by the thick smoke, the Pizarros have been forced to evacuate the superb Sumtur Huasi located at the eastern corner of the Plaza Mayor, a palace that Manco offered to Francisco when the vanquished and the victor went in for demonstrations of their good will.

When the situation seems hopeless for those besieged, a "miracle" occurs which all the chroniclers present describe poetically: The archangel St. James, mounted on a white horse, pursues the Indians with his flaming sword while the Virgin Mary descends from heaven to spread her glorious mantle of dew over the city. The fire is extinguished immediately, and the Virgin envelops the Sumtur Huasi in a radiant cloud which hides it from the eyes of the infidels.

---

[8] This huge painting was cut from its opulent frame at the end of the nineteenth century by an Indian priest who refused to concede that the Virgin could have come to the aid of the foreigners rather than to those of his race. He tossed the painting into one of the church's storerooms and replaced it with a painting by Delacroix. Who found the original painting and took it to Argentina? No one knows, but it was acquired by an antique collector from Tucumán, Juan A. Ambrosetti. The painting had a counterpart in Cuzco, another canvas evoking the "miracle" and representing *Santiago matador de indios* (St. James, Indian-Killer).

More down-to-earth, modern historians assume that a violent storm—like those which often descend over the Andes near Cuzco—accompanied by a providential rain extinguished the flames on the thatch roofs.

Comparing the round building in the picture, painted in the sixteenth century, with that of Machu Picchu, and noting the striking similarity in the architecture of the two buildings, Uriel Garcia therefore "unbaptizes" the Torreón and gives it the name Sumtur Huasi, "in accord with the political, artistic, and religious tradition of Inca-Quechua linguistics."[4]

This investigator makes it out to be the center of numerous activities connected to the successful municipal administration of the "Lost City." Perhaps it was also used as a storage place for rich liturgical ornaments, the gold idols and vessels of the Sun, and particularly, as at Cuzco, the Suntur Paucar, "a pole adorned with a gold scepter, which the Inca held in his hand like a king with a banner. Three feathers crowned the shaft and the imperial standard *in the colors of the rainbow*, which was the symbol of his authority and the government of the Incas," who had been handing down the insignia of the omnipotence of the Sons of the Sun ever since the reign of the Ayar Manco Capac.

GATEWAY OF GOLD, OF THE SACRED SERPENTS . . . OR OF THE RAINBOW?

We perhaps find the multicolored, iridescent symbol of the rainbow in one of the most abstruse mysteries of Machu Picchu, the unusual Portada of the Amarus which, while conforming to the Incan trapezoid, otherwise presents a geometry so strange that it baffles all the archaeologists, without exception.

But is it a door or a window? Both, simultaneously! A door on the inside, and a window when seen from the outside, for it overhangs the stairway-street of the "baths."

---

[4] Huaman Poma specifies that *sumtur huasi* means "round house." Father Domingo de Santo Tomas indicates that *suntuni* and *sumtusca* apply to things that are "connected, adjoining, close," as the Torreón and the Nusta's Palace are at Machu Picchu. The old Sumtur Huasi is no more. The Spaniards built the church "El Triunfo," the first cathedral in Cuzco, on the site.

The mysterious Portada of the Amarus
(Torreón of the Sun)

Or is it something else entirely? From a false threshold made from a hollowed-out granite cube in the center of a rectangular canal rise three monoliths on each side, facing one another, on separate tiers, and receding on a slant. One could designate them neither as "steps" nor as "benches"— functions quite removed from the mythical mode of the builders, who thus reproduced the well-known, intriguing American scalar symbol.

The first two tiers are strangely pierced (what incomprehensible technique was used?) by circular orifices that are extended within by canals that follow not a straight line, but a sinuous curve, which further complicates the mystery.

Bingham was the first to wonder about this "window," which would be called "problematical" in archaeological jargon. He thought about it for years before he dared advance an opinion. Three solutions came to mind. His colleagues considered the first as strange as the opening itself: The high priest of the Torreón kept *snakes* in these labyrinths of perforated stone. According to the way the "sacred vipers" entered or came out of these holes, he deduced and predicted future events in the empire[5]—"like a fakir," a Peruvian archaeologist would exclaim.

Since this theory seemed to him to be ultimately debatable, Bingham envisaged a second possibility: Did the ancestral spirits of the deities worshipped in this temple perhaps speak through these orifices, by means of a ventriloquist's voice?

But in that case, why do several of the "undulations" pierced in the granite have no exterior outlet? Unable to answer, Bingham essayed a third hypothesis: Was corn *chicha*, a beverage relished by the ancestral "spirits" as well as by the living, perhaps poured into these cavities, to slake—symbolically—the thirst of the god of this round temple?

Collating the chronicles, the Americanists tried in vain to formulate an opinion in turn. Bingham himself finally reverted to his original lucubrations, after having noticed similar cavities in the wall of the Temple of the Sun in Cuzco (he was unable, however, to check their interior shape). Had these not been contrived "to facilitate the exhibition of the gold ornaments and plaques of the Sun," which, according to the sixteenth-century texts, illumined all the solar temples?

By questioning the very old *quipucamayocs* who "read" the entire history of the empire on knotted cords, the chroniclers learned that "to commemorate certain events, the Incas had golden gateways placed at the openings of Tamputocco," the legendary cave. Might they not have done the same for the Torreón? Given the striking similarity of the round temples of the capital of the Andes and those of Machu Picchu, it is quite possible that the great golden image of the Sun—the famous Punchao—was, for a long time, guarded and exhibited in the Torreón by

---

[5] In regard to "prophetic" serpents, Bingham published a photograph of a "snake rock" near the Sacred Plaza. There are several such rocks at Machu Picchu. He also shows the "curious and indecipherable figure" carved in the stone, of a sun beaming among small serpents.

Manco Inca and his sons in exile. The idol—rather than serpents!—must have been solidly wedged, as if "seated," in the problematical Portada of Gold.

Although he repudiates Bingham's "considerations of a magical, metaphysical, or theological nature," Uriel Garcia reconciles his own deductions with the latter hypothesis of the American scholar. He pictures a structure composed of gold plaques, fashioned by the Incan goldsmiths, "set in the stone matrix prepared for this purpose by the architect." On it, by means of tension, a gold pedestal was set up as well, and the whole shone over the "Lost City" from sunrise to sunset.

What did this magnificent altarpiece contain? "The insignia of divine authority, kept in the tabernacles of Coricancha, at Cuzco, and elsewhere," explains Uriel Garcia: that is, the idol of the day, Illa Ticsi Viracocha,[6] an immense gold plaque on which, sculpted in relief, were the figures of the Sun, the Moon, the stars, the seasons, earth, water, the Andes, the first inhabitants, animals, and plants, "as a summary of the Andean genesis which explained the cosmogonic conception of the Quechua world, and which the people could thus see represented permanently."

The chronicler Betanzos provides us with an interesting clue: "The Punchao idol," he declares, "was placed on an *escaño* [small bench or stool] made of wood, very prettily covered with feathers from shimmering birds, of various kinds and colors . . . And the [golden] Sun was given to eat and drink by placing a gold *brasero* in front of the idol; into the fire were thrown small birds, kernels of corn, and *chicha*"—a rite repeated daily.

Pedro Pizarro also mentions a stool which he describes as being made of gold, "embedded in a great stone carved in the shape of an *escaño*,"[7] on which the Sun was said to

---

[6] Uriel Garcia confuses the Punchao (the idol of the day), Illa Ticsi Viracocha (the supreme god of Lake Titicaca, and later of the Incas), and the gold plaque of the cosmogonic genesis which adorned the altar of the Coricancha in Cuzco. He also throws in the Sumtur Puacar, the insignia of power!

[7] Francisco Pizarro, a general in the Conquest of Peru, appropriated this *escaño* as his personal booty. His cousin Pedro Pizarro estimated its value at 60,000 *castellanos*.

sit, in the form of a gold statue, which, he says, "was never found."

Finally—an important detail—Gutierrez de Santa Clara and a few others remarked with wonder that the walls of the great *cuzqueño* solar temple and this *escaño* were "subtly perforated" and that in the holes shone many emeralds, turquoises, and other precious gems. Thus, one can imagine, along with Bingham, that a similar dazzling spectacle diffused the golden reflections of the Sun through the mysterious scalar "window," out over the city, and as far as the valley—which induces Luis Pardo to view this opening as "a *mirador*," modeled on "the stones for nests of the snakes domesticated by the ancient inhabitants of Cuzco, who observed a totemic cult regarding ophidians."[8] Serpents symbolized wisdom, according to Angles Vargas, and they were represented abundantly, particularly on the walls of the Yachay Huasi, the school for young nobles, which this investigator in fact places, at Machu Picchu, in the upper part of the rows of the central group, where the Torreón is also found.

For his part, Jorge Cornejo Bouroncle states that when he visited the "Lost City" in 1928, the orifices pierced in the tiers of the Portada of the Amarus were closed off by stone plugs which he could pull out as easily as "drawers" and which hermetically sealed the niches of the "sacred vipers."

But there remains one final hypothesis, the most surprising of all, advanced by Antonio Santander Cascelli. For this connoisseur of "lost secrets," the mysterious opening must be called Kuichi Puncu, "Gateway of the Rainbow." Cavities drilled in the monolithic frame, he points out, spouted "fine, multicolored jets of water," as in the cult devoted to Kuichi, the Quechua deity of the meteor, connected with the water cult, as the latter was to the cult of the serpent.

Santander Cascelli claims that a *chiuka* (unseen canal) 3 centimeters in diameter runs along the entire inner wall of the Torreón; through it water arrived from a distance of

---

[8] Melchor Enriquez Tapla, who supervised the restoration of Machu Picchu, found in the ruins a snake *champi* alongside some *tumis* (blades shaped like half-moons) and disks made from the same alloy.

25–30 meters. The micrometric precision of the stonework, he believes, prevented the water from seeping to the outside. Echoing him, Alfonsina Barrionuevo writes, "The Portada of the Amarus opened by means of a complicated jet of water."

At first glance, this hypothesis might appear revolutionary. However, we must recall that the perplexing scalar *portada* overlooks the principal liturgical fountain of the "Lost City" and the Stairway of Fountains. Coincidence or connection?

THE INVISIBLE *CALVA*

But this is not everything strange and incomprehensible connected with the famous Torreón! A new mystery awaits us on the upper part of the enormous boulder supporting it.

Describing this rock as being carved into seats or platforms in the guise of an altar for placing offerings or burning sacrifices, Bingham notes that the surface must have been subject to "a really extraordinary amount of heat," for it flakes off the way granite does when subjected to great heat. Was this flaking caused by a single fire or rather by repeated fires--from the roof burning, for example, or from a fire made of logs, with the fuel being replenished? It is hard to believe that the damages observed by Bingham could have been caused by the ignition of a mere thatched roof. On the other hand, the chroniclers inform us that sacrifices were celebrated during the solar festivals of the Inca calendar. At these times the Virgins of the Sun were burned, as a magical incantation, so that the Sun, pleased by these handsome gifts, would in return provide the people with abundant harvests, the most beautiful mantles woven of vicuña or alpaca wool, and fine colored garments.

Hence, it is clear that the central rock cradled by the Torreón's curved wall may have been a "sacrificial altar." Perhaps, according to Victor Angles Vargas, "the time was calculated there, in conjunction with the priests and scholars of the Intihuatana."

A few paces away, the Portada of the Amarus seems also to have undergone a deflagration so extreme that its heavy granite lintel cracked, then broke, partially crumbling. Let us recall that storms rock the Picchus daily. Now, if the walls were once covered with gold, would they not have attracted lightning all the more?

The better to revere the deified rock (a miniature Picchu), says Uriel Garcia, *checocs* and *lucrics* encased it in the most marvelous monument in the "Lost City." The entire structure of the Torreón revolves around this "talisman of the builders, a form of exorcism, so that the raw materials with which they built grandiose works would never be exhausted."

Indeed, rock was the source of the exceptional artistic genius of the Incan architects, and the rock of the Torreón "symbolizes the fecundity of stone."

As the German archaeologist Ubbelohde Doering points out, "Natural sacred rocks, surrounded by walls, dedicated to the cult, exist not only at Machu Picchu but also at Pisac in the Sacred Valley, on the Island of the Sun in Lake Titicaca, and at Moche, on the Pacific coast." Such consecrated rocks "demonstrated a veneration which must date back to the earliest prehistoric epoch of the South American cordillera, to a preceramic era when man left no sign of his passing other than the megalithic constructions."

And from there back to the myth of Atlantis. The German Karola Siebert, who devotes all her efforts to the search for an "unknown" Peru, believes that it is possible to read, in the form of the Torreón and its captive rock, "the Egyptian hieroglyph of the Deluge, constructed in stone, with the monster inside, awaiting the time to come out."

Indeed, the curvilinear wall wraps around the rocky pivot as if it wished to block the sight of the secret *calva*, the bald head of a giant, carved by hand and so hard to see that Bingham never suspected it was there! Nor did any of the investigators who flocked to the "Lost City" during the half-century following his discovery. All of them passed by the macrocephalic rock of the Torreón without noticing the strange, angular face, invisible at the level of the outcropping in the rock but clearly outlined at a height of 5 meters, from the top of the overhanging wall.

That the *calva* should have remained unknown for so long seems inconceivable to some. Astonished that he never discerned it, the archaeologist Julio Espejo Nuñez suspects that the artificial "head" of the Torreón was "an alteration made after the discovery of Machu Picchu." The work of a guardian of the ruins, perhaps?[9]

Others believe it to be an "optical illusion," or even the result of trick photography. These accusations crumble in the view of tired tourists, who are often photographed seated on the tiers sculpted at the location of the "giant's eyes"—there where high hierarchical priestesses, Mamacunas of imperial blood, no doubt once sat. Moreover, when studied under a magnifying glass, the photographs taken at the beginning of this century by the members of the Yale Peruvian Expedition to Machu Picchu show that the giant "face" already existed at that time. Could it date from the troglodytic era?

Under the mother rock, in fact, lies one of the most splendid prehistorical caves in all Peru!

THE ROYAL MAUSOLEUM

"Even though an exact inventory of the caves in Peru has not been drawn up, the accounts of the reliable explorers and scientific voyagers who have studied the country enable one to assume that the number of caves and caverns—some of which are quite large and have great geological, anthropological, and archaeological value because of their contents—is considerable," declares Cesar Garcia Rosell of the Geography Society of Lima. In ancient Peru, he adds, "The cave is a mythical element connected with the origin of primitive man and his social evolution, including the formation of the Incan Empire, as shown by the legends: the legend, first of all, of the four Ayars and four Mamas who founded the Tahuantinsuyo, starting from Pacaritampu and Tamputocco, as well as the legend of Kon Tiki Viracocha, who, in order to create the

---

[9] Espejo Nuñez assumes that many of the pictographs and paintings said to be prehistorical were made in Peru after the Conquest. As for the *calvas*, or ornamental heads keyed in the megalithic walls, he happened to discover, he says, that once the soot covering them was washed away by spraying water on them, these walls revealed the engraving marks of modern forgers!

pre-Inca world, caused the first men to leave the caves of the high plateaus, starting from Titicaca and heading in the direction of the rising Sun."

The ancient Peruvians demonstrated a profound veneration for the Andean lairs called *machay* and for the *toccos* (natural faults) converted into sacred sites, where they placed the bodies of the deceased along with their offerings. Thus, the caves came to be richly accoutered with altars, porticos, and niches, and the walls were lined with finely carved stone.

The majority of the great American caves favored, therefore, the study of the appearance of humans in the New World and, before them, that of animal species now extinct, the whole enabling archaeologists to establish a basic chronology.[10]

"The belief in a subterranean, all-powerful world of the dead dominates all these caves," notes Doering, "and the sculptures found in them must be connected with this belief. The shapes carved in the stone—steps, tiers, platforms, altars, cones, cylinders, thrones—have a meaning, a magico-religious significance," which unfortunately we cannot understand. But they constitute *the only monolithic hieroglyphs in the entire world*.

At Machu Picchu, Hermann Buse declares, "Because the city is to be the great center of contact between men and gods, all its buildings will have to be adapted to the rocks and caves."

In the famous cave that Bingham discovered thanks to the Quechua child, under the enormous rock protruding from the Torreón, the Incan architects lined the walls with "the finest cut stone" in order to transform it into a superb

---

[10] About 50,000 caves dating from the paleolithic epoch have been counted in North America. The largest are found in Cuba, where Nuñez Jimenez has indexed one hundred, noteworthy for their fossilized remains of prehistoric animals and cave paintings; these caves extend under the sea and contain marine fossils from the Miocene Epoch. In Venezuela, human occupation of the caves of El Jobo dates back 16,000 years. The best-known caves are, in Brazil, those of Lagao Santa (9,000 years); and, in Ecuador, those of Alausi; as well as the caves of Patagonia, containing Mylodon fossils, remains of prehistoric Patagonian men, etc. In Peru, the painted caves of Mazo Cruz, Lauricocha, and Toquepala date from 7,000 to 10,000 years ago.

sepulcher. The corners and interior folds (including the ceiling) were admirably crafted by the hands of magician-artists who adapted the granite blocks to the capricious irregularities.

"It looks as if a giant squeezed into the hole," writes José Gabriel Cosio, "and, raising the rock on his back, shattered it, the better to mend the cracks with polished stone. Thus the ancient lair of pumas and other wild animals of the Andes became one of the most curious monuments in Incan art."

Two short flights (of four steps each) descend to the cavity that hollows out the entrails of the deified rock, where semidarkness reigns, evincing, for Buse, "some mysterious cult." To the right of the entrance, which traces a triangle, a gigantic granite panel must have blocked the passage almost completely. Successive tiers outline here the most grandiose scalar Greek key design that I have ever seen in the Americas, where this *siglum* was common to all the ancient peoples. Thirty angles were cut right into the living rock, from the base to the ceiling! The work of an Inca, which represents, in the view of Luis Pardo, "the petrified hieroglyph of Mama Pacha, Mother Earth."

The inner walls of the cave were carved with trapezoidal niches of an ideal precision and carefully finished; they are surmounted by cylindrical stones which protrude 20 or 30 centimeters. Three of the niches, as tall as an upright Indian, were perhaps destined for the Ayacamayocs, or guardians, of a royal mummy placed in the fourth niche, which was shorter but large enough for a body curled up like a fetus, in accordance with the ancient American custom of mummification. Other small niches must have contained the ceramic *conopas* (or ex-votos), idols and effigies of the lares in gold and silver, and chased vessels and plates for the mummy's formal table setting, which his servants filled with victuals so that he would not be irritated by some oversight on the part of his survivors.[11] Even today, the curse of the ancient mummies is as feared by the Quechua and Aymara Indians of Lake Titicaca as it was in Egypt during the time of the pharaohs.

Embalmed according to natural or chemical procedures,

---

[11] See my book *Masks, Mummies, and Magicians* (Edinburgh: Oliver & Boyd, 1965).

the mummy retained a curiously lifelike appearance. At Machu Picchu, as at Cuzco, it was probably removed from its rocky sarcophagus and taken to the Sacred Plaza to participate in the festivities organized on the occasion of great seasonal, civic, military, or religious feasts. It was a mummy whose eyes were covered with gold, who listened to chants spoken to the rhythm of the tom-toms, and to the sonorous hymn singing its praises, celebrating its successes and virtues, as it quivered in the Andean wind—but, in this case, whose mummy?

THE MUMMY OF PACHACUTI VI?

Hiram Bingham attempts a retrospective leap back 3,000 years, to the reign—according to Montesinos, his favorite chronicler—of the sixth Pachacuti, King Titu Yupanqui, one of the great leaders of a dynastic line who has never ceased to arouse controversy among the Peruvian and foreign historiographers. Was he hypothetical or real? For a long time the first view was favored, but currently it is necessary to reexamine Montesinos' writings carefully; they have been cast in a new light by the modern discoveries and radiocarbon datings, which bring him increasingly into accord with archaeology.

Under attack from hordes descended from the high Aymara plateaus of Colloa near Titicaca, King Titu Yupanqui (who was much more religiously than militarily minded), terrified by grim omens, ordered that the bloody sacrifices to the gods be stepped up. But the barbarians from the south kept advancing irresistibly, pillaging and razing the rich cities of the Amautas. Defeated in the Pass of La Raya, Titu Yupanqui, borne aloft on a golden litter, was struck by an enemy arrow. The 500 survivors among his decimated troops brought his remains back "to a place located in the Andes and hid him in a cave."

For Bingham, all the requirements described in Montesinos are met at Machu Picchu: natural defenses; ideal climate; numerous windows; the structure of a sacred city, with temples of the Sun and all the Incan pantheon. One can predict the conclusion made by the scholar from Yale: Pachacuti VI was buried here in the cave, the Torreón's belly, which was naturally the most venerated place in the "Lost City." This is why, he notes, its construction was seldom equaled in the world, and never surpassed in beauty and majesty.

If this is so, it would place the occupation of Machu Picchu much earlier in the pre-Columbian era than the majority of archaeologists are willing to admit is possible. And some of them prefer to place in the niches of the "Royal Mausoleum" (Bingham's term) the mummies of the master architects who elaborated the dizzying mathematical plans of the incomparable "Lost City." Each to his own truth! Influenced by the sinister appearance of the cave, others see it not as a mausoleum but as a "place of punishment and cruel tortures." Cosio, for example, thinking of the unyielding justice of the Incas (among whom any crimes against the purity or chastity of the Chosen Women or against the holiness of the cult were punishable by the atrocious agony of immurement), wonders about the four niches in the cave: Were condemned nobles exposed there until they died?

Worked (once again) in the scalar pattern, a mass of granite emerges from the floor of the cave. To what esoteric or mystical cult was it dedicated? What bloody sacrifices were conducted here? Could it have been related to the Intihuatana at the top of the city? From his conversations on the site with the archaeologist Manuel Chavez Ballon and his assistant Valencia (two specialists from Cuzco in charge of clearing and shoring up the ruins at Machu Picchu), my co-researcher, the ethnologist Bernard Lelong, got the impression that "while the first Intihuatana, located on an artificial protuberance of the religious section of the Hanan district, perfectly fulfilled its role as a solar instrument, the second, situated beneath the Torreón, in the darkness of the cave, must have been connected with the Mother Earth or the chthonic forces." This idea coincides with the opinion held by Luis Pardo, mentioned earlier.

According to Valencia, "In the Inca epoch, an anthropomorphic gold idol was transported from the Intihuatana above to the one below, so that the message recorded on high would be transmitted to the earth, which was responsible for the harvests."

I noted another version, which holds that the cave burrowed directly beneath the *calva* was propitious to the word of an oracle which the believers came to consult loudly. To this day, according to my informant, the Indians of the Peruvian and Bolivian sierras continue to go to "magic" places to speak with a deity, questioned by the "moving spirit."

If the result of the excavations carried out in the cave had been known and divulged, the problem would have been, if not solved, at least cleared up to some extent. Who made this cave? Luis Pardo accuses Hiram Bingham of having found "some tomb" here. But today the mystery is complete. Amautas, kings, nobles, priests, mamacunas, *quipucamayocs* have all left this place, taking with them, into other tombs, the secret of what their eyes beheld.

Will the esoteric message of the great cave at Machu Picchu remain indecipherable forever? It is risky to speak at length about the secrets of this unusual mausoleum. Did it in fact serve as a ritual "display case" for the imperial mummies? Did the cavernous voice of the oracle answer the pilgrims who flocked to it by way of the Nan Cuna? Or, rather, did high personages meet there to conduct a silent rite with hieratical gestures? A small building, located opposite the cave, and the neighboring *cancha*, where the pilgrims bearing offerings could gather, would seem to indicate that this "resting place of the soul" (as Luis Pardo calls it) was designed thus in order to make it "an eternal mausoleum that would speak to the generations to come of a grandeur never lost."

As I pondered these questions on the threshold of the cave, it occurred to me that, hidden there, are the ancient roots of the Peruvian people.

Might there not have existed a "sieve," an invisible gap that permitted only the initiates, equipped with a secret fluid amplifying the body's vibrations, to communicate with a world parallel to our own? Is there perhaps a tunnel hidden beneath the cave, where the high priests conversed with the cosmic and telluric forces? Everything points to this conclusion.

THE NUSTA'S HOUSE

Adjoining the Torreón on the south side is a magnificent residence whose two superimposed levels, each composed of a single room measuring about 3 by 5 meters, are not connected interiorly.

No one knows what material was used to separate the first story from the second; though nothing remains of it, one can picture a "floor-ceiling" made of tree trunks supported by the projecting *mensole* that is still in place, 2 meters above the floor. But to reach the upper part, one must, on the outside, use the ceremonial stairway with eight megalithic steps carved at right angles into a single block of stone. One thus ends up in the raised patio, next to the *calva* and the Portada of the Amaru, access to which, from the first floor, is afforded by a large trapezoidal opening. This suggests the close connection that must have existed between the person occupying this upper room and the cult.

On the lower level, the bottom of the chamber is equipped with a large, long, solid stone platform, 30 centimeters high, which was perhaps used as a bed for lying in state. But by whom? By the Nusta or the Coya, daughter or wife of the Inca? By a sibyl? Or else by a prominent figure in the city—a governor, a *sinchi*, or a high priest who was the guardian of the Torreón?

There is nothing to inform us. The name "Princess's House" or "Princess's Palace" still remains, the product of the imagination of the Indians who frequent the ruins; but they cannot—or do not care to—justify their inspiration.

Only one certainty emanates from this splendid building: With its perfect monolithic assemblage, remaining intact over the centuries, it demonstrates the fantastic antiseismic skills of its builders.

Below, gardens (where—who knows?—flowers for bouquets for offerings were perhaps grown), *andenes*, and a few outbuildings (to house courtesans?) complete the central group and the ceremonial center. Hiram Bingham swears he found nothing in the buildings that make up the ensemble. But beneath the terraces of the princely dwelling place, the Indian *peones* with the Yale Peruvian Expedition find piles of old broken pottery: over 200 shards, many of which were pieces of jars. "Evidently," says Bingham, "the former owners were good housekeepers and insisted on broken pots being taken away to the rubbish piles."

THE HUAIRONA

Machu Picchu displays, in several places, a new architectural element, which archaeologists designate by various names: *huairona* (or *huairana*), *masma*, or simply "corridor." The term *carpahuasi*, says Uriel Garcia, would be more suitable for buildings without a facade, as the chronicler Huaman Poma explains.

Located a few strides to the west of the Torreón and the mysterious Portada of the Amarus, the Huairona, the most beautiful of the *huaironas* in the "Lost City," deserves a special mention: covered by a steep, thatched roof, its three walls are adorned within by a long granite couch, 60 centimeters high, which crosses the back wall. Sitting there, one has a spectacular view of the Torreón, the entrance to the Inca's palace, the series of "baths," and the main stairway—that is, the stairway of the royal and ceremonial sector associated with the Temple of the Sun and the water cult.

Pleasantly ventilated, this type of shelter is suitable for the special climate of Machu Picchu, tropical at midday but suddenly glacial as the sun sets quickly behind the sierras. Hence the invention of this type of open gallery, which lends itself easily to talk and is as well protected from heat as it is from intemperate weather. But was this merely a resting place, a place to pass the time, a place for gatherings, or was it a place for contemplation as well—where the Indian might spend hours meditating, across from the peaks of the Andes? Was the Huairona—wide open facing the east, with a view overlooking the most elegant liturgical fountain—perhaps reserved for the meetings of the civil or religious authorities of the city? Did they, for example, observe, at sunrise, from this shaded belvedere, the lustral ablutions of the Virgins of the Punchao, haloed by the reflection of Father Sun on the gold idol—as the idea occurred to us while we were studying the famous baths?

INCA HUASI: THE ROYAL PALACE

The "king's group"—thoroughly imbued with nobility and a powerful austerity by the magnificence of the architecture in the imperial Inca style—is located at ten paces

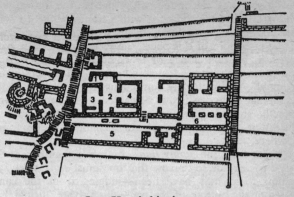

Inca Huasi: king's group
1. Hanging rock. 2. Interior patio.
3. Huairona. *4.* Huairona. *5. Interior*
garden. 6. Servants' quarters.

from the Torreón, on the other side of the great stairway, a sort of "royal road" transecting the Hanan sector.

"King's group," says Bingham, "because of the extremely solid character of the walls which enclose it, and also because it seems as though no one but a king could have insisted on having the lintels on his doorways made of solid blocks of granite each weighing about three tons." By what technique were they hoisted and fastened above the monumental doors? "Even had [the owner] possessed cranes, pulleys, and steam winches," Bingham observes, "he would have found it no easy task." Armed with patience, the builders of Machu Picchu "built up a solid inclined plane" against the walls, the American explorer thinks, so that they could gradually raise the monoliths with levers until they could be set in place.

The walls of the Inca Huasi rival those of the Torreón and the Nusta's Palace in beauty, indicating a very prominent social and political position.

Once one has crossed the entrance *portada* and then traversed the vestibule, an interior patio affords access to the various sections of this group.

Did visitors on official business from Cuzco wait, in the two *huaironas* set opposite each other, to be received by the Inca? These two vast rooms faced north and south respectively; one was decorated with niches, the other with windows. The first, equipped with a stone *petate* (a solid platform serving as a bed), seems to have been reserved for the great lord of this place; the second appears to have served as his conference or work room. The *portada* of each room measures 2.4 meters high by 1.3 meters at the threshold! Architecturally sumptuous, the walls are in the rectangular style, with rows of carved stone a meter thick, perfectly aligned. In a few corners the polygonal style is substituted—the most painstaking example to be found anywhere.

Not far from the *puñuy huasi*, or Inca's chamber, at the end of a corridor so narrow that one must walk sideways, a small room may have been—judging from the canal located at the bottom of the wall—his private "urinal."

All the dwelling places in the "king's group" were covered with a roof, including a sort of alley preceded by two steps set far apart. In the middle of the wall, a large, curiously shaped stone is provided, in the middle of its upper surface, with a perforated prismatic projection—hence the name *roca de ahorcado*, or "hanging rock." In fact, total mystery envelops its real function. Was this monolith connected with a ceremonial, imperial, or protocolar rite? Was the ring which pierces it used to restrain a sacred puma, guardian of the great entrance *portada*, as Luis Pardo suggests?[12]

A passage leads to the servants' outbuildings, grouped around another interior courtyard. These servants were no doubt numerous and carefully selected; they moved about quietly, their eyes respectfully cast down. Garcia imagines the young and very beautiful Acllas, destined exclusively to serve the sovereign, "representing the Incan hetaerism then customary in the social tradition."

What really happened behind the wool tapestries so smooth that they looked silken, adorned with feathers sewn on with gold thread? Who, then, was received in these imposing salons? Was it the Inca, listening to his high

---

[12] Machu Picchu is located at an altitude favorable to these felines of the Andes. Recently, on the path that descends from Huayna Picchu toward the Temple of the Moon, some French tourists were surprised by the appearance of a puma blocking the path; but it simply let them pass.

priests—or enjoying himself with his dark-skinned seraglio of Chosen Women?

But was this palace really the Inca's residence? Or was it, rather, a cenoby reserved for the communal life of the ascetics of the solar cult?

And who, then, walked in the peaceful garden that extends the entire length of the building, bordered by a stone bench?

INTI CANCHA, THE SACRED PLAZA

"Surprise followed surprise in bewildering succession." Leaving the Inca's Palace, Hiram Bingham climbed, by way of two fragments of a monumental stairway, toward Inti Cancha, the Sacred Plaza.

"Made to be admired and contemplated," writes Hermann Buse, this new group forms an eloquent "cosmic trinity" which spreads out on two levels.

The enormous principal temple, with a great monolithic altar adjacent to the long hall of the beautiful wall called the Wall of the Three Windows and facing the sacerdotal house, constitutes the lower level.

These monuments are distributed around the Sacred Plaza, "the setting of the cult of the major gods, Illa Tiki Viracocha and Pachacamac," according to Angles Vargas.

The western side of this great ceremonial terrace overhangs a fantastic cubic pyramid of gardens "hung" in space by prodigious illusionists. Incredibly vertical, the *andenes* plunge steeply into the precipices of Colpani and San Miguel, joining, far below, the silvery curves of the Rio Urubamba. In order to avoid a fatal fall due to vertigo caused by the view of these gigantic agricultural tiers, a semicircular balustrade borders the plaza. Certain investigators think they see in it the base of a monument which has since disappeared; perhaps it was dedicated to Mama Quilla, the Moon Mother.

Much higher, on the steep upper level, "chapels" guard the vicinity of the mysterious Intihuatana, which overlooks the "Lost City" and crowns the artificial pyramid composed of fourteen platforms covered with green grass.

All the buildings of the sacred group, in the cyclopean style, are so much more carefully constructed that they are very likely connected with the astral cult.

THE CARPAHUASI, OR PRINCIPAL TEMPLE

When he reached the principal temple, facing the north-west, Bingham says, "It nearly took my breath away." The northern wall, which has undergone some dislocation, contains blocks that weigh, he calculates, "several tons" each.

This rectangular monument, 11 meters long by 8 wide, never had a front. The two lateral walls, which stem from the back wall, are joined to it like huge open wings reaching toward the Sacred Plaza. They are supported by colossal stone blocks, one on each side, 2.4 meters high; one is 3 meters long, the other 4. Arranged like a rhythmical frieze, exquisitely worked niches adorn the upper part of the walls, whose parallelepipeds of light-colored granite decrease in size and are intentionally inclined 40 degrees inward.

It is thought that, in order to make such walls, which astound modern architects, the best engineers and stone-cutters in the Incan Empire came especially to Machu Picchu.

But in the place of the missing front, it seems that a long wooden rod—supported by a central pillar now missing—was embedded in the cavities bored on each side, beneath the first row of parallelepipeds. This system

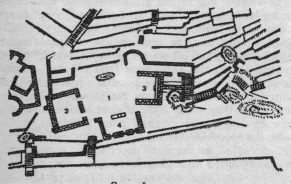

Sacred group
*1. Inti Cancha, the Sacred Plaza. 2. Palace
of Willac Umu. 3. Principal Temple. 4. Wall
of the Three Windows.*

would have made it possible to close off, at will, by means
of a large tapestry, the entire interior of the temple and
the great altar adjoining the back wall.[13] The altar is composed of a single rectangular megalith over 4 meters long.
In the center and at the base of this block, with its excep-
tionally rectilinear cut, a flat slab served as a pedestal for
the officiant who conducted rites and sacrifices.

Smaller blocks flank the altar on either side. Gleaming
gold idols and ornaments, offerings for the totems lodged
in the niches, must have been displayed here—or else, as
Uriel Garcia imagines, "gold statues, realistic works of art
reproducing portraits of Incas and Coyas—naked, or
dressed in sumptuous garments copied from those which
the reigning imperial couple wore."

For this historian, the principal temple of Machu Picchu,
exposed to the south wind and to the zenithal sunlight, was
a *carpahuasi*, a sort of sanctuary for audiences as well as
religious acts, in the sense of an Indian "basilica," used—
as were those of the Romans—as a tribunal or "house of
covenant."

More than at any other date, it is on the day of the
Raymis, the opulent solar feasts of the solstices, that this
monument experienced the hustle-bustle, lively but silent,
of the Acllas and Mamacunas, Virgins and Abbesses of
the Sun, preparing the ritual for the visit of the Inca and
the extremely opulent court of Cuzco. Choruses and dances
performed in the Sacred Plaza must have then charmed
plenipotentiaries and distinguished guests, seated on poly-
chromatic tapestries in the shade of walls covered with
magical flowers and illustrated hangings celebrating the
life of the Inca and of the gods.

Everything in this imposing temple suggests a credo,
and one imagines one can hear the prayers addressed to
the Supreme Creator. If "there exist places drenched in
mystery which wrench the soul from its lethargy"—as
Maurice Barrès declared—this is certainly such a place.

[13] Father Eduardo Villar Cordoba thinks that it was a question, rather, of a "large plate of gold sculpted in the image of
the supreme deity—symbolized by the Sun, some mystical bird,
or the anthropomorphic feline—that was embedded in the
lateral walls."

THE TEMPLE OF
THE THREE WINDOWS: TAMPUTOCCO?

The second temple also lacks a front; it is flush with the Sacred Plaza and wide open facing it. It overlooks on the east (by way of three trapezoidal bays—the largest and most sublime in ancient Peru) the vast grassy esplanade of the Intipampa, which separates the upper and lower cities. The temple overwhelmed Hiram Bingham. Dazzled by the sunrise as seen through these openings onto the wild *cañon* and the distant ice-covered peaks, the American explorer exclaimed: "Nothing just like them in design and execution has ever been found . . ." They seemed to him "too large to serve any useful purpose, . . . beautifully made with the greatest care and solidity."

But above all, he noted, "Nowhere else in Peru, as far as I know, is there a similar . . . *masonry wall with three windows.*" Now, that is what is described, word for word, in the information provided in 1620 by Juan Santa Cruz Pachacuti Yamqui Salcamayhua, in regard to the works that the first Inca, Manco Capac, ordered to be executed *at the place of his birth*, the name of which unfortunately is not specified.

"A great enemy of the *huacas,* Manco Capac," the Indian chronicler relates, "destroyed all those of the Pinaocapac *curaca,* along with all their idols, and he did the same when he conquered Tokay Capac, the great idolator,[14] whom he then ordered to execute works *at the place where he was born.* By Manco Capac's order," he continues, "the Indians tore the house down and with quarry stones they built a stonework structure in the form of three windows, which represented the *toccos* of the house of his forefathers . . ."[15]

Confronted with the mysterious polygonal wall resting

---

[14] Tokay Capac, a close relative of the Incas, appeared on Lake Titicaca at the same time as Manco Capac; he was the great leader of the Tampu realm, which includes Machu Picchu.

[15] According to the version of the *quipucamayocs* of Cuzco, Manco Capac emerged from a "window" of Tamputocco, engendered by a ray of sunlight or a sunburst which penetrated the opening.

on imposing megaliths, Bingham wonders: "Was that
what I had found?" If he is not mistaken, he has discovered
not only the capital of the last Incas, but the birthplace of
Manco the Great!

The area does, in fact, correspond strikingly to the basic
characteristics of Tamputocco, the site of a salubrious
refuge for a civilized populace forced to flee before
barbarian tribes with the body of their king. Was he perhaps buried here, in the Royal Mausoleum, a century
before Christ? Everything in the Yamqui's account seems
to Bingham to apply to the magnificence of the white
granite wall, whose three openings expose, like a belvedere,
the beautiful countryside of the Tampus, awash in an azure
transparency, suffused with all the sensuality of the
Andean tropics.

Confusing the tale of the legendary cave with what
Montesinos reports with regard to the predynastic Amauta
kings, Bingham forgot that all the chroniclers placed
Tamputocco a few leagues southeast of Cuzco, whereas
the "Lost City" is located to the northwest and at a much
greater distance.[16]

However, it may be that Bingham had very nearly hit
upon the truth, on at least two points. The first concerns
the birthplace of Manco Capac, which is unknown. All we
know is that the first Inca emerged from the Island of the
Sun, but where was he coming from? We do not know.
Sent forth on the path of the Sun by Viracocha, the
civilizing hero who divided the world among four cultural
heroes (one of whom is in fact Tokay Capac), Manco
Capac reappeared in Tamputocco. No chronicler ever
claimed that he was *born*. We see him only "emerging,"
along with his brothers and sisters, the Ayars and the
Mamas.

---

[16] Sarmiento de Gamboa specifies that "Pacaritampu and
Tamputocco are 5 leagues southeast of Cuzco"; Garcilaso de
la Vega places them at 7 or 8 leagues south of Cuzco.

The viceroy Toledo was informed that the Incas had sprung
from a crevice, or *tocco*, "the den that quickens"; Cristobal de
Molina indicates that Viracocha ordered Manco Capac to walk
from the banks of Lake Titicaca, by way of a subterranean
path, whence he emerged . . . in the cave of Pacaritampu,
"waystation of the dawn" or "daybreak."

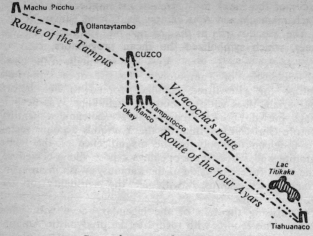

*Legendary sacred itineraries of
Viracocha and the Inca
"Sons of the Sun"*

Did Manco Capac and Tokay Capac, king of the Tampus, perhaps return, after a long journey and separation, to their ancestral birthplace—that is, Machu Picchu? The "Lost City" is in fact located in the small realm of the Sacred Valley, for which, we are told, Manco Capac fought with Tokay Capac and won. This hypothesis—which I am advancing, I believe, for the first time here—would explain, better than any other hypothesis heretofore put forth by researchers, why the "Lost City" on the Old Peak is the most beautiful city in all Peru.

As for the second point, if Machu Picchu had been connected to the family tree of the Incas, it would be plausible that, after having triumphed over his Tampu relative, Manco Capac had a wall with three *commemorative* windows erected there, as a "label" of origin—that is, to recall the cave of genesis and to mark the survival of the cyclopean style from distant epochs.

If this were so, if the wall that is the "wonder of wonders" of ancient Peru—the wall that obsessed Bingham and, after him, never ceased to intrigue archaeologists—corresponds to the Yamqui's account, two extraordinary trees must have been planted in the same spot (again, by order of the Inca) to "represent his mother and father," Pachamamachi and Apu Tampu, the "Great Tampu."

The Yamqui tells us that Manco had the roots of these trees, which symbolized the Incan progenitors, covered with gold and silver. From their branches hung "fruits and gold nuggets, all as if they were the fruits of the trunk and roots of the Incas." There was talk of "the sanctuary of the garden of gold and silver." Now, immediately beneath the three windows of the open temple there extends a large *anden* which could have been this magical garden!

Sarmiento de Gamboa instructs us that the Inca Pachacutec, "curious to know the story of the past and wishing to record his name for posterity, visited the mountain of Tamputocco in person." He entered the cave from which Manco Capac and his siblings were thought to have emerged when they first set out for Cuzco. After having visited it, Pachacutec worshipped the site and showed his feelings by conducting feasts and sacrifices there. "He had gold doors installed on the central, most beautiful window, known as Capac Tocco, and ordered that henceforth the place was to be the huaca of orisons, where one would come to consult the oracles."

Is this another possible reminiscence? A great granite mass, oriented east-west on the Sacred Plaza, located a few paces from the magnificent "commemorative wall, has all the characteristics of a sacrificial altar."

Were the three intriguing bays of the "Lost City" once sheltered in gold as well? Other mysteries remain to be solved! For example, when it was built, did this unique wall perhaps include five openings instead of three? Today, near the inner corner, at each end, one sees something that looks like two niches not quite as high: are these ancient windows, now blocked off, of the "house of Tokay Capac"?[17]

A pillar that rises in the center of the terrace, opposite the "symbolic" wall, also poses a problem. Did it support a thatched roof? A flat slab, juxtaposed in front of it, suggests, moreover, a cult stele. Close by, a block of faced

---

[17] This detail in no way means that Machu Picchu cannot be an allusion to Tamputocco, which modern researchers think they have identified; there they have noted the presence, not of three natural caves, or *toccos*, but five.

granite, with three scalar steps with carefully polished faces carved on each side, recalls simultaneously the pyramidal stone lodged beneath the Torreón, in the Royal Mausoleum; the stone of the same shape in the "princess's bath" at Ollantaytambo; and a third, identical monolith located in the "sacred group" of the ruins of Pisac. Are these stoneworks related to the Mama Pacha, to the great personages of Incan society, or to the personality of Viracocha? At the very most, one can assume that they were erected for cult purposes.

Finally, does the name "temple" suit the monument? Uriel Garcia acknowledges that it could have been modeled "in memory of the fable of Tamputocco, but for reasons of work and social life." As for José Mendoza del Solar, he notes, above all, *the frequency of the figure three* in the itinerary of the Inca Adam and Eve. To cite only a few examples:

- Three rows of "flying kings" on the famous gateway of the Sun at Tiahuanaco, near Lake Titicaca
- Three *toccos* in the legend of the Ayars of Tamputocco
- Three disciples of Viracocha who will teach the Indian people to worship him
- Three windows in the "beautiful wall" of Machu Picchu

This investigator deduced that no one particular Inca monarch resided in the "Lost City" (where many buildings also have three windows or doors, including the Torreón with its three openings). He sees here, rather, "a council of three Mancus, leaders of the three Ayllus Capacs [the three great groups of the Inca Genesis], in honor of whom were built the palace with the three windows, from which the inheritors of Tamputocco formed a *confederation of Machu Picchu* and from which they governed a second Quechua empire."

In fact, Mendoza del Solar denies that the countless ruins of utmost beauty in the Sacred Valley and everywhere else in the Peruvian Andes could have been built in only five centuries, with such aesthetic progress; it must have taken, he says, periods not measurable in decades. And one is tempted to agree with him.

THE RESIDENCE OF THE WILLAC UMU

Opposite the principal temple and adjoining, in part, the wall of the three windows, a rectangular building occupies the southeast side of the Sacred Plaza. Provided with two *portadas* and nine trapezoidal niches, it must have been designed to be used and inhabited by the high priest of the solar cult, the Willac Umu, the "inspired head" who speaks—a figure as powerful as the Inca (often his brother) and supreme leader of the church of the Sun and of the religion, but also the greatest magus in the Incan Empire.

One sees him represented on the *keros,* or ceramics: He has long hair and is dressed in a knee-length white tunic fringed with red wool and adorned with gold plaques and jewels. He is usually wearing a high tiara made of gold disks, crowned by a gold sun surrounded by feathers, attached under the chin by means of a gold half-moon.

A CAPITULAR CHAMBER

To ascend ever higher toward the Intihuatana, the culmination of the "Lost City" and of the religious thought of the Incas, we use a passage about twenty paces long which, on the left, borders the vertiginous pyramid of *andenes* already described.

At the junction of the monumental stairways, on the right, a large *portada* opens onto a small rectangular room; one of the lateral walls adjoins the wall of the main altar of the principal temple. Displaying an architecture equally refined, the back wall is adorned with a flawless row of identical niches and underscored with a long stone bench which covers the entire base to the floor. It is possible that artistic *cumbi* carpets made of vicuña wool were thrown over this monolithic couch to palliate the hard stone.

But the most striking aspect of this room consists in the fact that each lateral wall is composed of *a single solid megalith,* carved into *thirty-two angles* which join it to the neighboring blocks perfectly!

At first Hiram Bingham thought this room was "the High Priest's house." Then, after further study, he thought it might be a chapel for mummies, who were lined up on the bench for a "sun bath." Or else it was used to display the old busts that the Inca Pachacutec caused to be made, "as many as there had been Lords who had succeeded Manco Capac down to his father, Inca Viracocha."

For Uriel Garcia, this was the "checkpoint for traffic to the Intihuatana, the most sacred place in the city." Here one kept track, he believes, of the sun's progress, and of astronomical observations of the "celestial family" who ruled the passage of time; here, also, one could find out the solar time. Perhaps a town crier even announced the time from a rock that stands nearby; sculpted in it, to the top, are seven steps where astronomers could have stood.

Other versions make it out to be "the room where liturgical ornaments were kept" or the "antechamber of the solar cult," or else, like a capitular chamber, "the place where Amautas and patriarchs of the sacerdotal group deliberated." Also, offerings could have been collected here before the daily solar "mass"—unless it was in fact an alcove dedicated to some lesser deity, such as Illapa, wielding the thunderous weapons of the Storm, or Chasca, the attractive Venus, both of whom had, at the Coricancha in Cuzco, chapels next to the altars of the Sun.

THE INTIHUATANA, SUPREME SOLAR OBSERVATORY

The sacred zone of the Intihuatana starts at the very exit from the small room just described, at the foot of the great pyramid. Did the Tarpuntaes—priests of the Sun and Incas by blood or privilege, who, at certain times of the year, would head for the mysterious Casa del Sol, following the course of the solar rio—climb this stone stairway, which Bingham considered to be the most carefully constructed in Machu Picchu? Bordered on each side by low stone walls, the steps—designed both for isolated individuals and for groups (as in spiritual processions) climbing the steep slopes—are intersected by three flattened landings, which facilitate the ascent toward the observatory.

Viewed from the temples of the Sacred Plaza, or from farther away (from the Nan Cuna, for example), the artificial hill—with its fourteen tiered platforms, getting smaller toward the top—outlines the most impressive irregular pyramid of the "Lost City." It reaches a height of some 25 meters.

From the crowning terrace, the view plunges 500 meters below, to the bridge of San Miguel and the abyss, carved into vertiginous "hanging gardens"; from the other side, one looks out across the city stretched out at one's feet.

Having mounted the seventieth step of the stairway of the Intihuatana, the pilgrim ascends—by way of four patios, made slightly uneven by three large, low landings—toward the artistic culmination of a quasi-theatrical setting. Like stage flats, small buildings (called "chapels" for lack of a better word) stand beside the upper platform; their trapezoidal doors were two-thirds filled in and converted into *mirador*-windows. What mystical acts of telluric worship, what dances accompanied by chants or poetic hymns to the Sun took place here?

At the center of this "acropolis" of Machu Picchu, rising opposite the apocalyptic horizon of the blue-tinged cordilleras, an enormous boulder was completely cut geometrically, on the horizontal and vertical planes. A prismatic, somewhat trapezoidal gnomon emerges from it. This is the famous Intihuatana, considered a veritable "astronomical observatory" and "sundial," which—according to the opinion generally voiced by the investigators—dictated the dates of the calendar of agricultural tasks and festivals.

Inti, the god-star and Father Sun, in fact directed the work of the farmers of the Quechua-Aymara world, and the Intihuatana, apotheosis of the builders of the "Lost City," allowed the officiants of the cult to rule the celestial forces of a magical world, by communicating intimately with the universe. One senses here—more than anywhere else in ancient Peru, so rich in admirable ruins—an aura of cosmic eternity.

Four steps appear in the surface of the capriciously cut rock. If one heeds the legends related by the chroniclers, the Willac Umu symbolically "tied" the Sun to the gnomon with a gold chain, so that it would not go farther north and risk getting lost, condemning the Indians then to die of cold and hunger. The shadows cast by the prism, which is 36 centimeters high, indicated the month, the season, and the year.

Huaman Poma tells us that "the Indians, philosophers and astrologers, knew how to determine the movement of the stars, as well as the Sun's daily itinerary . . . calculating time like a clock . . . determining, through the rotation and displacement of the stars, summer and winter and the beginning of the year."

The position of the Sun (the "Inca of the sky") in relation to the Intihuatana must have then been recorded on the knotted *quipus* and on *quelcas*, a type of chiseled or engraved slate which has disappeared from Machu Picchu.

The exact function of the Intihuatanas found throughout ancient Peru[18] is the subject of much debate.

During the Conquest the chroniclers indicated that the very name "Intihuatana," derived from the Quechua verb *huatay*, meant "to tie"—whence the theory that the Sun was attached to it on the evening of Inti Raymi, which initiated the agrarian year, and on other feast days related to the seasons. However, modern linguists are reluctant to confirm this version. Some hold that *huatana* derived from *huata*, "year" or "solar cycle." In this case, it would be necessary to interpret "Intihuatana" in the sense of *recording* the movements of the Sun, rather than tying it.

Moreover, some Americanists deny that the structure had any astronomical function. They prefer to view it solely as a sacrificial stone, where the propitiatory victim destined for the solar holocaust (a young child or animal) was "tied," with its back to the stone gnomon—which also justifies the Colonial translation. Luis Alayza y Paz Soldan pictures this victim seated on the prism, offering its naked chest to the Sun, in a position convenient for the extraction of the heart and viscera, in which the diviner-priest would decipher auguries.

Others saw the rock, carved "in the rhythm of an imaginary spiral," as an *usnu*, or throne, of the Sun; sheathed in gold plaques, the gold statue was placed on the stone "dado." Thus "tied" to the prism, the Punchao (the Holy Grail of the Incas) presided over the ritual festivals; "Inti Huatana" must have stood for "the place where the Sun celebrates."

Horacio Urteaga examines the subject in greater depth. The Intihuatanas, he says, were nothing of the sort; rather, they were "altars dedicated to the funerary cult." In fact,

---

[18] Other Intihuatanas exist in the Sacred Valley, at Ollantaytambo, Pisac, Intihuatana, etc. Those of Cuzco—which are mentioned by the chroniclers were destroyed by the Spaniards.

he notes, these so-called astronomical "dials" turn out to be surrounded by walls which, for example, would have blocked the rays of a star as it set. Thus, he sees the archaeological complex crowning the great pyramid of Machu Picchu as an "oratory for the prayers of the deceased."

Which version is correct?

"Jealous guardians of the esoteric doctrine and of the mysteries of the Andean culture, the Amautas have long since crossed the frontiers of life," writes Luis Pardo, regretfully. And the sanctum sanctorum of the Incas will no doubt guard the secret of the dead gods forever.

CHAPTER SIXTEEN

Hurin, the Lower City

> *Too high to be a citadel responsible for guarding the pass, too far away from the roads to serve as a place of commerce, too vast to be a sanctuary, this city . . . with no raison d'etre, lingers in the memory of those who have seen it, like a strange hallucination.*
> —Louis Baudin, 1947

THE INTIPAMPA,
GREAT PUBLIC PLAZA AND FORUM

Hanan, above, and Hurin, below, are separated—along their entire length—by the unique flat part of the rocky outcropping upon which the marvelous "Lost City" is tiered.

The vast esplanade—rectangular, oriented south-north in the direction of Huayna Picchu, conforming to the irregular surface of the terrain, and carpeted with vivid green grass—unfolds on three slightly staggered horizontal levels. The plazas thus formed, bordered by *andenes* which outline aerial Greek keys, must have seen, unfolding amid the brilliance of helmets adorned with multicolored feathers and gold-embroidered garments, the grandest ceremonies in the entire empire, and solemn processions. Perhaps, as at Cuzco, the sportive trials of the *huarachico* were held here: armed like medieval knights, young nobles on the verge of receiving the costume and insignia that would confer manhood, competed in swift races. No doubt dramatic and folkloric presentations were performed here as well.

The larger section, the Intipampa (or "Field of the Sun"), forms a splendid proscenium. Some time ago a *huanca*—a raised stone with a serpent carved in it, before which offerings were placed—rose in its center. The archaeologists had it removed.

From the tiered terraces, which held the crowd, and the three windows of the open temple on the Sacred Plaza, which look out directly over the esplanade, the sight of the festivities probably alternated, according to the date, with commercial *ferias* in which the natives took part, having come up from the Urubamba Valley or down from Cuzco by way of the Nan Cuna, bearing articles for barter to the plaza transformed into a *catu*, or Indian market—like those seen today in the center of every Andean town or village, swarming with a technicolor multitude.

Perhaps, also, as at the Forum in Rome, public matters were sometimes debated here. These great plazas, modeled after the Huacaypata (Sacred Plaza) and Cusipata (Plaza of Joys) of imperial Cuzco, to which was added the Rimacpampa (Plaza of the Town Criers), are characteristic of Incan cities.

Determined to convince the scholarly world that the "Lost City" of the Old Peak is the ancient site of the "University of Idolatry and Abominations," Hiram Bingham proved that Machu Picchu was *Vilcabamba*, the place where the magic tree grew! He writes that it was probably here that *huillca* grew.[1] And he speaks at length about the seeds being made into a powder, which produces a narcotic (known as *cohoba* in Cuzco), which the Indians inhale

---

[1] *Huillca* (or *vilca*) means, in Quechua, "something sacred." The shrub—*Piptadenia colubrina Benth*—belongs to the mimosa family. It grows at altitudes of up to 1,500 meters and abounds in the tropical valleys of the ancient Incan province of Vilcabamba. It is also found at the foot of Machu Picchu, at Huadquiña. Its roots have narcotic properties known to the Indians. The hard, heavy wood is reserved for the opulent staffs of alcaldes, encrusted with silver. The seeds are purgative; the infusion made from them is used as an enema. To this day the Andean *brujos* (sorcerers) continue to intoxicate themselves for magical purposes, using the juice, bark, or root of the *huillca* mixed with corn *chicha*. The word *vilca* is found in many names in the Valley of the Incas: Vilcanota (House of the Sun), Vilcamayo (Rio of the Sun), Vilcapampa (Sacred Pampa), Vilca Umu (the high priest of the Sun), etc. It is also the ancient name for the idols.

through the nostrils by means of a bifurcated tube made out of bone. Now, among the artifacts found at Machu Picchu there is, in fact, a "nasal tube," like those used by the priests and diviners to plunge themselves into a hypnotic, divinatory sleep. Necromancers, magicians, and sorcerers, experiencing supernatural visions, thus communed, they claimed, with the invisible powers. To this day, their incoherent babblings are interpreted as occult revelations and prophecies. In this altered state of ecstasy, they discover the cause of illnesses and the name of the enemy or evil spirit who has caused them, by casting spells.

PRISONS, TORTURES, AND THE CONDOR OF SACRIFICES

Other sights—horrible ones—must have unfolded in one of the districts of the lower city, located at the foot of the "Stairway of the Fountains." Hardly consistent with the rest of the "Lost City," the jumbled layout here evinces a disagreeable sensation. The name of what Hermann Buse calls "the place of infamy" varies according to the author consulted: *chinkana* (underground labyrinth "where one gets lost"), Sankay Cancha, or Phinay Huasi (prisons).

Jailers, judges (*michocs*), and executioners (*tocricocs*), and other officials and servants, occupied the two-story building under which the dank, humid cells unfold.

A monumental rock 6 meters high, carved on several planes, supporting a rustic *torreón*, seems ready to crush the group. Beneath it, in a disturbing semidarkness, a *chinkana* contains niches and scalar stones. At the back, a passage burrows into the earth. How far? Apparently, no exploration has yet been authorized, under the pretext of the risk of suffocation and cave-ins. Have the treasure-seekers respected the taboo?

And Bingham? He never mentions the passage.

Chavez Ballon estimates that "at least a third of Machu Picchu is still hidden, in the form of intricate underground passages." In 1970, Germain Alatrista, a Peruvian journalist who visited the site, identified, together with this archaeologist, "five doorways leading to the underground passages of the city." One was located next to the great stairway that descends to the bottom of the Hurin district; it had a "clearly visible" lintel and "a solidly secured stone doorway . . . in accordance with the order received to block off all the *chinkanas* before abandoning the city for unknown reasons."

Like the passages that I visited at Sacsahuaman, Kinko, Chincheros, and elsewhere in the vicinity of Cuzco, most of these megalithic passages are equipped with altars, benches, platforms, and lateral niches.

In front of the *chinkana* in the "prison" district, in the very floor, there lies a flat, triangular slab, in the simplified shape of a recumbent condor. Sculpted so that it faces the rising sun, the head of the allegorical bird of prey is underscored by a semicircular ruff, composed of two white stones that suggest the "neck ribbon" of immaculate feathers of the "Birds of the Sun"—its messengers.

The curved stone beak points toward an orifice and conduit which surely lead to the unexplored underground passage, symbol of the Mama Pacha. The blood of victims laid across the megalithic condor ran into the gutter enclosed between the head and the collar, then streamed through the beak into the entrails of the Mother Earth, which it thus fertilized, fecundated, and vivified.

Was the solar predator—under whose symbol the pre-Inca complex of Chavin de Huantar north of Lima was placed—also the totem of the "Lost City"? Did Manco Capac, a direct descendant of the terrible "Condor Men" of Lake Titicaca and Tiahuanaco,[2] introduce it to Machu Picchu when he returned there?

Recesses and dark pits commence at the back of a triangular chamber, preceded by a cramped entrance leading to a low antechamber. Water seeps through the vault composed of long slabs sloping toward the floor, and drips monotonously into puddles. Moss, inching up the walls, fills the cracks in the rock and the joints between the stones. The gloom of this squalid prison is almost unbearable.

Hermann Buse pictures "a totem with a terrifying mask" guarding this place from atop the high niche that flanks the entrance, on the left. Eight steps rise toward an inner chamber pierced with nine other niches, in which a man can stand upright. What is inexplicable is that at the back

[2] See my book *Tiahuanaco, 10,000 ans d'énigmes incas*, Chapter 4 ("Hommes-Soleil et Hommes-Condor"), pp. 62–85.

of each there is a quadrangular opening at the height of the prisoner's face. Bingham makes note of these *nichos raros*, without, however, finding any reason for them. Some researchers imagine horrible torments for those condemned to a slow death. How many prisoners must have pined away in these sinister cells, which preceded the *huaytay-huan*, or "torture chamber," embedded beneath the boulder overhanging the *chinkana*?

Hermann Buse explains that the condemned were seated, with a board pressing their throats against the back wall of these "death niches," their arms inserted and firmly fastened in the cavities bored in each side. Thus, a single jailer would have been able to guard several captives, some of whom may have been women—dishonored Virgins of the Sun.

Other cells must have corresponded to the Sankay Cancha, where the Iscay Sonco Auca (double agents and traitors) were imprisoned for life, and to the Phinay Uatay Huasi, or common prisons, mentioned by Huaman Poma. The first type (which, constructed underground, was very dark) served as a place in which to raise venomous snakes, pumas and jaguars, bears, foxes, wild dogs and cats, eagles, vultures and owls, toads and lizards, "responsible for punishing and devouring alive the great evildoers and criminals, or Hatun Huchayocs." The terms of those in the latter group of prisons, used for prominent citizens and simple Indians, lasted no longer than it took to pronounce the sentences, which ranged from a whipping to forced labor in the gold mines. A few prisoners risked being subjected to torture, or *chancnay thocllauan chipanay uilla conanpac*.

Inexplicable also are the seats carved in the rock and a toboggan of polished stone.

CATACOMBS AND SARCOPHAGI

Below the preceding group, an axial path skirts the abyss, on the sloping flank of the mountain which overlooks the Rio Urubamba and the Puente Ruinas at the bottom of the *cañon*. Intersected by narrow paths, this sector underscores the lower city.

Defying vertigo, the houses are scattered on various levels. Daring ramps provide access to terraces and *andenes*

hovering over the beckoning void, and to numerous furnished funerary caves. All were ingeniously lined with
carved stone and decorated with niches and Greek-key-
type steps. Luis Pardo considers them to be "superior to
the mastabas and hypogea of ancient Egypt." Set amid
their precious possessions, huddled up and masked in gold,
"the mummies of great personages rested in these sepulchers, clasped to the warm bosom of Mother Earth."

It is in this area that Bingham discovered and explored
the greatest number of mausoleums fashioned by the Inca
architects in "every accessible—and many seemingly inaccessible—parts of Huayna Picchu and Machu Picchu."
The leader of the Yale Peruvian Expeditions notes: "As the
burial caves occurred generally on very steep rocky slopes,
more or less covered with dense tropical jungle, the work
of visiting and excavating them was extremely arduous.
Nevertheless . . . practically every square rod of the ridge
was explored . . . More than fifty caves were opened under
Dr. Eaton's personal direction and fully as many more by
his Indian helpers . . . the last caves opened being very
near the Urubamba River."

According to the rumors that I heard in the Sacred
Valley, one of the *chinkana* caves led to "royal tombs"
still being guarded by the Indians; in them several pillagers
of treasures had disappeared without a trace.

PUCAMARCA, THE GROUP
OF THE TWO *MORTEROS*

From the bottom of the central stairway of the "Lost
City," eleven gently graded ramps rise toward the imposing
double-framed monolithic *portada* of the district known
as that of the *morteros*. A colossal wall 6 meters high
hermetically seals the complex, which is ranged in three
tiers, the first two residential and the third, above, probably reserved for the cult. All the doorways of this group
are equipped with the "safety locks" previously described.

The various rooms are connected, by means of stairway-
passages, to interior patios and to a central room for the
head of the community, as well as to double *huaironas*.
Arising here and there, blocking the passage and forcing
one to retrace one's steps to find another outlet, are giant
rocks sculpted into seats or altars with totems.

There is one peculiarity: The windows, *grouped in threes*, all face west.

This group owes its name to two circular, concave mortars carved directly into an outcropping of the rock, which—set close to each other, "like two eyes raised to the sky"—rise about 10 centimeters from the floor, practically in the corner of one of the seven spacious dwellings that form the group. *In situ*, these mortars scarcely interest Hiram Bingham: "The wife of the chief of this group must have enjoyed a sense of superiority over her neighbors who, in making their corn meal, had no such permanent conveniences built into their kitchens."

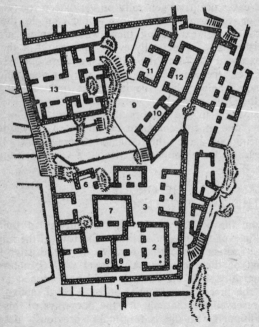

Pucamarca: group of the two morteros
1. Entrance portada. *2. Room of the* morteros.
3. Interior patio. 4–5. Great open hall. 6. Chapel with altar. 7. Great central room. 8. Double huairona.
9. Triangular patio. 10–12. Long open rooms. 13. Raised district.

This must be the largest, most beautiful *kitchen* in the world! Actually, it is an immense monolithic hall, with three large *portadas*: it measures 12 meters long by 7 wide! But Bingham's ingenuousness is infinite: "The privileged cook," Uriel Garcia quotes him as saying, "there ground corn, preparing a soup or beating *tamal* (corn paste)."

A good number of archaeologists have ridiculed the Yale scholar. Uriel Garcia observes, "These immovable, unbreakable *morteros* are not found on any private property, but rather in a workshop for collective labor." In his view, they were not "designed for culinary preparations but for grinding vegetable or mineral matter for dying the wools that the Acllas of the Sun used in their fine weavings." This version will not find many supporters.

Nevertheless, Uriel Garcia insists. He bases his personal conviction on the old coloration of the walls, which still retain traces of red stucco, and which Bingham noted in 1911. He therefore proposes the name "Pucamarca," or "Red Group," for this urban sector, because of the reddish clay used, "which shows that the buildings were dedicated to the task of extracting pigments and to the actual dying."[3]

This original hypothesis may agree with Bingham's on one point: Machu Picchu was a city of Acllas, Virgins of the Sun, skilled textile workers consecrated to Father Sun and to the Inca. For Uriel Garcia the "Lost City" was even—after Cuzco, the model of the genre—the principal Acllahuasi of the Chosen Women of the Incan Empire, that is, "a communal center specifically devoted to the laundering, dying, spinning, and weaving of guanaco wools; its cooperative organization was set up by the Incas."

But few Americanists agree on the "industrial" character of this majestic group in a city that apparently was not industrial either! After extensive study, moreover, Bingham decided that it was "the group of the intellectuals and the Amautas, the famous great thinkers of the Tahuantinsuyo." Chavez Ballon prefers to see it as "the royal district of the lower city, or *Inca Cunaqhuasin*."

[3] To this day, in Cuzco, an important block of buildings (near the Acllahuasi, or House of the Virgins of the Sun, and the Coricancha) shows similar colored walls. Called Pucamarca, this group belonged to Tupac Inca Yupanqui and contained Chuquilla, the idol of thunder (water cult).

Rebecca Carrión-Cachot, who was a famous Peruvian archaeologist, suggests another hypothesis. The "basins" hollowed in the rock floor are actually *pacchas*, or ceremonial bowls. To attract rain by means of magic or magical mimesis, she explains, the high priests kept sacred receptacles in the temples, always arranged in pairs. Through secret rites, they studied the precious celestial liquid collected and, according to the quantity, predicted good or bad years, abundant harvests or impending famine.

In each temple there was a special open chapel consecrated "to the cult of the celestial water"—"like the Hall of the Morteros at Machu Picchu," this investigator notes; like the "reflection of the pitcher which the moon goddess carried in the sky and which a god, her brother, struck in order to break it and free the beneficent rains."

During their recent explorations of the paths of Machu Picchu, Victor Angles Vargas' expedition discovered a monumental boulder located at Intihuatana, near the "Lost City." The granitic silhouette recalled a giant's cranium over 1 meter high. Now, the round eyes on the rock face "are two receptacles for rainwater that were connected with the liturgy."

THE ACLLAHUASI, OR PALACE
OF THE VIRGINS OF THE SUN

A stairway with sixty-two steps and three landings, which skirts four pyramidal *andenes* rising above the main plaza of the Intipampa, leads to the level of what Bingham calls the "private garden group," otherwise known as the "Group of the Three Gateways."

An elongated platform "enabled the tenants to participate in the celebration of the great ceremonies of the imperial liturgy as if from atop a balcony," writes Hermann Buse. It is true that, ordinarily, the occupants of this group must have lived cloistered in the interior, which no window illumines on the side of the plaza—which is unusual. Now, on this upper terrace, two "proscenia" pierced by bays, look out directly over the public plaza and, beyond it, the sacred group of the temples with the three symbolic windows, and as far as the pyramid of the Intihuatana.

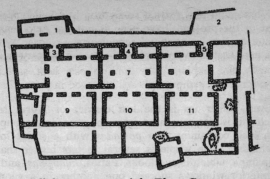

*Acllahuasi: group of the Three Gateways
1–2. Annexes shaped like stage flats. 3–5. The
three entrance gateways. 6–8. Patios and
double* huaironas. *9–11. Great workshop-halls
with three doors.*

This district is named after the three imposing *portadas*
with double stone frames, which can be closed off at will,
using the locking mechanism exclusive to Machu Picchu.

Inside, three spacious halls open onto large patios
separated by double *huaironas*. The walls contain four
aligned windows. Numerous small rooms, toward the rear,
suggest a particular density of inhabitants, whence the name
occasionally used, "the popular district." All the rooms are
interconnected, which evinces a typically Incan society,
familial and coherent: an intimate, harmonious life-style.

An architectural peculiarity gives this group a physiog-
nomy all its own: The walls are shaped like capital T's, in
order to separate patios and rooms set opposite one
another. These are, according to Uriel Garcia, the *ahuay-
huasi*, textile workshops attended by spinners and weavers,
under the watchful eye of the Mamacunas; here artistic
finery was manufactured for the Inca, the Apus, and the
Sun.

Open spaces between the buildings were used for llama
parks and reserves of provisions, or *colca-pata*. On the
eastern side the mountain drops away abruptly. Other
buildings and *andenes* of the Acllas are suspended over
the void.

What could this district, so rigorously shielded from the sight of the profane, have been if not the Acllahuasi, the mysterious phalanstery and school of the Chosen Women? It is here that the very core of the sacred mystery must lie.

THE UPPER GROUP

Even higher up is the last district of Hurin Machu Picchu; it is also separated from the preceding group by a high wall containing two *portadas* with a secret locking mechanism. The whole is several meters higher than the Intipampa, which it overlooks. Patios, *huaironas*, and rows of interior windows succeed one another in a geometric rhythm. But on the west side, again, no opening gives onto the upper city and the sacred groups—which proves a certain "shibboleth" of a mythic and religious nature.

One senses here a sudden desertion, as if the inhabitants had evacuated the city hastily, without warning, and with no hope of returning. Were they unaware of this?

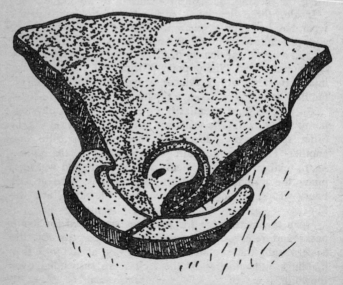

The sacrificial condor

CHAPTER SEVENTEEN

Huayna Picchu,
Cosmic Mountain

*The ancient Peruvians climbed to the very
top, in search of the horizon . . . because
they understood that the soul needs more
space than the body.*

—Fernando Belaunde Terry

PACHAMAMA HUASI, OR THE SACRED ROCK

Underscoring the base of the Huayna Picchu (the Young
Peak, which is "still growing"), an elongated, light-colored
rock assumes—naturally?—the shape of a huge fish; it is
positioned as if it had been laid out on a platter, and it
has human features. Set on a monolithic pedestal, this is
the Pachamama Huasi, the venerated dwelling place of
Mother Earth. This sacred boulder measures up to 3 meters
high, 7 meters long, and nearly 1 meter wide. It is thus the
largest of the thirty-odd divinized boulders of the Picchus.
And yet, despite its dimensions, this isolated boulder cannot be seen from the "Lost City"; it is intercepted by the
walls of the upper group, a jumble of fallen stones and
lush vegetation.

It suggests, with its two flat sides facing east and west, a
great "altar" against or upon which cult objects or—who
knows?—some "hieroglyph" or ideographic message could
have been displayed.

It was seen only by those intrepid enough to undertake
the frightening climb up the Huayna Picchu, draped in the
evanescent mists which constantly rise from the depths of
the *cañon*.[1]

[1] The ascent of the Huayna Picchu cannot be undertaken
alone, without an Indian guide. Many tourists have met with

It is rumored that, because of the taboo protecting the Acllas of the Sun, the Old Peak and Young Peak were once cut off from all contact with the world and connected solely by means of the secret underground *chinkanas*. For a long time archaeologists refused to believe this, until one day some Argentinian university students accidentally discovered, near the Sacred Boulder, the entrance to a deep labyrinth, which they succeeded in penetrating to a depth of about 7 or 8 meters. At that point cave-ins blocked the passage. They observed, however, that the walls of the tunnel were lined with finely carved stone.

THE MARQUIS DE WAVRIN'S "FIRST"

The path that goes from the Pachamama Huasi toward the granitic spearhead of the Huayna Picchu must be modern. But an ancient route could be traversed starting from Mandor Pampa, in the hollow of the valley.

A pioneer in the "scientific" exploration of the Young Peak, the Marquis de Wavrin was the "first" to reach it during the time when it was known only to the treasure-seekers of the Sacred Valley of the Incas. He thus became convinced that the ancient Peruvians regularly frequented this apparently inaccessible slope.

This access route was discovered by three adventurers, one of whom, Valdivia, agreed to guide the foreigner to the steep peak only after having solemnly warned him of the mortal dangers awaiting him: loss of equipment at every step; a fall, to hundreds of meters below; so many swarming serpents, one did not know where to place one's feet. The marquis was required, moreover, to give his word of honor that he would maintain absolute silence concerning the adventure upon his return to Cuzco.

Engineers with the department of bridges and roads, who at that time were overseeing the construction of the Cuzco–Santa Ana railway, had Indian *peones* set up in advance a cable as a handrail in the most dangerous spots.

---

death there—for example, in 1963 the American Mormon Philip Terry Stile, whose body was found in the Urubamba, after a vertical fall from the great Temple of the Moon. Three Frenchmen were recently found drowned at the same spot.

Suspended from an iron hook and sliding along in a crudely constructed seat along the steel cable of an *oroya,* the explorer crossed the Rio of the Sun and began the ascent.

A series of steep walls supported by boulders near the bank, superimposed and perpendicular, fortify the piedmont. Huge piles of slingstones still await the Inca warriors.

His hands bloodied, de Wavrin clings to the thorny shrubs, slipping on the humus soaked with rainwater from constant downpours. A few "flying" *sarutas* sticking out from the walls enable him to regain his footing on higher ground. Valdivia leads the marquis to a cave which a "spectacled bear" (*Tremarctos ornatus*) has only just abandoned, leaving fresh tracks. Several other caves with stone-lined walls have entrances protected by a "screen" or "rain shield" made of stone.

About 300 meters from where they started out, a gigantic boulder is pierced by the most notable cave, known today as the Temple of the Moon. The interior layout represents an art as austere as it is admirable and mysterious.

Valdivia interprets these various "arranged cavities" as "a city of cavernicolous troglodytes from the prehistoric era." When he first inspected them, he was surprised to find, he says, "no trace of smoke or a cooking hearth; no ceramic shards (not even utilitarian ones) or stone axes or other weapons; no tools or instruments; not even any human bones."

However, these caves were *inhabited* in the very distant past. De Wavrin hunts down, close by, a reservoir of spring water, where he quenches his thirst and discovers "a flat stone" for grinding (by rocking), along with the pestle of the archaic mortar.[2]

The explorers climb three graduated *andenes,* which are surmounted by small cubic rooms with *vertical walls* (they do not slope inward, Inca-style)—watchtowers, no doubt—

---

[2] In 1934 the engineer Jacobo Rauss carried out the only excavations conducted on the Huayna Picchu thus far. He unearthed ceramics and metallic objects in the form of *champis,* in the classical Incan style.

set up at regular intervals. These are succeeded by a new row of shelters beneath the rock.

With his index finger, Valdivia points out to de Wavrin "the stairway with *600 steps*" that they are about to tackle! A veritable Titan's ladder, heading straight up, scarcely wide enough for both feet—and sometimes only wide enough for a single foot, placed at an angle.

Many slabs are loose, and de Wavrin will christen this acrobatic structure a "stairway of death." Exhausted, the men spend the night 50 meters from the peak, beneath a rocky gable. The next morning the marquis will discover, at the very top, "an admirable throne carved nearly 1,000 meters over the void."

A few paces farther, an opening in the ground intrigues him. He penetrates for about 20 meters, but the air becomes unbreathable. Outside again, he notices that the orifice could have been sealed with a round stone, still standing nearby.

THE THRONE OF THE SUN

What superhuman race of equilibrists succeeded in carving out a passage to the very top of the Young Peak, sculpting "thrones on top of the clouds"? One of these, solid, lies overturned, its seat and back upside-down the result of lightning or some Dantesque cataclysm? Valdivia identifies it, perched at an altitude of 2,700 meters, as "the throne of the Sun." The panoramic view from this throne, overlooking the entire Sacred Valley as far as Ollantay-tambo, is one of the most magical sights in the world. It would make an excellent lookout point for a sentinel who did not suffer from vertigo. Turning around and facing in the other direction, de Wavrin discovers, stretched before him, all the jungles of Vilcabamba and Quillabamba, in what is now the province of La Convención.

This inconceivable "astral observatory" is bathed in a disorienting, nearly intolerable glare, reflected from the surge of the eternal glaciers opposite. When the sun shoots its rays over the Huayna Picchu, an extraordinary phenomenon occurs.

The three Indians accompanying the explorers, whom thus far nothing has seemed to impress, tremble with fear. They interpret this luminous phenomenon as a bad omen:

Suddenly the shadow of de Wavrin, seated on the "throne of the Inca"—who must have watched the sunset from this site—is cast on a cloud clinging to the peak, and haloed in all the colors of the rainbow: an intense blue at the edge, turning orange toward the center. This "specter" projected onto the cloudy screen flickers in response to the shifting winds, which push it first eastward, then pull it back westward. Thus, the marquis' aerial image is by turns diffracted in the sky, then re-formed when more mists rise from the *cañon*. The effect is truly fantastic, but startling.

De Wavrin takes delight in an enchanted view of the "Lost City." He even perceives, in the distance, three unexplored archaeological groups, built atop a bluff which is inaccessible because of its steepness. And beyond, he sees a paved road, very long, which trails off into the clouds.

If he looks down at his feet, the marquis is no less dazzled by a sense of *jamais vu*! Everywhere, defying the laws of equilibrium and gravity (not to mention mountain sickness and vertigo), there loom walls, *andenes*, short stairways, buildings, and mausoleums.

On this peak, which is known for having always attracted lightning (as is shown by the jumble of hewn, cracked, or completely shattered rocks), pieces of the mountain have crushed splendid polyhedral walls under construction. And the marquis wonders: To what use could the flawless walls crowning this terrible place, blasted by fire from the sky, have been put? And, above all, by what inconceivable prodigy were they conceived and executed?

He is unable to reach a high, uncompleted trapezoidal niche which opens out over the abyss. Elsewhere, the lintel of a monumental *portada* has collapsed, but under a ridge smooth and straight as the letter I, the rock was leveled and encrusted with carefully joined stone cubes. Only a daring mountaineer, suspended from the end of a rope, would be able to reach it. Decidedly, on top of this cosmic mountain anointed with divine "solarity," the Inca magicians had no sense of what was impossible.

THE TEMPLE OF THE MOON

Currently, no one attempts to climb the Huayna Picchu by way of the slope perched perpendicularly over the

Urubamba. However, the path now used to climb the granitic needle—praying to the Inca gods!—is still hard to believe.

Ligneous plants, swarming with butterflies and flying ants, cover the *cuchilla* where the path insinuates itself, zigzagging. Out of sight, under cover of the woods, wild animals often escort the tourists. These are generally spectacled bears who send stones rolling and snap branches —or, more rarely, a puma.

Ancient "resting places" were carved in the bends in the path, which is sometimes interrupted by a dark tunnel, carved into steps, which one must enter on all fours.

Having, with considerable effort, reached the summit, one can never forget the view of the "Lost City" stretched at the feet of the Young Peak. Then, turning one's back on it, one sees the path redescend—whipped by a harsh wind— toward the enigmatic "Temple of the Moon," which was, Hermann Buse declares, "a monument raised to the secret powers of the world."

Indeed, this cave looms here, where we least expect it, like a triumph of human daring, and of a technology which almost smacks of science fiction.

Set in front of the entrance, an outdoor throne sculpted in the rock allows one to watch the sun sink abruptly behind the screen of the folded cordilleras.

Inside, to a depth of seven paces and along a width of twelve, the walls of the mountain have been quilted with blocks carved and imbedded with utmost care, from the floor to the ceiling, which, in the corner, slopes and rests against a low rock. In the back, three false *portadas* and six false trapezoidal windows with double monolithic frames adorn the puzzle; there is also a niche.

Opposite the outdoor throne, a raised *tiana*, with a back, is wide enough for two or three people to sit on it. To the left is an altar with empty niches for idols.

Adjoining the "sacred chamber," a second cave, located on a higher level, is illumined by a fissure. One reaches it by way of three steps. From a "deified" boulder there emerge strange protuberances. Here, again, the desertion must have been rushed, for altars and walls were never finished, and carved stones lie about on the floor.

An investigator from Cuzco, Jorge Cornejo Bouroncle, has made a curious observation concerning the Huayna

Picchu: *Pircas* (low walls made of pebbles) stand before the entrances to the caves and dwellings. And behind these screens made of piled-up stones, the thresholds were sprinkled with ashes—a custom that the ancient Peruvians observed, he explains, "to indicate their absence and to say that no one might enter but that they were coming back."

What is the derivation of the name "Temple of the Moon"? Once again, it originated with the Indians, who observed that, on the night of the full moon, the cave's interior is illumined to an almost unreal brightness, emanating from the rays of Mama Quilla, the "mother of the Incas."

These same Quechua Indians believe that at sunset, the Machus, or ancestors, emerge from the mausoleums of the Andes to warm themselves at their evening fires. This might explain the numerous outdoor "thrones" of the Young Peak, on which, on certain dates, the noble mummies were exposed at the highest points, so that they would be closer to the great celestial deities.

ESOTERICISM AND MICROCLIMATE

Given the altitude and the microclimate, which one feels more intensely at Machu Picchu than anywhere else, "the telluric forces," says Bernard Lelong, "emanate more than they do in any other place." It is quite possible that the sages discovered and selected this work of nature, and exploited and extended it in their constructions and instruments. Therefore, he believes, the Incas must have located "their center for esoteric teachings at Machu Picchu," and had the buildings here constructed in accordance with a design that enabled them to harness these exceptional telluric conditions, for the benefit of master and student.

Lelong also mentions the "potential of negative ions," which may have enabled the builders of the "Lost City" to restore their vital forces without feeling fatigue. "This potential, currently being developed by western man," he notes, "has been known to the sages of all traditions and civilizations."

Pursuing this hypothesis further, Lelong adds, "If we perceive an indefinable something in certain places, nega-

tive ions are usually one of the elements of that perception."
These "hot points" produced by the microclimate may have
been reinforced "by specific shapes"—pyramids, trapezoids,
scalar symbols?—and by "waterfalls, the very basis of life."
Although today the Inca's hydraulic system for collecting
and distributing the precious liquid has fallen into dis-
repair, "The channels for alimentation, the irrigation of the
terraces, the baths, and the distribution posts—all of which
formed indispensable cascades—still exist and demon-
strate," he concludes, "the influence of negative ions."

THE COSMIC MOUNTAIN, AXIS OF THE INCA WORLD

A Venezuelan scholar, Dr. José Manuel Estrada, who,
as an observer, attended the World Congress of Philosophy
held in Mexico in 1963, states, "Since the tellurico-
magnetic center of the planet has shifted 30 degrees to the
south, it is now located in the heart of the Incan ruins of
Machu Picchu."

Was the Huayna Picchu—a magnet for the "fire from
the sky" both feared and revered by the ancient Peruvians
—the *axis mundi*, the axis of the world, the supreme
cosmic mountain of the fabulous mythology of their
Olympus, from which there streamed over the incomparable "Lost City"—as Samivel writes in connection with
the Egyptian pyramids—"torrents of inexhaustible energy"?

It cannot be denied that the exhilarating double panoramic vision of sunrise and sunset that one enjoys from
the top of the Young Peak placed the Picchus of the
Sacred Valley in an absolutely unique position, one all the
more special in terms of the esoteric and religious cult of
the Incas.

Another fascinating theory has been put forth by Dr.
Eduardo Galleani Viacava, a Peruvian of Italian descent.
His theory is based on the natural pyramidal shape of the
Huayna Picchu.

In the eyes of the pre-Columbian peoples, as for other
vanished civilizations, the pyramid symbolized the structure
of the cosmos. It served as a "pattern" for religious
architecture, and the Greek key and scalar symbol represent its "scale-model" reproduction. Galleani Viacava,
taking into account the traditional astrological and cosmo-

graphic conception of the peoples who inhabited the Andes countless millennia ago, believes that in a distant era (perhaps at the beginning of time) the true pyramidal shape of the Young Peak—which at that time was much more pronounced than it is today, planed by erosion—was interpreted "as a symbol of nature," around which the earliest inhabitants of the Sacred Valley settled. "With patient hands," he says, "they accentuated its geometrical shape, sculpting this 'natural temple' so as to convert it into a sublime, ideal sanctuary."

THE EXTRAORDINARY "PYRAMIDIZATION" OF THE MUMMIES

Later, Galleani Viacava believes, the entire mountain of the Sun was reserved for the high priests and the Acllas, who alone had access to the divine city. He therefore thinks it probable that many of the elect lived here and were buried here, along with all their treasures.

A supporter of an extraordinary thesis, according to which the age-old pyramidal shape was inspired by "the polyhedral cluster of light which, by revolving and condensing, formed the universe," this investigator suggests, "If one holds the 'key' to the rectilinear propagation of light and its spectrum, which was known to the Ancients,

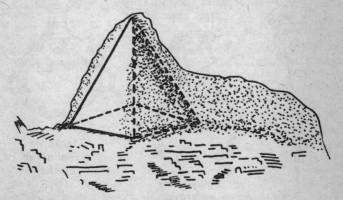

"Pyramidization" of the Huayan Picchu
(by Dr. Eduardo Galleani Viacava)

it should be possible to locate, exactly, the position of the mummies entombed beneath the Huayna Picchu," along with the fabulous ritual offerings, which constituted "important messages for humanity."

"This 'key,' " he continues, "enables one to study the orientation of the mountains, which give off superimposed layers of luminous vibrations of the various rays of the spectrum; these rays are directed toward the monuments, which symbolize the prism."

Having perfected "a personal method" for "pyramidizing" the space and area to be prospected, Galleani Viacava is convinced that gold and silver statues, precious crockery, and bas-reliefs constituting a sort of glyptic or hierographic language are still hidden in the subterranean *chinkanas* that burrow deeply, for several kilometers, beneath the cosmic mountain—hidden along with the most fantastic mummies, in places that were not selected at random, but specially chosen by the Inca magi. His pyramidization of the Huayna Picchu, he believes, has enabled him to detect them—at least in theory.

Will he someday undertake excavations that will reveal to the world "the golden book" of the marvelous Incan culture, along with the famous, mummified Acllas of the Sun, who disappeared without a trace nearly 500 years ago?

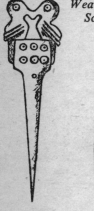

Weaving tool—Machu Picchu Sculpted wood with two urpis, *or doves*

Ppuino *(jar) with royal necklace*

Makka, *or aryballus for* chicha

PART FIVE

Virgins of the Sun
and
Archaeological Mysteries

By the Inca's order, hundreds of virgins consecrated to the Sun, chosen from among the most beautiful in his lands, were gathered in buildings near the royal palaces . . . The young women live out their lives in a chastity respected by the people. Nevertheless, their perfumed bodies aroused sensual desires . . .
—Charles Wiener, 1875

CHAPTER EIGHTEEN

The Acllahuasi and the Chosen Women

*To the east of Amarucancha, traversed by
way of the Road of the Sun, is found the
district known as the Acllahuasi, which is
the abode of the Chosen Women, where
the convent of the maidens dedicated to the
Sun is found . . .*

—Garcilaso de la Vega, 1609

THOUSANDS OF COURTESANS

The Inca's most precious possessions were not—as we
would tend to think—gold or silver (the pure tears of the
Sun and the Moon), but the famous solar Virgins. Great
was the surprise, as well as the lust, of the conquistadors
when they found out that the Inca—rivaling the greatest
voluptuaries, from the sultans of the tales of Arabian
nights to Solomon, King of Kings—still had at his bidding,
throughout the Empire of the Tahuantinsuyo, thousands of
courtesans.

Cloistered like hetaerae, the very lovely Acllas led the
life of high-born ladies, revered by the people and the
nobility alike, in sumptuous Acllahuasis, palaces which
were protected from the eyes of men; the Spaniards, mad
with desire, broke down the doors to these palaces, hitherto
rigorously guarded.

The chroniclers, who witnessed the rape of the "women
of the sun" and of the Inca, and the pillage of the Incan
convents, indicate that there was an Acllahuasi in every
major town, even in the provinces farthest from Cuzco, and
that it was considered a supreme honor on the part of the
Inca when he built these cloisters surrounded by window-
less, cyclopean walls—in a region he had recently conquered and incorporated into the empire.

Some Acllahuasis housed 200 "virgins," others 1,000 or even more—the number was unlimited. To these must be added the attendant Acllas (often as many as 500) and the Mamacunas, or "mother superiors," along the lines of "abbesses"—daughters or close relatives of the reigning Inca, who were responsible to the Willac Umu (high priest of the Sun) for running the house.

These Incan "convents" lived off the revenues and yields of the Inca's regional haciendas; their lands were cultivated right after those of the sun and before the *chacras* (plots of arable land allotted to the people). The administration of each Acllahuasi was entrusted to an Incan governor, assisted by a steward who attended to financial matters. The Yana Willcas of old, "doctor-scholars" advanced in years, saw to the health of the recluses.

Like the vessels used in the Temple of the Sun, the Acllas' tableware—pitchers, jars, goblets, platters, and plates—was all made of finely worked gold and silver. The Virgins bathed in gold-plated basins and strolled in gardens where every living thing had been reproduced in molten gold, fashioned by the most skillful goldsmiths in the country.

THE GREAT GYNAECEA OF THE EMPIRE

The greatest and most competitive Acllahuasi (which only princesses of the highest imperial lineage could hope to enter) sheltered, a few days before Pizarro's raid on the Incan capital, 3,000 Acllas consecrated to Father Sun, in the manner of vestal virgins.

A little while earlier the 1,500 Chosen Women of Huascar (one of the rival heirs to the empire after the death of Huayna Capac) were all assassinated in the Acllahuasi of Pucamarca, by Quizquiz, Atahualpa's deputy, and by his order.

Imprisoned by Francisco Pizarro in Cajamarca, Atahualpa kept with him over a hundred concubines, who soon suffered all manner of humiliations at the hands of the Spaniards. Two of his favorite Huarmi Palli Cunas were raped by drunken conquistadors. Rather than live on in disgrace, one of them killed herself, honoring the ancestral laws which forbade—under penalty of a cruel death——any Chosen Woman who had shared the Inca's bed to belong to another mortal.

Atahualpa appeared infinitely more pained and angered over these sacreligious acts than he was over the pointless loss of the fabulous treasures he handed over for the illusory ransom. When he learned of the suicide of his favorite, the beautiful Morning Star, the Inca was wild with rage. Invoking the god Pachacama, he entreated him to transform the spirit of the dead Aclla into a bolt of lightning that would strike the transgressor and reduce his body to ashes. By a curious coincidence, Atahualpa's curse was carried out a few days later. The Spanish knight was in fact struck by lightning on the road to Quito.

Many virgins managed to flee the great Acllahuasi of Huaylas when the conquistadors invaded, and escape to the Cordillera Blanca. Others were spared "because they were thought to be witches." They were quick to be "baptized in order to become the Acllas of Christ," a missionary tells us.

From the accounts of Father Calancha, we are able to deduce that a great number of Acllas and priests of the Sun lived in the "abominable University of Idolatry" at Vilcabamba. For this reason, Hiram Bingham never doubted for an instant that the Chosen Women who had escaped from Cuzco in time hid, until their deaths, in the inaccessible "Lost City," which was, as we have learned, "the secret of the Acllas."

THE CREATION OF
THE INCAN "HOUSES OF PROSTITUTION"

We must look way back to the protohistoric centuries of Peru to find a trace of the first Acllahuasi. Montesinos associates it with the name Lloque Yupanqui, "the Left-handed," third Inca of the so-called legendary empire, who must have reigned sometime around the seventh century (or the eleventh, according to certain other chroniclers).

Lloque Yupanqui had four types of "houses" built, in which lived the chaste and reclusive Chosen Women. The most beautiful women, in form and features, were dedicated to the Creator. All the others who became the servants of the deity could belong to the Inca. Finally, he offered the less lovely Acllas to his great chiefs and allies as a reward.

By deciphering the ancient *quipus,* it was learned that the fifth Inca, Capac Yupanqui, was a *capacome*—that is, a great womanizer—and that he had a weakness for the virgins of Collao cloistered in one of the most famous Acllahuasis, that of the sacred Island of the Sun in Lake Titicaca.

The wife of the Inca Viracocha, Mama Runtu (who was so well versed in gastronomy that she boasted she had never eaten the same dish more than two or three times, so varied were the number of dishes that she knew how to prepare), ordered that the Acllas and Mamacunas study the art of cooking in the Acllahuasis so that they might serve delicacies at the frequent banquets held for the court of Cuzco.

The religious institution of the Acllacunas was later reformed by the famous Inca Pachacutec, lord of Pacaritampu, who established a three-year "novitiate." He is the Inca responsible for the majority of the houses reserved for the Chosen Women and particularly the immense Acllahuasi of Cuzco, which served as a model throughout the empire. Detailed descriptions of it are scarce, but its impressive ruins can still be seen in the capital of the Andes.[1]

Not far from the solar Temple of Gold, the Acllahuasi, which covered a vast quadrangular space, formed a veritable district bordered by two parallel roads leading, at one end, into the ceremonial esplanade of the Coricancha and, at the other, into the great plaza of festivals known as Cusipata. The house of the Chosen Women constituted an autonomous, central town in the heart of the city. A single monumental *portada* adorned

---

[1] After the booty was distributed among the Spanish conquerors, half of the Acllahuasi reverted to Pedro del Barco, and other parts of the monument to the licentiate de la Gama and Francisco Mejia, before falling into the hands of Diego Ortiz de Guzman, knight of Seville. Later the convent of Santa Catalina was built on the site, and other virgins, replacing the priestesses of the Sun, came to serve the new God.

its facade; it was opened only for the Coya, the Inca's wife, and to welcome the women who were entering into the service of the gods.

The Acllahuasi was a dwelling place so sacred to the Incas that when Manco decided to burn Cuzco, he gave the order to spare this district, even though he knew that many of his enemies were lodged there.

A long interior street in the form of a corridor divided the building along its entire length. Two people could walk down it side by side. On each side of the axial way there unfolded cells and workshops. The openings, covered only with opulent hangings, were watched over by extremely vigilant guards. At the entrance to the corridor, twenty porters ran back and forth, carrying in and taking out everything that had to enter or leave the Acllahuasi, but everyone was forbidden to cross the threshold, under pain of death. And it was only at the very end of the interior road that there stood the district of the virgins in perpetuity, the sight of whom was even more taboo for profane eyes, and even the eyes of the Inca.

Moreover, the discipline imposed in the Acllahuasis forbade any novice to enter the part reserved for the Acllas of the Sun, where each category also lived isolated from the others.

Tupas Yupanqui, the tenth Inca, had a convent for Mamacunas built in the "holy" city of Pachacamac, on the Pacific coast, about 30 kilometers from Lima; facing the fields and gardens cultivated in the desert, the convent lay in the shadow of the Temple of the Sun erected atop a pyramid which overlooks the sea and the oasis of Lurin.

Huayna Capac, his son and successor, ordered the construction of a Temple of the Sun at Tumbes, near the present Peruvian-Ecuadorian border, which was attended by 200 virgins chosen from among the most captivating in the region. An extremely ferocious jaguar and puma guarded the entrance.

SACRED HETAERAE OR SLAVES?

While the expression "Chosen Women" cannot be applied to the Acllas as a synonym for "whore," neither should the Acllahuasis be confused with "houses of prostitution" in the sense currently ascribed to establishments where common prostitutes offer themselves to strangers for a fee.[2]

In pre-Columbian Peru it was more precisely a question of a form of imperial hieroduly, as well as hierogamy or sacred prostitution, practiced by other ancient peoples— a purely gratuitous hieroduly reserved solely for the Inca, who, in deflowering a virgin, inseminated her in the name of the Sun, to perpetuate the solar lineage.

I have read that in order to ensure the Incan dynasty perfectly pure eugenics, the virgins initiated by the Inca must have first been plunged into a "magical" sleep and then inseminated as if by an incubus.

Quite the reverse of a "house of prostitution," the Acllahuasi should be considered as a sacred college where beautiful young women were schooled in refinement under the strict supervision of the Mamacunas. Also unlike the harem or seraglio of eastern princes, where the hetaerae led a lazy, leisurely life, the Acllahuasi of the Incas overflowed with variegated, incessant activities. From the moment they entered the "house," the young "chosen women" learned not only good manners and the ritual of the cult (including the maintenance and decoration of altars, prayers, offerings, and sacrifices), but all the handicrafts assigned to their future rank. The Mamacunas taught them to spin wool, to weave and embroider the geometric or totemic designs, and to sew more artistically than anyone else in the world. One year was scarcely enough time for one of them to make and finish a vicuña wool garment for the Inca or Coya, magnificently adorned with gold plaques and jewelry—clothing so elegant that "Verily," Cieza de León acknowledged, "the clothes sewn by the Acllas outshone those of the Spaniards."

Only the Acllas could make the *paicha* (the short fringe of red and yellow wool mounted on a thin braid, which the lords of the blood royal wore on their heads) and, in particular, the *llautu* of the Inca, made of red wool and

---

[2] Prostitutes and "ladies of the night," known as Pampacunas, did exist in Incan times. But, the object of general contempt, they were not allowed in the cities: they were exiled to the country.

as thick as a finger, which was wound around his head five or six times, like a turban; his forehead was draped, from temple to temple, with a fringe with gold tassels.

They also wove the *chuspas*, little pouches for coca carried—slung over the shoulder—by the Inca and a few captains whom he singled out for distinction.

They were also instructed in the art of decorating with feathers.

One of the major daily occupations of the Chosen Women involved the careful preparation of monumental jars of corn *chicha*, for the court, the college of young nobles, the sacerdotal group, and the warriors in the garrison or in the field—the recipe varied according to the use. The intoxicating *yamor toctoy asua*, the divine drink of the Inca, was fermented for a month before being served to him.

With their brown hands, the Acllas kneaded corn flour dampened with human blood (obtained from bleeding the brows of newborn babies) to make *zancu*, the "blessed" bread for the sacrifices to the Sun, rounded and the size of an apple, which they cooked and distributed during the great ceremonies of the Raymi and of the Citua, the feast of purification.

Other recluses roasted ears of corn and tender meats destined for the table of the sovereigns, as well as for the mummies, whom the smoke from these foods nourished symbolically.

Some women cultivated the fields, tended the orchards, looked after the sacred llamas of the Sun, and raised hummingbirds or baby pumas.

Some, finally, became *taqui-acllas*, musicians who performed at the celebrations of the imperial court of Cuzco; they played the tambourine or flute, or sang hymns to the glory of the incandescent Sun and of the Inca.

The calm of the Acllahuasi seems to have been frequently disrupted by amorous intrigues, and numerous were the concubines of the Inca who paid for his passion and their haughty beauty with their lives. This happened to Chumbillaya, the most bewitching of Huascar's favorites (she was also poisoned), and to many others, whose names have been handed down by tradition.

Disobedience remained the exception in the ingenious

mechanism of the Incan regime. It was a question, not of a slavery[3] (in the general sense of the term) in the service of the state, but of a voluntary tribute, a sort of "tax" which the parents of the young recruits who were chosen consented to most eagerly. They considered themselves honored—in view of the religious aspect of the choice involving their daughters—to see them pass into a high caste in which, in addition to being maintained like princesses (housed, fed, and magnificently dressed), they would enjoy—for life—the greatest honors and the respect of the people. Some parents even went so far as to beg that one of their daughters be accepted, even though they knew that they would never see her again.

The social position of an Aclla was such that, if one of them left a convent to visit a sanctuary and, on the way, some offender was fleeing, justice could not pursue him, since the presence of a Chosen Woman was sufficient to protect him. Few were the dissidents among the great provincial *curacas* who would refuse the Inca the gift of a wealthy heiress, so desirous were they of gaining the monarch's favor. But, to cite only one, Tumpalla, the great lord of the island of Puna off the coast of Eucador, refused even to receive the emissaries of Huayna Capac, whom he suspected—judging from this Inca's reputation— of wishing to take away the most beautiful women and girls in his territory.

The yearly tribute of the adolescent girls pledged to the gods and to the Inca was exacted every November (or Aya Marcay), in all the provinces of Tahuantinsuyo visited by an imperial delegate: the *apupanaca* (judge), *tocricuc* (or provincial governor), or else—lacking these—the *huarmicac*, his principal official. Heralded by the town crier, the envoy from Cuzco was empowered to choose, according to his own taste (which was undoubtedly very eclectic), the shy candidates who were presented to him in the central plaza of the villages. Nonetheless, not everyone

---

[3] For E. Choy, "The status of the Aclla was that of a slave of the State; she ceased to be one only to become the slave and private property of some official or specialist, similar to a chattel."

who wished to be an Aclla got to be one, however great her wish. But, on the other hand, anyone attempting to force one of the young girls into service was severely punished, and the girl was immediately returned to her family.

In December the "chosen" girls left the provincial Acllahuasis and, at the Inca's expense, traveled to Cuzco, accompanied by old guards and warriors who were probably eunuchs. Having passed the initial test, they were then definitely accepted; they received a dowry (that is, all the necessities—an income, essentially) and were assigned a *china*, or lady's maid.

ACLLAS OF THE SUN AND ACLLAS OF THE INCA

There were strict requirements regarding the age, social position, and, above all, the virginity of the candidate before her admission into an Acllahuasi. No "natural" or illegitimate daughter could hope to enter (whether she would be destined for the Sun or for the Inca). It was necessary to guarantee the purity of the union, whether symbolic (with the deity) or consummated (with his representative, the sovereign). Each girl therefore underwent a sort of "prenuptial examination," conducted by the Mamacunas, before she finally pronounced the vow of chastity—temporary or perpetual.

The preliminary selection often was made well before puberty, starting as early as four years, or, more often, between eight and ten years—never later. The young girl chosen for her beauty or lineage could belong to any social class whatsoever, noble or plebeian, as long as—this condition was the *sine qua non*—she was not disfigured by any flaw or bodily imperfection. A relatively light skin counted for a great deal in the "ranking" of the Acllas.

The adolescent girl accepted in the Acllahuasi assumed the label of Huiñay Chichuy Aclla ("Chosen Child"); her growth and aptitude for feminine tasks, as well as her religious tendencies and deportment, were carefully observed.

The initial ceremony consisted in cutting the hair of the novice (now classified as a Humac Aclla), leaving only short locks braided across her forehead and temples.

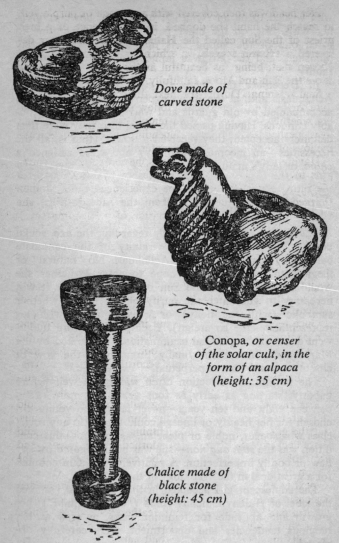

Dove made of
carved stone

Conopa, *or censer
of the solar cult, in the
form of an alpaca
(height: 35 cm)*

Chalice made of
black stone
(height: 45 cm)

*These three stone objects, unique in America, must have
been found at Machu Picchu by treasure-seekers*

Her head was then covered with a maroon or purple veil, to match the habit she donned, in the presence of a high priest of the Sun called the Hatun Willca. The latter delivered a solemn speech, in which he informed all those chosen that, being "as beautiful as the stars," they should serve the Sun and Moon faithfully. Then he left them with a final warning: During the next three years of the noviatiate, or *huanac*, they should "follow their hearts" in deciding whether to remain in the temple for the rest of their lives, perhaps renouncing—depending on a later choice— the joys of human love and of maternity.

Having delivered these warnings, he remanded the young girls to the care of the governesses of the Acllahuasi, in the ratio of ten novices to one experienced older women charged with inculcating in them the sacred tasks; she herself was subject to the supervision of a "headmistress," who in turn was under the direct orders of the "abbess" or "mother superior" of the House of the Virgins.

Certain Acllas became the vestals of Nina Willca, the sacred fire of the Coricancha, the great solar temple, which they watched over and kept going day and night, tossing into the flames, as sacrifices, the most colorful weavings or fledglings.

Once their long, elaborate, and instructive novitiate had been completed, the Huanac Acllas could dream of the splendid ceremony that would soon take place in Cuzco, after the harvest season, when, according to their inclination, they would choose—this time irrevocably—their unusual fate.

The Inca and the Coya, along with the gleaming gold idols of Illa Tiki Viracocha, the Sun, the Moon, Venus, and the god of thunder and lightning (set up on splendid altars decked with flowers and adorned with rare gold and silver objects), presided over the ceremony held in the atrium of the Temple of the Sun.

Next to the imperial couple (who were seated on golden thrones, dressed in multicolored garments, and sheltered under a dais of brightly colored feathers) stood the Willac Umu, and behind him were gathered all the ministers of the cult, magi and diviners, proud captains, the members of the Incan council (or Hunu) and its president (the Capac Hunu), plus the Inca's honor guard in dress uniform, all positioned in accordance with the hierarchy and their seniority.

Clustered a little farther away, the Indian crowd could admire at leisure the cohort that turned out for these "beauty queens," who were led before the impressive Areopagus; they appeared with the governesses, teachers, and "prelates" who had thus far been responsible for teaching them and carefully watching over them.

After having questioned them on how they liked the reclusive life they had just led for three consecutive years, the Willac Umu enjoined them one last time "to think it over before deciding." Henceforth, no one could change her mind and get married—whether publicly or secretly— without incurring death, both for her and her accomplice.

Thus, on that day, each Aclla had to choose and become either the wife or the servant of the Sun (Nusta or China del Sol) or else of Quilla, the Moon—that is, the Chosen Woman of the Inca (without, however, knowing for certain whether she would ever actually share the Inca's bed). Or else she could still give up becoming a "nun" and marry the man to whom the Inca assigned her—a young man over twenty-three years old, of a social standing which corresponded to her own.

As long as she acceded willingly to the imperial laws, no nubile girl could be recruited by the Acllahuasi by force. That is to say, having reached the age of eighteen, she could not refuse to take a husband, or else the law dictated that, as a result, she would be placed in a "reserve" of Chosen Women, in the service of the stars or as an actual servant of the Acllas, depending on her rank.

It seems highly doubtful that the virgins who refused to marry were, "according to tradition, dishonored by a high priest of the Sun." Nevertheless, it may be that in the early days of the institution, the sacred hetaerae were "initiated" by the magi.

In any event, few of them dared protest the implacable laws of the empire. The historian J. V. Larrabure reports that the most beautiful Nusta among all those belonging to Huayna Capac, Huiñay Cusi ("Always Cheerful"), violated this law by refusing to marry, so profound was her love for the young and already powerful Inca. Huayna Capac was not unaware of her affection; however, every time he was about to embrace her, an ill-fated event occurred:

either he was suddenly called away to subdue a rebellion breaking out in a far country, or, at the moment he was about to possess her, a violent earthquake would tear her from his arms. Finally, a solar eclipse was interpreted as so bad an omen by the oracles that, resigned, Huiñay Cusi begged the Inca to allow her to withdraw into the Acllahuasi. But she had just turned twenty, two years past the age limit where she could have chosen to dedicate herself to the Sun.

Huayna Capac wanted neither to punish her nor to send her away, and this angered the queen, Rahua Occlo, not solely because this degree of clemency violated the law. Fearing that her husband preferred the rebel to her, she had the famous sorcerer Supay-Sua poison Huiñay Cusi.

Once the speeches had been delivered, the prayers to the Sun recited, and the sacrifices conducted, each Aclla donned a white habit woven from the wool of rare vicuñas and embroidered with red thread. On her head she wore a white veil held in place by the *cori huicha*, a golden garland. Then, after each virgin grazed the hand of the Inca, then the Coya, with her lips, they marched out in groups of fifty, escorted by guards, and served a colossal banquet on immaculate cotton tablecloths prettily decorated with flowers. At the end of the feast each girl distributed among the guests a treasured "host" of Illai Tanta bread. Finally, they offered the finery and ornaments that they had made during their long novitiate: sandals adorned with gold and silver, embroidered headdresses and belts, carved *tupus* to pin lovely striped mantles. In exchange, they received valuable presents: livestock, lands, wool, precious objects.

Changing from novices into confirmed Acllas, they would henceforth live in a "convent," leading the life of a "Carmelite"—to use the terms used by André Lefèbre to emphasize their obvious similarity to Christian nuns.

Replacing the graduated novices were the Sayapallas, from twelve to fifteen years of age.

BRIDES OF INTI AND ROYAL CONCUBINES

In the lustful eyes of the conquistadors, every Chosen Woman was a Virgin of the Sun. But it appears that the Chosen Women should be divided into several categories.

I attempted to find the characteristics and names of these categories amid the gibberish of the chronicles from the period, which are so confused—indeed, contradictory—that the classification of the residents of the Acllahuasis remains unreliable.

First of all, it appears that we must establish a very clear distinction between Intip Acllas, consecrated solely to the Sun, and Incap Acllas, dedicated to the Inca.

Once the rites had been completed, the *apupanaca* and the *tocricuc* first chose the four or five most outstanding candidates and offered them to the Sun. Then they chose three or four who were only slightly less beautiful, yet still very attractive and desirable, for the Inca. All the candidates for this supreme selection were taken from the highest social ranks. Women of baser extraction, even if they were very beautiful, were excluded, in the belief that "the Sun god slept with the women consecrated to him," according to Santillan.

Cloistered forever, the Intip Acllas would never again see the outside world, not even their relatives. No man could lay eyes on them, let alone approach them or speak to them, without dying forthwith.

It seems that the Intip Huarmin and the Punchao Huarmin, the "women" or spouses of the Inti, should be distinguished from the Intip Chinan and the Punchao Chinan, his servants, who, though extremely beautiful, were uniformly condemned to perpetual virginity.

Pity the unchaste woman who did not keep her vows of reclusion, abstinence, and chastity! No doubt very few succumbed to the temptations of the flesh; they were too well guarded to commit such a sacrilege. However, several legends deal with Acllas seduced by love or magic, by a prince as well as by a guard or a simple shepherd of the Sun. This is what makes us wonder about the strictness of the guard kept by the *huasicamayocs* and *puncucamayocs*, servants and gatekeepers who watched over the Acllahuasis—and about their status as eunuchs, even if we find it equally difficult to believe that the Incas, so careful when it came to the sexual integrity and purity of the Chosen Women, would have assigned them virile men for attendants.

The fact remains that, during the reign of the Inca Viracocha, four virgins of Inti fornicated with the porters of the Acllahuasi of Cuzco. Submitting to the implacable Incan law, they were buried alive, and their lovers were hanged—an insufficient punishment had not the relatives, servants, and neighbors of the guilty parties also been wiped out, by being stoned and left to the wild beasts and predators. The holocaust included babies and old people, as well as all the inhabitants and livestock of their respective birthplaces. The houses were destroyed, the trees torn up, and the entire villages were covered with stones or salt so that no one could ever again tread the ground of these cursed sites.

Another legend relates the love at first sight between Sinchi Paco, one of the Inca's favorites, and the virgin Ticana. Assigned to lay out the aqueduct of the Acllahuasi, but dazzled by the statuesque beauty of the Aclla whom he managed to glimpse, Sinchi Paco diverted the canal and made it lead under the monolithic wall of the forbidden district. Making a hole, he led out the beautiful Aclla, and together they fled toward the high plateaus of Lake Titicaca. They got as far as Chuquiabo, where they disguised themselves in Aymara clothing. But the Indians of the Sacred Lake, thinking they were spies, clubbed the wrongdoers to death.

Better known is the legend that relates the irresistible passion of a shepherd of the Sun, Akoyturpo, who enchanted the royal virgin Chuquillantu with his magic flute. The adventure takes place amid the majestic setting of two glaciers in the Yucay Cordillera, Sawasiray and Pitusiray, which still symbolize for the Quechuas the lovers, petrified as the Sun's revenge. Their crags must have contained the ruins of the principal house of the Mamacunas dedicated to raising white llamas, reserved for propitiatory sacrifices to the star of the day.

A "mitigating circumstance" granted a brief reprieve to any pregnant virgin who swore she had been "impregnated by the rays of the Sun." She was allowed to stay alive until she gave birth; then she was buried alive. As for the offspring of the divine union, if a girl, she was made an Aclla of the Sun; if a boy, he was pledged to the priesthood.

Even though Garcilaso de la Vega, speaking of the Inca kings, remarks philosophically that they were "given no opportunity, and they lacked passion with regard to women, since they could easily have the most beautiful women if they desired them" (which, in his view, explains the absence of sexual transgressions), one of them was certainly an exception to the rule. The young Urco, Viracocha's son, was known as "a man of great vice, given to lust, dishonesty, and public drunkenness," and he was accused of having "corrupted Mamacunas in the Temple of the Sun."

THE RITUAL SACRIFICE OF ACLLAS

Did the Incas ritually sacrifice Acllas? Some chroniclers affirm that they did, others deny it, and Americanists are doubtful. However, it is hard to imagine that they did not, since Max Uhle, carrying out extensive excavations at Pachacamac at the beginning of the century, showed that human sacrifices were indeed conducted there, and en masse.

Between the pyramid of the Sun and the Acllahuasi (now reconstructed—but in reinforced concrete!), which were built by the Incas near the ancient monuments dedicated to the deities of the Pacific coast by ancient peoples, the German archaeologist exhumed *a hundred female mummies* whose ceremonial garb and funerary ceramics proved that they belonged to the Incan high society of Cuzco. Now, their faces powdered with red cinnabar for a "deluxe" holocaust, these Chosen Women—tightly bound by cords which bit into their flesh—had their throats slit or were strangled before being buried in the necropolis whose desert sands (it never rains there) preserved them miraculously for hundreds of years.

Moreover, working with Peruvian archaeologists on digs around and even in Lima, I had a chance to see numerous mummies frozen for eternity in a typical gesture of terror, their hands cupped over their faces and their mouths wide open as if still screaming. The museums contain edifying examples.

However, these horrifying sacrifices were certainly less frequent—especially in the days before the Spanish Conquest—than was true in ancient Mexico, where they constituted veritable human hecatombs. All the same, they did take place in pre-Columbian Peru, as a bloody offering to the Sun, no doubt as the result of exceptional circumstances, or during the great feasts of the solstice, or to mark the accession of a new Inca, if the sovereign became seriously ill or grew weak. Like many vanished peoples, the Incas harbored the belief that human blood fortified the Sun and thereby its earthly delegate—hence the immolation of pure, innocent creatures, accompanied by expiatory rites.

It is known that the Incas valued—above all other gifts or virtues—youth, beauty, chastity, and perpetual virginity.

Sacrifices of the Virgins of Inti were also perpetrated whenever the empire was in grave danger, and during the construction of imposing sanctuaries dedicated to Father Sun or to the tutelary deities that protected the empire; these sacrifices were accompanied by ceremonies conducted with great pomp by the sacerdotal clan.

Polo de Ondegardo suggested that the Acllas who refused to remain in the temple were earmarked for these pagan sacrifices and given priority—an assertion repudiated by the Peruvian historians. In any event, it appears that the sacrifice of a Virgin took on the significance of a supreme tribute to the gods she was setting out to join and serve forever.

PURE VIRGINS OF THE IDOLS AND HUACAS

Among the pure virgins who died in a state of sanctity in the course of their religious ministry, we should include the Yurac Acllas, virgins of the idols, who had extremely light skin and wore immaculate garments. One of them— almost always a sister of the reigning Inca ruled the house of the Chosen Women. She played the special role of the "bride of the Sun" in the ceremonial festivals and perhaps ran the terrible risk of being sacrificed.

Her companions prepared the Inti's repasts and offered them to him according to a dithyrambic ritual.

The first-class Huayruro Acllas Sumac, over twenty years old, were given to the principal *huacas*.

The Sumac Acllas, very beautiful Chosen Women, acted as "wives of the *huacas*" and served them.

The Sumac Acllas Catiquin, over thirty-five years old, remained in the service of the secondary idols and *huacas*, spinning and weaving wool to offer as sacrifices to these deities and to clothe them.

The Chaupi Catiquin Sumac Acllas, over forty years old, of average beauty, sewed and raised crops for tertiary idols and huacas.

The Pampas Acllas Cuna, over fifty years old, saw to the maintenance of the houses of the Moon, the stars, the Willacs, and common gods. They were divided into the Acllap Huasin, who worked indoors, and the Acllap Chacran, who worked in the fields and in the *tambos* on feast days.

The Intip Mayau bore the title of "noblewomen chosen by the Sun."

INDIAN POMPADOURS AND DU BARRYS

The Huayra Acllas with pretty bronzed skin and bright pink cheeks, so pleasing to look at, chosen from among the daughters of lords and royal princesses, were between twenty and twenty-five years old; they were consecrated simultaneously to the Sun, the Moon, the stars, the idols, the *huacas*, and the Inca. They could easily be recognized by the long *huincha* which they wound like a turban around their shiny black hair, and by the multicolored *lliclla* covering their shoulders, fastened at the throat with a gold and silver *quisqui* and adorned with two large *tupus* made of the same precious solar and lunar metals. As a special honor, they were entrusted with serving the Inca's meals, cultivating his gardens and fields, and leading his troops of llamas to pasture.

The Incap Acllas, potential concubines of the Inca, could belong to any social class, as long as they were shapely, gracious, and pretty, like the Shipa Coyas, who were not of royal blood. Each dreamed of one day actually being chosen by the Inca, the only man who could caress them, but outside the Acllahuasi. All of them spun and wove like Indian Penelopes, waiting to be summoned. If numerous Acllas must have been disappointed in their desires, many were indeed called to the imperial bed. The chroniclers cited the sizable figure of 700 concubines for one Inca at the apogee of the Tahuantinsuyo, some of whom gave him several "direct descendants."

Once noticed, the fortunate women chosen never returned to the Acllahuasi. This way, they could not tell their former companions about their amorous initiation with the Son of the Sun, nor about the "intimacies" of conjugal life. Their quasi-conventual reclusion ceased as soon as they were in the Inca's arms, and henceforth they passed into the no less envied rank of "ladies of the court and of the queen," leading a life of luxury in the royal palace, showered with honors and respect. Some even acted as Indian Pompadours and Du Barrys, taking a hand in politics and exerting sufficient influence on the monarch to alarm his entourage and create at atmosphere of intrigue, in which rivalries led to dark dramas. Several Incas died in this manner. On the other hand, certain exceptional favorites received the title Mamanchic, customarily reserved for the Coya, as a reward for their wisdom and good advice.

The Inca was so attached to his Chosen Women that he took his favorites with him everywhere he went—even to war, to the great peril of the soldiers, who, if they caught a glimpse of them, would be immediately executed. If one of the soldiers succeeded in sinning against the divine person of the Son of the Sun by seducing one of his female companions, an equally cruel fate inexorably awaited him. Debauching an Aclla constituted so great a crime that the offender was burned alive, and his entire family would meet with a cruel death.

Fidelity, on the other hand, was greatly rewarded, and the mistresses who could prove that they had been faithful received the title of Yamor Toctoy.

Every mature Chosen Woman assumed the name of Mama Aclla and passed into the active body of the Mamacunas, the matrons who gave orders to the young Incan "nuns" and instructed them in the cult of the idols or directed the work centers "like a loving but strict mother."

If the Inca died before they did, the Mamacunas who had enjoyed his special favors inherited lands and other goods. As concubines of the deceased Inca, they joined the ranks of "the court of the mummies," enjoying a bit more freedom while becoming the "mothers" of the successor and the "mothers-in-law" of his concubines.

A good many other names mentioned in the chronicles can be added to the list of the types of Chosen Women, the unique invention of the Incas. In the servant clan are classified

- Pacha Mamacunas, assigned to the Inca
- Laichailla Collanas, servants of the Acllas
- Acllas Pampa Sircuc, ordinary virgins who worked outside of the Acllahuasi, particulary in the countless waystations, or *tambos*, which lined the Nan Cuna and all the Inca roads
- Llama Acllas and Acllas Chacra, who tended the flocks of llamas and the storehouses, or "supply depots," adjoining the fields

The class of workers, divided into young and old weavers, included the Acllas Cuna Huiñay and the Purun Huarmi.

All of these second-class Acllas could leave the Acllahausi, but only in pairs and accompanied by their servants and old Chosen Women, and flanked by two warriors armed with spears, bows, and arrows. They traveled thus not to take a stroll or to visit people, but to get from temple to sanctuary, in order to see to their upkeep and decoration.

Except for the Acllas pledged to the Sun, any Chosen Woman remaining a virgin could be given by the Inca, as a present, to his vassals or to anyone who had served the empire, whether civilian or a military leader, noble or commoner. Countless were the Acllas from his own family —his daughters by sacred hetaerae—who were offered thus to avoid a war or to consolidate an alliance. In these cases, the young Chosen Woman could neither improve her lot nor refuse the union with the stranger without thereby choosing death, for having opposed the will of her master. But the situation was not such that his best general or strongest ally could request one of his concubines or daughters as a companion—as we saw in the case of the great captain Ollanta.

The Huasi Sipa, or "those whom the Inca had cast aside," became the mistress-servants of the regional *curacas*. The other Acllas and Mamacunas finished out their lives in the Acllahuasi, where often they provided their services to the age of one hundred or more.

Certain "jubilant" Acllas lived out their days in the provinces of their birth, enjoying general respect and living in opulent houses which the Inca ordered to be built for them. When they died, all the inhabitants of these lands came to the funeral. Borne by prominent citizens, they were buried with great pomp, on a sacred peak. The royal insignia were attached to the sepulcher, and they were surrounded by attendants and servants "made of wood."

Also found in the Acllahuasi were the daughters of high-placed officials and well-known personages; less than eighteen years old, they were authorized to board there for a while to complete their education. They would then return to their families, unless they decided to dedicate themselves to the Sun—or to the Inca. Old *quipucamayocs* said that widowed queens and virgin princesses were also allowed to live in the Incan convents, like the Acllas. They thus gave up any chance of leaving to marry. Finally, the royal princesses, known as Ocllo, sometimes took vows of chastity without, however, living in the cloisters; rather, they lived at home and were highly respected. If they broke their vows, the Inca ordered that they be thrown into a mysterious "Lake of Pumas" or burned alive.

THE HOLOCAUST OF
THE WIDOWS OF ATAHUALPA

According to a cruel law, upon the death of the reigning Inca, nothing could honor his memory better than the voluntary sacrifice of his favorites. Thus, when Atahualpa was assassinated, 5,000 Acllas wished to follow him into the beyond!

Miguel de Estete, recounting the imperial funeral rites for the Inca, wrote: "The strangest sight the world has ever seen took place here, and I saw it with my own eyes . . . The mass for the deceased was being sung in the church, over Atahualpa's body, when in came his sisters and wives, howling; they made so much noise that the funeral service was disrupted. They were shouting that we should wait and conduct an even greater mass, because it was the custom, when the Inca died, that all those who loved him be buried alive with him, in his tomb." And Cieza de León adds: "So profound was their grief that their lamentations seemed to rend the air."

One can imagine the Spaniards' amazement, confronted with such zeal to claim, as an honor, a slow agony and so horrifying a holocaust! Pizarro must have firmly opposed this mass sacrifice, but numerous anyway were the Acllas, lovers and servants, who strangled or hanged themselves with their long hair, saying that they were leaving to serve the Inca in the other life.

A conquistador who happened to be near Atahualpa on the road to the site of his execution saw him send away 300 of his favorites, including twenty of his sisters, saying haughtily, "Go!" and pointing to the Andes. "The 300 Acllas," he says, "hurled themselves from the peaks!"

How many escaped this holocaust, the last in the fabulous Empire of the Incas? We do not know, but we do know that on November 15, 1533, at the hour for high mass, there appeared on the heights of Carmenca, above Cuzco, the first three Spaniards to break down the *portada* of the Acllahuasi, seize the Acllas, and rape them. Sancho de la Hoz, Pizarro, and Estete did not learn until later that they had had their way only with house servants because the majority of the true priestesses of the Sun had been led away earlier by the Willac Umu.

And it was on the way to the celestial sanctuaries of the Sacred Valley that all trace of them was, until now, lost.

AND MACHU PICCHU CAME INTO THE LEGEND

It must have been on the advice of Mama Quilla, the guardian of the sacred fire of the Acllahuasi, that the Virgins of Inti and of the Punchao sought refuge in the city of the gods, "where they languished unto death." According to the legend, as recorded by Alfonsina Barrionuevo, Hernando de Soto penetrated the dwelling place of the "Chosen Women" on horseback and carried off Mama Quilla. But the Indians recaptured her and sacrificed her to the Sun, in order to obtain the star's pardon. From the sacrificial altar, the virgin addressed her companions, saying: "I die happy that my eyes cannot see the downfall of the Empire of the Sons of the Sun. The wings of death will soon envelop the divine sky of Cuzco, and its streets will run with the blood of its sons . . . Flee far from here, beyond the white mountains, so that you do not fall into the savage hands of these foreigners who respect nothing . . ."

Another tradition holds that the Virgins of the Sun disappeared without a trace because, as a group, they hurled themselves into the abyss, in multiple suicides which lit up the Moon and the stars.

Legends concerning the "Lost City" of the Incas are scarce. I did find a mythological version of its creation, however: In the beginning of time, each peak served as the divine throne of an Apu. Apu Picchu, the tutelary deity of the grand Urubamba Cañon, had two sons, named Machu and Huayna Picchu, who were rivals in love. The object of their contention, the princess Mumay Quilla, was none other than the daughter of Apu Ollanta, who was enthroned on the neighboring cordillera.

In order to decide between the younger and older suitor (one a master mason, the other an Amauta scholar), Apu Picchu advised them to vie with each other in art and learning, by each building a marvelous sanctuary. Thus there arose, above the abysses, the two twin cities. Who won the original contest? Huayna Picchu, says the legend, because, although Machu Picchu created a peerless masterpiece, his younger brother, with unparalleled daring, succeeded in enthroning his beloved on the highest point of the mountain, on the level of the gods.

In another legend, torrential rains inundated the pre-Columbian night of time and the Urubamba Cañon. The waters of the Sacred Rio rose so high, one old Indian recalled the Flood of which the ancients had spoken: the few survivors were spared only because they climbed the highest peak. Scanning it, he perceived, misted over in clouds, Machu Picchu. He led his *ayllu* there, and, on his advice, the men set out to build, on the Old Peak, a megalithic city which no cataclysm could destroy. But they were unable to complete it.

Many centuries passed, until the reign of Huayna Capac, when a spreading rumor again sowed panic throughout the Empire of the Incas: bearded white men wielding lightning, who were one with unknown four-legged monsters, which they fed gold and precious gems, were approaching the northern border. They could already be seen; they were just as the oracle of Pitumarca had described them. Also during this time, one day the Inca was celebrating the splendid solar festivals of the Inti

Raymi in the plaza at Cuzco and a *huaman* (divine falcon) fell at his feet: yet another grim omen. Fearing for the Acllas' lives, and recalling the refuge-city that his distant ancestors had started to build, he sent his best Amautas out to restore the ruins of Machu Picchu. All that was most beautiful and precious in the empire was confided to the high priests of the cult and to the Acllas, who abandoned Cuzco, taking along with them the invaluable treasures of the Coricancha.

Cut off forever from the world of the living and celebrating at each dawn the appearance of the first rays of the Sun, the exiled nobles died out, one by one, in the conspiratorial silence of the Andes. But the Quechuas say that, to perpetuate their memory, the spirits of the Virgins of the Sun still roam the phantasmal white city, in the form of iridescent hummingbirds, pale orchids, golden serpents, and trailing clouds.

One final belief of the Indians of the Sacred Valley takes us back to the moment when, with Huascar and Atahualpa dead and the Incan legions scattered, the conquistadors are storming the gates of Cuzco. Gods more powerful than the Sun seem to render them invulnerable, and the Willac Umu is in despair: How to preserve the purity of the virgins of the Inti? Hastily he has arranged for a long caravan of llamas, laden with the sarcophagi of dead emperors, to head for the impregnable snow-covered peaks of the Ausangate, and he has had the great golden images of the Sun copied, to replace the real idols, which are buried deep beneath the mountains. But what about the Acllas?

Death would be the best refuge for them! However, it is forbidden to spill the blood of a virgin not guilty of one of the offenses covered by the ancestral laws. To immure them alive in the secret *chinkanas* of the Ucu Pacha, the underworld, would be to extinguish the Sun, for their eyes represent its light.

The Willac Umu consults the old *quipus*. One of these knotted cords, kept at Poquen Cancha, reveals that an untouchable city, which the Sun ordered the Apus to build so that those of his divine race might take refuge there in times of danger, remains hidden beneath the flowering jungle, guarded by abysses, adjoining the sky.

The secret must be kept forever; so the high priest burns

the miraculous *quipu*, then leads the Acllas to the gleaming retreat of the Old Peak. All the roads are blocked off, the bridges are sundered, and the golden vipers raised in the Amaru Cancha are released around the outer walls.

Thus, along with the Virgins of the Sun, Machu Picchu vanishes in the night of time.

150 MUMMIES DISCOVERED

When the Spaniards questioned the Indians concerning the mysterious disappearance of the highly coveted Acllas, those in Cuzco answered that "Father Sun took his Chosen Women to an inaccessible place so that they would not be attacked by the white foreigners."

Took them, that is, to Machu Picchu? *Therein lies the entire question*, ever since the discoveries made by Hiram Bingham and Dr. Eaton in the funeral caves and beautiful mausoleums of the "Lost City."

Their findings suggest that Machu Picchu was probably, toward the end, simultaneously a female cenoby and phalanstery for a special group of very beautiful Virgins of the Sun and Mamacunas, who found refuge there, along with a few high priests of an elevated sacerdotal rank, during the death throes of the Tahuantinsuyo. It is in this undiscoverable shelter that they all perpetuated, up until their deaths, the ancient solar religion and the idolatries with which the worshippers of Christ reproached them.

The proof? Of the 173 mummies discovered at Machu Picchu by the Yale Peruvian Expedition, 150 belonged, according to the osteologist Eaton, to young women—an astonishing percentage. The others (some of which could not be identified for certain) revealed "effeminate" individuals, a far cry from husky warriors or herculean builders—more like priests diminished by an austere life of privations. This hypothesis is further bolstered by the fact that none of the twenty-three skulls that may be masculine bear any trace of trepanation, unlike the human remains found on the outskirts of the "Lost City."

But is such a small number of skeletons not surprising, when it is generally estimated that 1,000 people, on the average, lived in Machu Picchu? Victor Angles Vargas provides us with a sagacious reply: "The quantity of human remains discovered," he believes, "cannot be a valid index for calculating the demographic density or the number of inhabitants in the city—no more than the small proportion of hammer stones could correspond to the thousands of tools used to build it. The interpretations drawn are thus highly debatable."

Moreover, the initial excavations carried out by Bingham were deceptive. At first he found only potsherds decorated "in the Inca style," which lay at the foot of the famous wall with three windows of the Temple of the Sacred Plaza—as if they had been thrown through these unusual openings, he believed, as a form of "house cleaning."

Then Recharte and Alvarez showed him the funeral caves on the western side, which contained the mummies: "Here were the bones of a woman about thirty-five years old, a representative of the middle coast region of Peru, and possibly one of those attractive types who were commanded by Inca Titu Cusi to attempt the seducing of the Augustinian fathers," Bingham declares. "She had been buried in the usual contracted position, the knees drawn up under the chin. With her were buried the remains of her cooking pots and food vessels."

Another cave provided "an excellent specimen of a two-handled dish, nicely decorated . . . a perfect piece of Inca pottery." Unfortunately, most of the sepulchral caves had been looted or disrupted by bears and wildcats. And these natural cavities, propitious for the preservation of the mummies, did not prevent the fabrics and clothing of the funeral *fardos* from being destroyed by humidity.

A few rare objects—llama bones carved into a point, others made of bronze—lay near the bodies.

Some fifty mummies watched over by four men, discovered on the edge of the precipice northeast of the "Lost City," were those of the famous Chosen Women, as were fifty others found in a second necropolis located below the Hurin district, near six guards.

Near a large ledge carved with snakes at the top of the central stairway, a cave contained—along with a piece of red paint and an inexplicable quantity of pebbles from the Urubamba riverbed—the most remarkable archaeological artifact found at Machu Picchu: an artistic bronze knife decorated with a fisherboy stretched out along the slightly curving blade. So far, this specimen is unique in all of ancient America.

Three hundred and fifty pottery specimens were found: *chicha* jugs (on one of which a "grotesque fat man" is modeled in relief); cooking pots blackened by hearth smoke; liturgical objects; and a curious *janccana* with an ovoid body pierced with holes, on a tripod, with a large mouth—perhaps a *brasero* or a corn roaster, or else a censer.

A hundred bronze *champis,* or crowbars, must have been used by the builders of the "Lost City," as were axes, chisels for wood and stone, clubs . . . They also found shawl-pins, disks, and small bells, as well as links made of the same alloy. Among the objects made of wood they found shuttles, hollowed-out plates, and carved and decorated crochet needles.

A profusion of llama bones, no doubt offered to assuage the mummies' hunger, and veritable collections of the bones of small deer were found in the tombs, along with awls and an agouti bone knife. a drinking cup, and guinea pig bones.

Among the mysteries figures the discovery, 200 paces in front of the entrance to the "Lost City," of two mummies of young men, one of whom wore a necklace of bone beads—and fused glass, which was probably of European origin! Were they spies sent by the conquistadors to track down and seduce the Virgins of the Sun? Why were they surrounded solely by *feminine ornaments* and with no tools or objects used by men?

One day Bingham discovered "the burial place of the High Priestess or Mamacuna, the Lady Superior of the convent, the person chiefly responsible for the training of the Chosen Women," on a rock-sheltered terrace 1,000 feet above the highest part of the ruins and agricultural terraces. With its magnificient view of the Sacred City, the marvelous *cañon,* and the snow-covered peaks, it was an ideal resting place for the Mamacuna.

Her personal belongings lay beside her: two large bronze shawl-pins and tweezers, a dainty and minute bronze curette decorated with a flying bird, and two needles made from plant spines, along with her guardian, a collie-type dog. The tomb also contained two beautiful aryballus jugs with human faces modeled and painted on the necks—a most unusual pattern—and a fine cooking pot decorated with a snake.

Chullanchaqui manca: *covered pot, perhaps liturgical*

Pucus: *dish and plate found at Machu Picchu*

Ovoid, tripod **janccana:** *censer or corn roaster*

The most interesting artifact among the Mamacuna's funerary accouterments was a concave bronze mirror with which the mother superior must have concentrated the sun's rays on a tuft of cotton wool to light the sacred fire. But, with all due deference to his Peruvian critics, Bingham says that "not a single article of gold was found."

Elsewhere he discovered terra-cotta ear plugs, disks perforated with small holes in which were inserted the feathers of birds from the Amazonian forest; these were worn by the Orejones of Cuzco.

The objects made of carved stone that were found included oval beads strung on a necklace, seven polishing stones, a curious checkerboard, meticulously polished round receptacles, corn mortars, obsidian knives, and weapons made of diorite and hematite.

The silver objects included large-headed *tupus* for pinning shawls, earpicks, needles, and crochet hooks.

Finally, small scraps of llama wool were found.

THE MYSTERY OF THE STONE DISKS

In 1911 Erdis, the archaeologist from Yale, revealed to the world a quantity of small stone disks discovered on the ridge of Machu Picchu. Some have the same dimensions as poker chips; others suggest coins of proportional value. All together, there are 156 pieces of dark-green (almost black) micaceous schist. Some of these "tokens" are perforated or notched; only one was incised with a cross in the center. Some were ground so thin as to be translucent. Their diameters range from 1 to 23 centimeters; there are more small disks than large ones, which according to Bingham, may show "the necessity of providing digits." Yet nothing seems to determine a fixed value; all are of the same color.

The larger ones, Bingham suggests, may have been used as "covers for chicha jars," although he doubts that they were.

Sixteen smaller disks, exceedingly well made, filled a hole near the Snake Rock, along with a pendant and a few discoidal beads. All of these carefully ground and polished pieces show "suspicious scratches," yet there is no way to ascertain whether these were "tally marks." They could easily have been erased by a slight amount of polishing.

Also in the upper Hanan district, Bingham collected "forty-two oblong stone counters" and "nineteen triangular 'chips,'" as well as "irregular chips," incised or pierced, which may have been used as amulets. Four green stones represent the silhouettes of jungle animals: a peccary, an anteater, an otter, and a parrot. Two others were miniature Australian boomerangs. Some are shaped like a pipe, the head and shoulders of an animal, or else a "spool" on which thread could be wound. Several resemble bronze knives or axes; "these might well have been used as offerings to the god of metallurgy, in the hope that the bronze castings would be successful."

Near the ceremonial gate of the "Lost City," twenty-nine obsidian "marbles"—originally from a meteoric shower—may have been used to keep a tally on the quantities of llama or alpaca wool delivered to the Chosen Women.

In addition to these collections, which are *unique* in pre-Columbian America, equally rare chips and "counters" of baked clay were unearthed, as well as a few pentagonal clay disks made of rounded potsherds, polished and marked with straight lines and crosses on five sides, "so as to be used as counters up to five"; they were "clearly intended to represent a numerical tally."

Bingham assumes that most of these stone objects found near the older sepulchers "belonged to an earlier culture than that of the Incas"—an opinion shared by the Peruvian archaeologist Gonzalez de la Rosa, according to whom "the predecessors of the Incas kept their accounts by means of record stones."

However, the mystery thickens, because there is no archaeological reference that deals with similar specimens of "counting stones" in such great numbers, which seem to comprise series, and they are totally absent from the museums.[4]

Should one look for them outside of Machu Picchu? Bingham discovered similar stones in Ecuador, on the Island of La Palta, and in various archaeological beds on the western coast, not far from the southern frontier of Colombia, unearthed by Professor Saville and Dr. Dorsey.

---

[4] Father Acosta mentioned the use of disks of engraved clay. In 1956 Luis E. Pardo found slate disks 50 centimeters in diameter.

The author of a book on Ecuadorian history, Oscar Efren Reyes, informs us that "the Caranqui and Qillacinga tribes used, as monetary units, small clay balls called *carates*."

In a lost chronicle written by Father Marcos de Niza, as cited by Velasco, one may read that before being conquered and incorporated into the Incan Empire, the Caras, the old chieftains of Ecuador, kept their records by means of "little stones of distinct sizes, colors, and angular form." They thus kept a record of their kings and "with different combinations of these they perpetuated their doings and formed their count of all." This system proved to be rather flawed, since one of the collections of stones, referring to the eighteen Cara rules of Quito, was interpreted by some as a period of seven hundred years, while others reduced it to five centuries.

Velasco notes that a small stone of the same type was set in the niche above each of the mummies of the pre-Inca rulers of Quito, "which denoted his age, the years and the months of his reign."

Bingham concludes from this information that the discovery of stone chips, disks, and tokens at Machu Picchu may indicate that, at one point, the "Lost City" was inhabited by people who had not yet learned to use *quipus*.

These "record stones," Bingham feels, "were made here [from the] green micaceous schist . . . which exists at the foot of one of the precipices on Machu Picchu Mountain," unless they were brought from Ecuador—a deduction which would not surprise us at all today, since we know, from the later researches of Christian Bues in the Sacred Valley, that in fact the Ecuadorian Cañaris long occupied the slopes of the Salccantay, the mountain of Machu Picchu.

Hiram Bingham imagines that the niches of the Principal Temple may have been "intended to receive collections of record stones," which were removed by order of the Willac Umu, when the time came for the use of record stones to be abandoned in favor of *quipus*, and buried near the Sacred Plaza.

That is, unless the "Lost City" was a "city of accountants" who used a system of mnemonic annotations different from that of the Incas at the time of the Spanish Conquest. In that case, did one of the districts house the members of this group? These are questions without an-

swers, even though Luis E. Valcarcel is certain that the
stone disks and chips could not have been "monetary
symbols."

THE MYSTERIOUS "HOUSE OF
THE SUN" OF PITCOS

One last question remains with regard to the cult and the
Virgins of the Sun: It concerns Tupac Amaru, the last Inca
of Vilcabamba. Did he really live at Machu Picchu? Are
we overlooking a "revelation" that could solve one of the
most incomprehensible mysteries of the "Lost City"? Are
we making the mistake of not knowing how to interpret the
account of Baltazar de Ocampo?

After having listed all the places in the Sacred Valley and
in the region of Vilcabamba that we know were frequented
by the rebel Incas, Ocampo discusses the fate of Tupac
Amaru, who was held captive by his half-brother Titu Cusi,
"a cunning man, like all tyrants." Where, then, did he take
the young legitimate heir to the Tahuantinsuyo? "To the
House of the Sun, with the Acllas under the Mamacunas,
who were matrons to keep guard over them, for they were
very beautiful." To place him there followed "a most
ancient custom among all the rulers of these kingdoms
before the arrival of the Spaniards."

Then, describing the splendid imperial funeral, (or
purucaya) later held for the usurper, with the same pomp
as in the past, Ocampo relates that "dressed in all the
insignia of sovereignty, bedecked with his jewels, the embalmed Inca was carried by his warriors, great lords, and
captains in deep mourning, with muffled drums, and sounds
of grief; they proceeded to the House of the Sun where
was the Inca Tupac Amaru, in the fortress of Pitcos."

He specifies only that the fortress "was on a very high
mountain whence the view commanded a great part of the
province of Vilcapampa, where there is an extensive level
space with very sumptuous and majestic buildings erected
with great skill and art, all the lintels of the doors, the
principal as well as the ordinary ones, being marble
elaborately carved,[5] whence they led out the said Tupac

---

[5] This is not marble but a white granite used by the Incas
which deceived the chroniclers.

Amaru to pledge obeissance to him as their true and
legitimate lord."

Even though Ocampo regrettably provides no details
about the geographical position of the most important solar
sanctuary, do not all the details correspond to Machu
Picchu? This is true even of the name "Pitcos," a current
distortion of "Picchu" (I've given several examples of it)[6]
and the place explicitly named in the deed of sale for the
lands adjoining Machu and Huaynu Picchu discovered by
Uriel Garcia, as well as in another historical document.

This is also the authoritative opinion of the old Peruvian
historian Luis E. Valcarcel, who points out, "So far, there
exists no other site containing houses that correspond to
the description given by Baltazar de Ocampo, no other
site with the same geographical position, the style of architecture in . . . white granite, numerous sumptuous buildings, or the extensive level space"—or the same name, I
should add.

Nevertheless, many investigators doubt that "Pitcos" is
anything but a distortion of the name "Viticos" or "Vitcos."
They are, at any rate, unanimous in wondering whether the
Incas had any knowledge of Machu Picchu during the final
imperial period—which, we note, does not fit in at all with
their belief that the famous "Lost City" was in fact built
by the Incas, and during this same period.

I have partially demystified the inexplicable "silence"
of the chroniclers, but it must still be determined whether
the fantastic "forgotten" city was at one point abandoned,
and when, by whom, and why.

The Yamqui Salcamayhua proposes a solution: the great
terremoto, whose echoes he heard. The scene takes place
during the time when Manco Capac, scoffing at the idolators, had all the idols and *huacas* in the country brought
to Cuzco under the pretext of holding a "procession and
general festival for them." He used them, instead, to build
the foundation of the great Temple of the Sun! But many
of them, according to the chronicler, "fled atop the Vilcanota, the Putina, the Coropuna . . . and, because of this
wickedness on the part of the Inca, the earth quaked much

---

[6] Even today the Quechuas of the Sacred Valley pronounce
"Machu Picchu" as "Macho Pitco" or "Pitchu."

more than it ever had in the past. Entire regions," he concludes, "were depopulated."

At this time, had the "lost cities" of the Sacred Valley long been uninhabited, perhaps even prohibited by the magi?

As for the later silence of the sixteenth-century chroniclers, historians do not understand why the Indians who were allied with the conquistadors (such as the Cañari Chilche or Paullu Inca) did not give away the famous "secret." The only logical answer is that they were not in on it, because of the tragic events precipitated by Pizarro's arrival in Cajamarca. Panic and surprise may have clouded people's minds. Also, it may be that at that moment the sacerdotal elite of Cuzco, aware of the rapid approach of the foreigners and the exactions they made, had sent away the principal Virgins of the Sun and the Mamacunas once again to conceal them at Machu Picchu.

Was Manco himself taken into the high priests' confidence? Did they not have the impression that he was betraying his people and his gods by making a triumphant entry into Cuzco alongside the Pizarros?

Later, when he rebelled and switched tactics, he could have found out what had become of the Acllas, placed in the "Lost City" for safekeeping by the Willac Umu. Observing that many of his brothers remained loyal to the conquistadors, might he not have imposed secrecy himself in turn and—to save the Virgins of the Sun (the concubines whom he would take with him when he fled were probably Chosen Women and not untouchable priestesses)—decided not to retrench in the impregnable Sacred City?

CHAPTER NINETEEN

The Americanists' Point of View

> *Machu Picchu is an open book—with un-*
> *decipherable letters! From the archaeological*
> *point of view, it is an extremely rich source*
> ✺ *of knowledge; in terms of the art and science* ✺
> *of engineering, a problem; in terms of his-*
> *tory, a question mark . . .*
> —Victor Angles Vargas, 1972

THE ANCIENT CIVILIZATIONS OF PERU: 20,000 YEARS AGO

Is it possible to locate Machu Picchu in the fantastic symphony of the lost civilizations of Peru?

The constant progress of the various modern sciences which permit an autopsy of ancient peoples has led some renowned investigators to attempt a provisional chronology. They have established that, if man is allochthonous, Peruvian culture is autochthonous and the result of a patient multimillenary evolution.

The archaeological sequences revealed since the beginning of the twentieth century have not ceased to push further back in time the mysterious appearance of the "first" American.

One pioneer, Max Uhle, showed that 2,000 years ago ancient fishing tribes, the Proto-Chimu and the Proto-Nazca, lived on the Pacific coast of Peru, to the north and south respectively.

Julio Cesar Tello discovered that the Chavin (possibly originating in the Amazonian jungles) settled in the Cordillera Blanca 3,000 years ago.

Junius Bird exhumed from Huaca Prieta the 4,000-year-old remains of fisher-gatherers from the Chicama Valley.

Recently Frédéric Engel pushed these dates back further still by unearthing the semisubterranean villages of the Paracas, dating back 5,000 years, then those of the horti-culturists of Chilca, between 6,000 and 9,000 years old.

While excavating the painted caves of Lauricocha, (at the source of the Marañon, at an altitude of over 4,000 meters), Augusto Cardich found the stone instruments of hunters who took shelter there 10,000 years ago; these hunters were contemporaneous with other clans identified in the south, at Toquepala, and near Lake Titicaca, at Mazo Cruz.

Near Lima, Edward Lanning unearthed—at Chivateros, in the Chillon Valley—stone tools used between 10,000 and 14,000 years ago. Finally, MacNeish recently opened up some prehistoric caves in the Ayacucha region, where preagricultural and preceramic groups took shelter 14,000 to 15,000 years ago, and even older caves at Paccaycasa, rich in paleontological associations, dating back at least 18,000 years,[1] or, at Piqui Machay, 20,000 years.

PRE-INCA CUZCO: 3,000 YEARS AGO?

The population of the Cuzco area should also date back to immemorial times. The fossilized teeth of pre-Columbian horses and of extinct animal species have been discovered alongside flint blades made by cave-dwellers.

Dr. Muller would date the "astronomical observatory" of Machu Picchu at 3000–4000 B.C.

Montesinos reports that when Manco Capac arrived in Cuzco, "a city already existed." Father Ambrosio Morales, who discovered fossilized carapaces of enormous chelonians at the site, thinks that this may indicate that, 4,000 years before the Incas, the area was filled by a lake, beside which lay a port and paths, or the Machu Nan, which followed the banks, converging on the lacustral piers. It appears that

---

[1] Not long ago Dr. José Felipe Valencia Arenas collected some arrowheads and paleolithic "knives" from the bed of La Huerta (on the road from Lima to Canta), which were from an epoch much earlier than that of the neighboring sites and similar to instruments found in New Mexico's Sandia Cave. Therefore, they may date, like the latter, from about 26,000 years ago.

torrential rains inundated this place, and because of the water pressure, a gap opened in the mountain, releasing the water so that it flowed forth and carved out the valley.

Rafael Aguilar Paez, the former vice-chancellor of the University of Cuzco, recalls that Walter Lehmann accorded Machu Picchu "a place prior to the Egyptian pyramids." As for the reason it was abandoned, he, like Bingham, supposes that violent seismic tremors, which jarred the colossal walls, caused breaks in the hydraulic system, or else—as was the case for the Mayas of the Yucatan—the lush forest conspired against the necessary expansion of the "Lost City."

In 1970 Dr. Luis Barreda Murillo discovered, on the southwest slope of Cuzco, the archaeological zone of Wimpillay, where he identified a citadel and a necropolis containing thousands of shards of utilitarian pottery, weaving tools made of bone, stone beads, metal objects, and textiles. He discovered thirty-two sites which he dated at 3,000 years old, an age that would correspond with the presence of Ayar Manco Capac, whom he thus placed much earlier than do the bulk of the Peruvian historiographers.

This is also roughly the age—this time indicated by dating with radioactive carbon-14—of the ruins of Chanapata, another suburb of Cuzco, rich in ancient black pottery of a very refined style, tools made of llama bones, javelin shafts with obsidian points, and figurines modeled in clay or carved in stone, specimens of which were found in the direction of the Sacred Valley. A magnificent chalice made of black stone, unique throughout ancient Peru, which was sold to a collector from Cuzco by pillagers working at Machu Picchu before Bingham's arrival, would justify the opinion that Machu Picchu dates from the same epoch as Wimpillay—that is, from 3,000 years ago.

Although the archaeologists criticize this hypothesis, one should heed a reliable witness, the geologist Carlos Kalafalovitch, who was assigned to study the cave-ins beneath the principal temple of Machu Picchu, which were threatening its equilibrium. In the course of his work, this specialist recently realized that this monument rests on a platform of cyclopean blocks buried 1.5 meters deep, which proves beyond a doubt that Machu Picchu was reconstructed on top of much older ruins! This means that at least one of the mysteries of the "Lost City" has been cleared up—and it represents one of my most important "revelations."

For his part, Victor Angles Vargas, while studying the cultural sequences of the central Andean area where the Incan civilization developed (and where Cuzco and Machu Picchu are located), became convinced that, influenced successively by the art and thought of the Chavin, the Tiahuanaco, and then finally—1,000 years ago—by the Wari, various small nations constituted "independent states which gradually turned into powerful regional states." This was the case, he says, for the "vigorous urban areas, the provincial capitals of Machu Picchu, Tamputocco, Ollantaytambo, Pisac, Chincheros . . . which, at their apogee and before they were confederated by the Incas to form the empire, constructed elegant temples, palaces, and buildings."

Although "the pre-Hispanic towns lack a birth certificate," Angles Vargas estimates that one can assume that over the centuries "demographic growth and progress achieved in the arts and sciences converted Machu Picchu into an important state, with a central government and judicial norms that made it a regional politico-religious capital of the utmost importance, possibly a sister and rival of Cuzco at the apogee of the Incan Empire."

If we heed this investigator, the antiseismic stone constructions of the "Lost City" housed the elite and the ruling class. As for the "common districts," consisting of thousands of houses made of crude clay bricks and huts made of wood or straw, scattered over the slopes of the Urubamba Cañon, they were destroyed by the elements.

As in Cuzco, the temples and palaces required a sizable staff. At Machu Picchu there were the groups of guards for the supply depots, the bridges, aqueducts, and roads; *chasquis*, farmers, potters, metalworkers, weavers, and spinners; builders; and a great number of people who prepared the food and drink.

Thus, in Victor Angles Vargas' view, the "Lost City" was not solely a sanctuary or "citadel," as many of his colleagues claim, but a large autonomous city. That it was temporarily unoccupied must have been due to a terrible, deadly epidemic which meant that it had to be rapidly evacuated, or else due to the downfall of its leaders, entailing a prohibition which turned it into a taboo city. This

event must have taken place, he believes, during the civil wars which broke out between Huascar and Atahualpa after the death of Huayna Capac.

Another Americanist, Victor Perez Armendariz, thinks it is possible to penetrate the mystery of Machu Picchu through the 103 reigns that, according to Montesinos, preceded the solar dynasty of the Inca Ayars. When the barbarian hordes rose up from the jungles of South America, destroying everything in their path, the men of a "megalithic empire" must have discovered this fertile valley, protected—by a *cañon*, a river, and the forest—from the invasion of great masses of people. These men were the founders of the "Lost City" which later became the secret refuge of the reigning family and the Virgins of the Sun.

José Gabriel Cosio, who accompanied the second Yale-Peruvian Expedition, appears certain that Machu Picchu had an enormous influence on the life of the peoples of the Vilcanota Basin. But he deduces that, given the silence of colonial history concerning this subject, "the Incas were not informed of this; otherwise they would have made this splendid fortress an instrument of Titanic resistance against any enemy army." As for its origin, Cosio speaks of "an early paleo-Quechua civilization dating back 2,000 years, whose work Machu Picchu must have been, and the memory of which was lost following the brutal invasion of the Aymaras, who pushed the peoples of this region in the direction of Lake Titicaca."

Luis Alayza y Paz Soldan does not hesitate to declare, "If the Incas did build it, it was certainly not those of the last dynasty, but those of the past eras mentioned by Montesinos."

Juvenal Jara makes it out to be "the first religious center dedicated to the astrological cults of the ancient Peruvians." And Max Jara Echea says it was "the creation of Andean man for the worship of the cosmos."

FROM THE "GOLDEN AGE" OR THE AGE OF PACHACUTEC?

Manuel Chavez Ballon, in charge of the restoration of the "Lost City," deals with a little-known aspect, closely related to the cultures and peoples who inhabited it and the age of their remains: the study of the pottery.

Most of the shapes, he tells us, belong to the classical and imperial periods (35 and 41 percent respectively), that is, to Inca eras. Some (12 percent) date from before 1450, but others correspond to the Colla, Chimu, Lupaca, and Lucre styles, which are much older. This is all the more revealing in view of the fact that, up until 1940, there was some doubt that vestiges would be discovered in the Cuzco region that could provide a historical basis for the legend that the Incas came from Lake Titicaca. But in the course of works carried out by the highway department, a layer of black potsherds appeared, which the American archaeologist Rowe classified among the most ancient pre-Tiahuanacoid shapes, hence pre-Inca by far. Nevertheless, Chavez Ballon believes that the "Lost City," as we know it, "was begun under Pachacutec and never completed."[2]

Dr. Toribio Mejia Xesspe, assistant director of the National Museum of Anthropology at Lima, prefers to stick with the modern scientific data which enable us to calculate the age of prehistoric monuments: that is, "the import and the quality of human architecture, which serves as a comparative basis and makes it possible to determine the style" and "the proportion of the refuse from daily life, the stratagraphic study of which attests to the respective cultural development."

However, he states, "At Machu Picchu we only have information concerning the architecture, pottery, and metallurgy, furnished in part by Hiram Bingham." From these documents one can conclude, he says, that "Machu Picchu belongs to the *golden age* of Incan civilization, that is, to the same cultural horizon as Tiahuanaco, Nazca, and Mochica, the ages of which are set at approximately 1,500 years, since these cultures flourished starting in the fifth century A.D."

For Alberto Jochamowits, cultural attaché of the Peruvian Embassy in Paris, Machu Picchu is "the marvelous city of the last Incas." In his opinion, "The conception of such a city could only represent the mind and the will of a single man." He noted that not only did setting up the

---

[2] Dr. Chavez Ballon informed me, through one of his assistants, Antuca Vega Centeno, that he had made no new discoveries at Machu Picchu: "neither Chosen Women of Manco nor vestiges of a Spanish occupation."

multiple dwellings required by such an unusual agglomeration call for a profound knowledge of urban affairs, the planner also had to know how to solve—in advance—all the problems posed by the location (on top of a nearly inaccessible rock face) and the very restricted space. It is in the Inca Tupac Yupanqui, who reigned from 1463 to 1471, that Jochamowits sees "the genius responsible for such a creation glorifying mankind."

Julio Espejo Nuñez, director of the Department of Explorations of the Museum of Anthropology and Archaeology in Lima, appears very cautious: "In view of the fact that no systematic excavation has taken place at Machu Picchu since 1911," he told me, "no professional archaeologist is, at present, in a position to provide a categorical answer. Moreover, all the known methods, as well as the instruments used, present serious problems—for example, the dates provided by the well-known carbon-14 chronometer, which, in many cases, lack proof. Even so," he concluded, "to establish basic frameworks on a single analysis would be absurd, given the possible error due to varying degrees of humidity and, in the Andes, to excessive radiations."

Since we are unable to find out the primordial opinion of the great Tello, the "king" of Peruvian archaeologists,[3] let us once again heed what Espejo Nuñez has to say; he was Tello's student and fellow explorer at Machu Picchu in 1941. Tello apparently expressed to him the idea that all the known ruins of the Sacred Valley belong to "the formative epoch," that is, corresponding to the age estimated by Chavin, or about 3,000 years. Tello noted, says Espejo Nuñez, "the later reusage of the carved stones, which indicates a superimposition of materials and technique according to a set plan."

THE TAMPU REALM OF TOKAY CAPAC

If the "Lost City" existed before the Incas, who built it and what role did it play? Here once again, archaeologists and historians disagree, and the very function of Machu Picchu remains as blurred at its correct age.

---

[3] Inexplicably, Tello's works concerning the Urubamba Valley have so far remained "secret" and unpublished.

Should one believe the old scholar from Cuzco who told me that the original name of the city was Willa Marca, or City of the Willcas, the great magicians and worshippers of stone idols, who built it? Could they have been the creators of the mysterious *calva*, the invisible giant head, much later enshrined in the Torreón by Inca architects?

Even to this day, the Quechuas are not without ancestral mythic ideas. My informant abides by the legend which holds that the sanctuary of the Willcas was burned by the rays of the Sun, who was jealous of the cult they dedicated to the stone idols. When one recalls that the *calva* bears the stigmata of a violent calcination, it indeed seems that here fiction and reality combine to make Machu Picchu the eponymous "city of the magi."

Since the solar cult was imposed by the Incas as a replacement for age-old beliefs, we ought therefore to find it centered in a territory adjoining Cuzco, the "navel" of the Incan Tahuantinsuyo. It is in this regard that Luis E. Valcarcel emphasizes two major points: the extraordinary importance of the Sacred Valley in the history of the Incas, and its magico-religious relationship to the solar cult, from before the time of the Ayars, the founders of the Tamputucco dynasty.

We find definite reminders of it in the old name of the Sun, which was called "Vilca" in ancient times and did not become "Inti" until the reign of Manco Capac. Likewise, ever since it originated in the glacier of Vilcanota, whose name signifies "House of the Sun," the sacred river has been known as Vilcamayo, or Rio of the Sun.

Valcarcel notes that, as an "intertropical labyrinth and the setting for the development of the final cultural phase of pre-Hispanic Peru," the Sacred Valley "links the two worlds of the Andean cosmos, the Amazonian forest and the high plateau of the lake of genesis, at the point where the rio and the mountain follow a similar course. In the valley and atop the peaks, both move toward the origin of the Sun, as if for fear of losing it, and in the direction of the Antisuyo, the country of the rising sun."

When the powerful figure named Viracocha carries out the quartering of the Andean world (whose "creation" is attributed to him, starting from Lake Titicaca), he distributes the north to Manco Capac and the east to Tokay Capac. Now, we have already seen this *sinchi*, king of the

Tampus, reigning over the middle course of the Sacred Rio, downstream from Yucay, toward Machu Picchu. As for Apu Tampu, Manco Capac's father, his name shows us that he was the principal leader of the Tampus. Thus, originally the noble caste of the Tampus preceded the Incan dynasty, as Huaman Poma confirms; he shows us "Manco Capac and Tokay Capac closely related." He describes the latter as "the last *sinchi* of the lineage of the Aucarunas, intrepid warriors of the fourth Sun," the sun that preceded the Golden Sun of the Incas. And he adds that the Tampus already worshipped the serpent Amaru, their "trademark," and the ice-covered Apus of the cordilleras, and that they bore the supreme title of Intip Churin,[4] or "Sons of the Sun."

Even more important, the Tampus boasted of having as a *pacarina*, or mythical birth place, the marvelous Casa del Sol,[5] the Sacred City which, according to the chroniclers, was built on the Vilcanota Nevado.

Finally, it was together that, invoking Father Sun, Incas and Tampus emerged from the cave of Pacaritamputocco and set out to conquer Cuzco. An oration to the Sun, recorded in 1575 by Father Cristobal de Molina, proves this: "O Sun, my Father, who said that there should be Cuzcos and Tampus, and that they should be thy conquering sons and dispossess all other peoples . . ."

Tampus and Incas are all Orejones with earlobes distended by thick, heavy, carved gold plugs. They speak among themselves in a secret dialect, forbidden and incomprehensible to their subjects, as Alonso Topa Atau would confide to the Jesuit Barnabe Cobo; he indicates, moreover, that Manco Capac lived in the palace of Tampucancha, next to the Temple of the Sun.

In 1572 several members of the royal caste of the Tampus still worshipped a rock symbolizing Manco Capac,

---

[4] In her *Historia de los Incas* (vol. 3, p. 14) Elizabeth della Santa notes that the Indians pointed out to her that in Quechua the exact term is not Intip Churin but *Intiq* Churin.

[5] This great solar temple, sought ever since the Conquest, has not been found, and one might well wonder whether the chroniclers were not mistaken and the temple in question was not Machu Picchu.

located in an *anden* on Colcampata, where the first Inca
had ordered a splendid castle to be built in the high part of
Cuzco. We can read their names in the *Informaciones*
requested by the viceroy Toledo, where they are inscribed
as "descendants of the Incas Mayta Capac and Inca Roca."

However, Tampus and Incas figure throughout Peruvian
protohistory as rival "brothers," alternately allied and at
odds, combatting a common enemy together or fighting to
the death over the temperate valleys of the heart of the
Andes.

Ultimately, Tokay Capac was routed by Manco Capac,
and no doubt it was then that, fleeing to the Sacred
Valley, he must have "torn down the house" and built in
its place a magnificent "wall with three windows" com-
memorating their common ancestors.

This, in brief, is what takes us back to Machu Picchu a
few centuries before another famous Tampu, the proud
prince Ollanta, and later Tokay Capac were finally killed
by the Inca Pachacutec.

All this opens up a new horizon for us: Ollantaytambo
must have been the Tampus' military and political capital
and Machu Picchu their religious capital, which was
"suddenly abandoned at least 3,000 years ago," if we are
to believe Manuel Suarez Polar. Much later, both were
enclosed and remodeled in the Inca style by the "Reno-
vator" of Tahuantinsuyo, who reconstructed Cuzco—and
probably all of the fortified cities of the Sacred Valley—
during this same period.

Concerning this point, the Peruvian historiographers are
agreed that the classical embellishments of Machu Picchu
and its "satellites" should be ascribed to the glorious reign
of Pachacutec. Connected by secret highways, these imposing cities, lost and rediscovered, must have been the
markers and stations of the Sun—or "holy places" along
its magico-religious itinerary—at its apotheosis.

On the other hand, several more objective Americanists
remain, like me, skeptical when confronted with the number and cyclopean size of the archaeological cities, the
extraordinary hydraulic systems, and the extent of the
terraces suspended along the sides of the Sacred Valley,
which, in this case, Pachacutec's marvelous architects must
have erected in less than thirty years! Dr. Enrique Soane,

for example, thinks that "two centuries would have scarcely sufficed, and 500 years would be much closer to the truth . . ." Or did it take much longer?

The liveliest controversy among the Americanists in fact concerns the time of the ruins' appearance. Some distinguish several styles, from the archaic formula of quarry stones merely stacked, to the ideal technique of astoundingly assembled polygonal walls. Others see in them only models varying in accordance with the building's function and the relative social position of the occupants.

As for the "regional characteristics" (doors and windows in much greater number than anywhere else in ancient Peru, open galleries, uncovered temples, two-story buildings, steeply inclined roofs), they must result from an intelligent adaptation to the temperate geographical environment of the Sacred Valley, as compared to the harsh climate of Cuzco and the Altiplano of Lake Titicaca.

Poetical fountains, niches, and countless "stone pegs" appear exclusively in the Tampu region. Returning one last time to the close kinship between the Tampus and the Incas, I think it is possible to conclude by stating that they created, *together*, a common aesthetic style and architectural "algebra," both admirable—and that, as in Hiram Bingham's interpretation, together they made the mountains of the Sun the refuge of the first and last Incas.

OMPHALOS OF ALL THE HIEROPHANIES

Luis E. Valcarcel considers the case of Machu Picchu very instructive in that it illustrates an important point: the coordination between the documentary and archaeological sources. Those who maintain that Machu Picchu is not Incan, because no description of it was given by the chroniclers of the Conquest, are, he declares, resorting to "an unsubstantial argument: Ignorance is no proof."

One thing is clear in this respect: The entire Amazon Basin was the center of a very dense and very active population, which contended with nature for enormous territories; today its ancient cities are "sleeping beauties."

A fervent partisan of the theory formulated by Uhle, Tello, Imbelloni, Bennett, Lothrop, Doering, and other professional archaeologists who do not hesitate to associate Machu Picchu with the apogee of the Inca Empire, he joins them in seeing it as the masterpiece, the supreme symbol, the city "at the frontiers of the impossible," which represented, on a reduced scale, the great ascensional empire, the natives of which, out of love for the Sun, reached the peaks of the cordillera, rising "toward a state of culture *in excelsis*."

Although the clearly religious buildings are grouped in four sectors, the "Lost City" is, as a whole, says Valcarcel, "a sacred entity," without being exclusively a sanctuary, much less a monastery. The political and economic institutions regulating the collective life of the inhabitants had their place, and the civil leader of Machu Picchu did not interfere, in Valcarcel's opinion, with the prerogative of the religious leader.

Proceeding from station to station (the "resting places" of the Sun, according to another author), then from sacred gateway to sacred gateway, the traveler—whether priest or official—penetrated with unction the zone forbidden to common mortals. He engaged in ritual acts at each stage, until he reached the fountains; their water purified him. He then climbed the monumental stairway to the high plaza of the temples, where his pilgrimage ended, since he was not allowed access to the solar observatory, or Intihuatana.

When he went back down to the city, he was directed to a house according to whether he served the Incan church or state.

Like this pilgrim, Valcarcel enters the "Lost City," partaking of the "divine inspiration" which animated its builders, experiencing their "cosmic ecstasy," and communicating with the sacred mountain, "*Imago Mundi*, prop of the sky, center, or omphalos, whence all creative power flows." For him, Machu Picchu has "all the characteristics of the supreme center or seat of all the hierophanies of the Tampu region, for which it must have been the sacred capital."

Restating in part the preceding theories, Chavez Ballon believes that Machu was "the last Inca bastion, built by 80,000 Indian artisans, as a replica—in miniature, but even more perfect—of imperial Cuzco, which was a small Tahuantinsuyo, or empire of four regions; from here Manco Inca planned to recapture the throne."

Garcia Rosell, of the Geography Society of Lima,

attempts to reconcile the various hypotheses by noting that Machu Picchu indubitably offer "examples of the Tampu style corresponding to a people of Incan culture."

For Frédéric Engel, the city of the Old Peak is "the frontier of the virgin forest" which Rivero Ayllon observes "frozen in a cyclopean stone sarcophagus which now holds only the ghostly memory of the Incas."

CITADEL, SANCTUARY, OR HAREM OF VESTALS?

The geographer Eduardo Rey Riveros bravely refutes the commonly held opinion, according to which, as in Tello's view, Incan culture originated in the Amazon Valley. He notes that a number of proofs, primarily linguistic, plead to the contrary: "The Incas populated the jungle only partially. The cyclopean, age-old stone ruins that look out across the Amazonian plain from the spurs of the eastern cordillera—including Machu Picchu—prove this."

Another dissenter, Carlos Troll, wonders whether the "Lost City" was not "a climatic prison colony for coca growers . . ."

The well-known architect and historian Hector Velardi sees "this city suspended over the abyss . . . as a cosmic vision of nature, and its character as sanctuary is particularly manifest in its ritual elegance and its sense of eternity. A form of architecture set in a peak of the Andes like a precious gem, it is one of the most impressive Inca monuments . . . to constitute part of a veritable chain of fortifications for defending Cuzco against powerful, unsubjugated tribes from the tropical jungles."

The archaeologist Arturo Jimenez Borja recommends that Machu Picchu be inscribed "in the Inca cultural patrimony." These ruins correspond, he believes, "to the later reigns, perhaps starting with that of Pachacutec, the epoch in which it should no doubt be placed with the greater probability."

Mejia Xesspe, examining the utilitarian purpose of the "Lost City," concludes, "The style suggests an essentially religious, artistic, and economic center: sanctuary, residence of Chosen Women, workshops for the ceremonial crafts."

José Uriel Garcia sees it as "an Incan center for feminine occupations . . . a stone document for history, a city of a civil nature rather than a military citadel or religious sanctuary." In his opinion, "Its construction dates back to long before the discovery of America." Its builders, he states, made it "comfortable, orderly, attractive, of an admirable geometric beauty, adapted to the needs of its inhabitants, and surpassing all comparable cities." He calculates that it took some fifty years to build it. The builders appeared to be "simultaneously sociologists, hygienists, geographers, engineers, architects, and, finally, artists to their very fingertips." For this investigator, Machu Picchu was particularly developed "following the Incan conquest of the Pacific coast." When they realized that the empire was dangerously extended, they built this network of cities to augment the sources of production. "Machu Picchu," he concludes, "was a marvel of art in the service of social necessities."

Luis Pardo holds that in Peru there is "no monument more complete as an ancient city whose constituent elements are quasi-intact, as if its inhabitants had just left." He finds there "the residences of the deities of the flourishing empire of the Quechuas, where felicity, pomp, and beauty once reigned." But Pardo does not wish to pass judgment on the theories put forth by his colleagues, "none of which can be confirmed at present." Machu Picchu is believed to have been, he notes, "the refuge of the vestals or the capital of a domain fortified against the armies of the jungle areas, or else the seat of the confederation of the peoples of Vilcanota" . . . and he observes, with regret, that the "Lost City" carefully guards "the sibylline mystery of an ancient race."

Eugenio Alarco thinks that Machu Picchu—which he feels was probably built by Tupac Inca and which marks the apotheosis of the style and refinement of Incan architectural art—constituted "the great ceremonial center, the most important and renowned in the entire complex of the Vilcabamba Cordillera."

Echoing him, Federico Kauffmann Doig, who admires both "the art of building evidenced by the Incas of the imperial period and their intense activity," sees in this important architectural development "the result of the political objectives of conquest and unification pursued by

the caste of Cuzco . . . which required fortresses . . .
impressive palaces, representing the hierarchy and power
of the Sons of the Sun."

While awaiting the day when "the pickax of seekers . . .
will open the door to vast mortuary halls and disrupt a
silent gathering of mummies," Bertrand Flornoy, imagining
the past, supposes that "this city existed as the simple,
rough capital of a tribe that emerged from the Amazonian
undergrowth. Then other peoples occupied it . . . The
entire massif, dominated by the snow-covered peak of the
Salccantay, was the refuge of conquered and rebellious
peoples. While pursuing them, the Incas surely climbed the
slopes of Machu Picchu and built, on this predestined site,
a fortress controlling both the cordillera and the entrance
to the virgin forest . . . Then . . . they set up a small city
behind the ramparts. Generations of builders enlarged it,
and astronomers, priests, and virgins were brought up.
Thus, it is not impossible that the last rebellious leader of
the Indians, Manco Capac, took refuge there with his
children, and that they spent their lives cornered in this
prison of the heights, where they had the illusion of
freedom."

Edgar Diaz, who belongs to an "esoteric school" established on the Old Peak, finds there "the educational center
of the Inca princes—where the Amautas and the astrologers
trained the members of the royal family in the art of
government—and a spiritual refuge for the sovereigns, in
close communion with the Sun."

Viewing them "from the perspective of urban affairs and
the science of the foundation of cities, which illustrate and
characterize the culture of their builders," the Peruvian
engineer Harth-Terré notes how the planning of the Incan
towns surprised the conquistadors, in the geometry and
regularity of their "patterns." The great public plazas,
streets and districts, houses and religious buildings struck
them, he says, "with their similarity to the old European
cities and those of the more ancient civilizations of Asia
Minor and the Roman Empire." However, Harth-Terré
deplores the fact that the reason for their cyclopean fortifications still remains a mystery. Fortifications against
whom? To protect themselves from small groups of savage
Indians, who had no military organization but were never

entirely subjugated by the Incas, and who may have sometimes emerged from the jungles, armed only with bows
and arrows?

Moreover, during the reign of Pachacutec, this investigator notes, it seems "that constant exchanges were
arranged with the forest-dwelling tribes and that the Sacred
Valley had become the magnificent and inexhaustible
granary of Cuzco."

Harth-Terré declares, "To deny the link that connects
the stonecutters of the walls of both Machu Picchu and
Cuzco would be to deny the very accomplishments of the
Incas." The style peculiar to the "Lost City" is obvious
proof that this monument was created by artisans who
possessed a highly developed artistic sensibility.

Based on economic and political criteria, Harth-Terré
discerns at Machu Picchu—as well as the thirty other ruins
surrounding it that have been discovered so far—"the
traces of intense commercial traffic and military transit
between Cuzco and the Amazon Basin, for the profitable
utilization of the abundant vegetable and zoological stores
of the nearby virgin forest, where the Incas stocked up on
manioc, peanuts, red peppers, coca, medicinal herbs,
precious woods, brilliant feathers, the hides of rare beasts—
all products unknown in colder regions."

Thus, for Harth-Terré, Machu Picchu was "a small,
integral, and autarchic city, a citadel in a sense, where, by
virtue of an agricultural area included in a circuit enclosed
by walls, a temporary defensive isolation was possible." In
sum, the "Lost City" played not a defensive role but, quite
the contrary, an offensive one, since it was created "for the
Incan penetration."

THE INCA VERSAILLES AND "EIGHTH WONDER OF THE WORLD"

Machu Picchu was, for Vincente Achala, "the resort of
the Incan leaders and nobles, in one of the most extraordinary landscapes in the world."

This is also the opinion of John Hemming, from whom
the "Lost City," like Pisac and Ollantaytambo, appeared
to be "one of the Inca's pleasure houses." And for Old
Hunter it was "the royal residence, in the style of Versailles

or Potsdam, as well as a sacred city, by virtue of its isolation and splendor, due to the altitude . . . [a] peaceful
[place] for observing the seasons and the course of the sun,
consulting the oracles, and conducting sacrifices, because it
was built, like Buddhist sanctuaries in Asia and the
Christian monasteries of the Near East, atop peaks which
ensured peace for the learned priests."

Nathan Wachtel defines Machu Picchu as "the high holy
place of the empire, a sentinel at the border of the four
worlds, between heaven and earth, mountain and forest."

Finally, as is only fitting, let us yield the floor to Hiram
Bingham one last time, who says, on the last page of his
book: "The story of Machu Picchu covers many centuries.
Undoubtedly in its last state the city was the carefully
guarded treasure house where that precious worship of the
sun, the moon, the thunder and the stars, so violently over-
thrown in Cuzco, was restored . . . where those Chosen
Women whose lives had from early girlhood been devoted
to all the duties of the Sanctuary found a refuge from the
animosity and lust of the conquistadors . . . [and where]
one by one passed away . . . and left no descendants
willing to reveal the importance or explain the significance
which crown the beetling precipices of Machu Picchu."

"It is a treasure of worldwide dimensions," exclaims
Hermann Buse, "which is to Peru and America what Egypt
or the Parthenon is to Europe."

For Alfredo Yepez Miranda it is "the emblem of Peru,
the triumph of Andean man, the image of the Incan past,
where the soul never grows old, where what is eternal is
worshipped, where the stones reach out to the cosmos."

And General de la Barra will have the final word, in
claiming for Machu Picchu—which stands in one of the
most splendid sites in antiquity—a place among the
wonders of the world.

"Of the seven acknowledged Wonders," he says, "the
hanging gardens of Babylon, the temple of Artemis at
Ephesus, the statue of Zeus at Olympia, the Colossus at
Rhodes, the Mausoleum at Halicarnassus, and the light-
house of Alexandria have been destroyed by the elements
or swallowed up by prehistory and legend. All that remains
is the famous Pyramid of Cheops! Alongside it, Machu
Picchu deserves the rank of Eighth Wonder of the
World. . . ."

Travel Information

LOCATION

Located in Peru in the southeastern cordillera of the Andes, at lat. 13° 07′ S, and long. 72° 35′ W, 112 kilometers northwest of Cuzco (by train), the "Lost City" of the Incas belongs to the province of Urubamba, known for the abundance of splendid ruins said to be "Incan."

The mysterious archaeological ruins of Machu Picchu, which stand at an altitude of 2,500 meters, in a magical landscape, on the slopes of the great Salccantay Nevado (6,271 meters), have been 50 percent restored.

TRAVEL

Jet airplanes—the Fawcett and Satco companies—ensure daily connection (flight time is one hour) between Lima, the Peruvian capital on the Pacific coast, and the Anta airport, near Cuzco, at an altitude of 3,400 meters.

The traveler who enjoys normal health, suffers from no respiratory illness, and is not particularly "susceptible," has a good chance of avoiding *soroche*, or "mountain sickness." It is useful nonetheless to carry Coramine glucose pills. A few hours' rest, which is indispensable, usually suffice for the body to adapt to the unusual environment of the high altitude. In case of sickness, an oxygen balloon can be used. At present, since the road ends at Ollantay-tambo (the great archaeological center 57 kilometers away) in the Sacred Valley of the Incas, the railroad is the only means of transportation between Cuzco and Machu Picchu—either the little "sierra train" packed with Indians, which stops in every village, where it is assaulted by picturesque native food-vendors, or by the tourist railcar. One takes six hours; the other half that time. Both follow the torrential course of the Rio of the Sun, between slopes covered with pre-Columbian ruins.

Trains depart every day, including Sunday, very early in the morning, from the Santa Ana Station, near a typical

Cuzco marketplace. The stop for the "Lost City" is at Puente Ruinas (a metal bridge where the Museo de Sitio is located), at the bottom of the wild, splendid Urubamba Cañon, which the nearly vertical "Hiram Bingham Road" climbs in steep zigzags. Cut through lush tropical vegetation, it was opened in 1948. The ascent, in minibuses, from the riverbank to the inn (*hotel de turistas*), takes a good quarter of an hour.

CLIMATE

Only two seasons characterize this temperate Quechua region: the dry, cold period (autumn-winter), from May through October, with violent storms breaking out in June; and the hot, humid season (spring-summer), from November through April. The average temperature ranges from 5 to 15° C.

CUZCO

At a distance of 1,168 kilometers by road from Lima (387 kilometers from Lake Titicaca), located in the heart of the Andes, and connected to Lima by planes, cars, and *collectivo* taxis, today the ancient "navel" of the Empire of the Tahuantinsuyo is the "archaeological capital of South America." Half-Inca, half-colonial, all the treasures of the history of the Incas, sons of the Golden Sun, evade —as if in a dream—the bold incursions of Pizarro's conquistadors, amid the enchanting daily life of the Andes Indians with their rainbow-colored costumes. Each year over 100,000 international tourists come to watch, during the entire week of June 24, the extraordinary performances reconstructing the Inti Raymi, the great solstitial festival of the Sun dating from the Incan era, which are held in the cyclopean ruins of Sacsahuaman, overlooking the city.

ARCHAEOLOGICAL RUINS

On the Outskirts of Cuzco

Sacsahuaman (2 km.): The largest megalithic fortress in the world.

Kenko (3 km): Remarkable monolithic amphitheater of the Chinkanas.

Puka Pukara (6 km): Bastion defending the pasturelands of the sacred llamas.

Tambo Mackay (7 km): Citadel and ritual bath of the Incas.

Ruins in the Sacred Urubamba Valley

Pisac (30 km): Immense "hanging gardens," famous Intihuatana. Sundays: Feria of the Varayocs.

Yucay (68 km): The "garden of the Incas." Palace of Sayri Tupac.

Ollantaytambo (96 km): Enormous tiered fortress defending the valley. The six "mirrors of the Sun," palaces, *andenes*, etc.

Ruins Near the Pampa de Anta

Chincheros (16 km): Ancient Inca town. Colonial church built on beautiful monumental foundations, with trapezoidal doorways. Sundays: Mass and barter marketplace.

Bibliography

MODERN AUTHORS

R. AGUILAR PAEZ. *Machupicchu*. Lima, 1961.

E. ALARCO. *El Hombre peruano en su historia*. Vol. 2: *Los Antepasados aborígenes*. Lima, 1971.

L. ALAYZA y PAZ SOLDAN. *Mi país: El Incanato de Vilcabamba*. Lima, 1944.

V. ANGLES VARGAS. *Machupijchu, enigmática ciudad inca*. Lima, 1973.

GÉNÉRAL F. DE LA BARRA. *El Indio peruano en las etapas de la conquista*. Lima, 1948.

A. BARRIONUEVO. *Cuzco mágico*. Lima, 1968.

L. BAUDIN. *La Vie quotidienne au temps des incas*. Paris, 1955.

H. BINGHAM. "In the Wonderland of Peru," *National Geographic*, 1913.

————. "The Discovery of Machu Picchu," *Harper's*, April 1913.

————. *Inca Land*, 1930.

————. *Machu Picchu, a Citadel of the Incas*, 1930.

————. *Lost City of the Incas*, 1948.

H. BUSE. *Antología de Machu Picchu*. Lima, 1963.

R. CARRIÓN CACHOT. *El Culto del agua en el antiguo Perú*. Lima, 1955.

M. CHAVEZ BALLON. *Cuzco y Machu Picchu: Waika N°. 4–5*. Cuzco, 1971.

J. CORNEJO BOURONCI E. *Piedras del Cuzco*. Cuzco.

J. G. COSIO. *Informe elevado al supremo gobierno*. Lima, 1961.

COSME BUENO. *Geografía virreinal siglo XVIII*. Lima, 1951.

F. COSSIO DEL POMAR. *El Mundo de los incas*. Lima, 1970.

R. CUNEO VIDAL. *Historia de las guerras de los últimos incas peruanos*. Lima, 1925.

E. DUMBAR TEMPLE. *Notas sobre el Virrey Toledo y los incas de Vilcabamba*. Lima, 1949.

O. EFREN REYES. *Breve historia del Ecuador*. Quito, 1934.

F. ENGEL. *Le Monde précolombien des Andes*. Paris, 1972.

P. FEJOS. *Informe de la Wenner Gren Expédition*. 1944.

GARCIA ROSELL. *Cavernas, grutas, cuevas . . .* Lima, 1965.

G. MONTOYA and A. GIESECKE. *El Misterio de Machu Picchu: « El Comercio »*. Lima, 1961.

W. GREEN. *Exploraciones arqueológicas de la Cordillera de Vilcabamba.*

E. HARTH-TERRÉ. *El Urbanismo en el antiguo Perú: Machu Picchu, ciudad autárquica.* Lima, 1961.

J. HEMMING. *The Conquest of the Incas.* London, 1970.

A. JIMENEZ BORJA. *La Danza en el antiguo Perú.*

J. JIJON Y CAMANO. *La Religión del imperio de los incas.* Lima, 1919.

R. KARSTEN. *La Civilisation de l'empire inca.* Paris, 1952.

F. KAUFFMANN DOIG. *Arqueología peruana, visión integral.* Lima, 1971.

GÉNÉRAL L. M. LANGLOIS. *Explorations archéologiques de la Vallée de l'Urubamba.*

J. LARREA. *Corona incaica: Machu Picchu, ciudad de la última esperanza.* Lima, 1960.

HENRY LEHMANN. *Les Civilisations précolombiennes.* Paris, 1953.

B. LELONG. *Cordillère magique.* Paris, 1955.

R. LEVILLIER. *El Drama de Vilcabamba.* 1935.

L. A. LLANOS. *Tampu.* Cuzco, 1944.

R. LOREDO. *La Crónica de Alonso Borregan.* 1940.

C. MARKHAM. *The Incas of Peru.* 1912.

V. M. MAURUA. *Juicio de límites . . . Vilcabamba.* 1906.

A. MÉTRAUX. *Les Incas.* Paris, 1961.

A. MIRO QUESADA. *Costa, sierra y montaña.* Lima, 1947.

L. PARDO. *Historia y arqueología del Cuzco.* Vol. I. *Machupijchu.* 1957.

FR. G. Y. PEASE. *Los Últimos incas del Perú.* Lima, 1972.

O. PECQUET. "Le Mystère de la Vallée Sacrée des incas." *Archeologia,* nos. 8–11 (1966).

R. PORRAS BARRENECHEA. *Mito, tradición y historia.* Lima, 1951.

E. PORTUGAL. "Hiram Bingham, el traficante de Machu Picchu." *Tareas,* n°. 6 (1961).

W. PRESCOTT. *History of the Conquest of Peru.* 1847.

S. QUIJADO JARA. *La Coca en las costumbres indígenas.* Lima, 1950.

M. J. QUINTANA. *Vida de Francisco Pizarro.* 1943.

A. RAIMONDI. *Itinerario . . .* Lima, 1916.

J. RASPAIL. *Terres et peuples incas.* Paris, 1955.

M. DE RIVERO and J. D. TSCHUDI. *Antiguedades peruanas.* Lima, 1851.

C. ROMERO. *Inédito sobre el primer Tupac Amaru.* Lima, 1907.

E. ROMERO. *Biografía de los Andes.* Lima, 1971.

A. ROSEMBLAT. *Campaña de Vilcabamba y muerte de Tupac Amaru.* 1966.

M. Rostworowski de Diez Canseco. *Pachacutec Inca Yupanqui*, 1953.

———. *Los Ayarmaca*, 1969.

———. *El Repartimiento de doña Beatriz*, 1970.

———. *Dos Manuscritos inéditos sobre Manco II*.

E. Della Santa. *Historia de los incas*. Vols. 1–3. Arequipa, 1970.

E. de Sartiges. *Voyage dans les républiques de l'Amérique du Sud*. Paris, 1830.

G. Savoy. "Imperio bajo la selva," *Caretas* (1966).

J. C. Tello. "Expedición arqueológica al Urubamba," *Pueblo y Cultura*, nᵒˢ. 11–12. Lima, 1942.

H. Trimborn. *Las Clases sociales en el imperio incaico*. 1925.

J. Uriel Garcia. "Machu Picchu," *Cuaderno Americano*, nᵒ 4. Mexico, 1961.

H. Urteaga. *El Imperio incaico*. 1931.

L. E. Valcarcel. *Machu Picchu, el mas famoso monumento arqueológico del Perú*. Lima, 1964.

J. J. Vega. *La Guerra de los Viracocha: Manco Inca el gran rebelde*. Lima, 1969.

H. Velarde. "Arquitectura incaica," *El Legado Aborígen* (1960).

N. Wachtel. *La Vision des vaincus*. Paris, 1971.

S. Waisbard. *Féerie péruvienne*. Paris, 1956.

———. *La Vie splendide des momies péruviennes*, 1960.

———. *Hommes, dieux et mages du Titikaka*, 1970.

———. *Mystérieux mondes incas perdus et retrouvés*, 1971.

———. *Tiahuanaco, 10,000 ans d'énigmes incas*, 1972.

Marquis de Wavrin. "Wayna Picchu," *Revista del Museo e Instituto Arqueológico*, nᵒ. 19 (1961).

C. Wiener. *Pérou et Bolivie*. Paris, 1880.

A. Yepez Miranda. *Grandeza de Machu-Picchu*. 1968.

CHRONICLERS OF THE CONQUEST

J. de Acosta. *Historia natural y moral de las Indias*. 1590.

J. de Arriaga. *La Extirpación de la idolatría en el Perú*. 1621.

J. de Betanzos. *Suma y narración de los incas*. 1551.

M. Cabello Valboa. *Miscelánea antártica*. 1586.

A. de la Calancha. *Crónica moralizada del Órden de San Agustín en el Perú*. 1639.

B. de las Casas. *De las antiguas gentes del Perú*. Circa 1561.

P. Cieza de León. *La Crónica del Perú*. 1553.

———. *Del Señorío de los incas*.

B. Cobo. *Historia del Nuevo Mundo*. 1653.

Titu Cusi Yupanqui. *Relación de la conquista del Perú y hechos del Inca Manco II*. 1570.

M. DE ESTETE. *Noticias del Perú.* 1535.

F. DE OVIEDO. *Historia general y natural de Indias.* Circa 1535.

D. F. DE PALENCIA, el Palatino. *Historia del Perú.* 1572.

GARCILASO INCA DE LA VEGA. *Comentarios reales.* 1609.

D. GONZALEZ HOLGUIN. *Vocabulario quechua.* 1608.

GUTIERREZ DE SANTA CLARA. *Historia de las guerras civiles del Perú.* 1544.

A. DE HERRERA. *Historia general de los hechos de los castellanos.* 1615.

F. HUAMAN POMA DE AYALA. *Nueva crónica y buen gobierno.* Circa 1613.

FR. DE JEREZ. *Verdadera relación de la conquista del Perú.* 1534.

M. JIMENEZ DE LA ESPADA. *Relación del sitio del Cuzco.* 1539.

R. LIZARRAGA. *Descripción de las Indias.* 1605.

P. LOPEZ. *Relación inédita.* 1570.

FR. LOPEZ DE GOMARA. *Historia general de las Indias.* 1552.

J. DE MATIENZO, *Gobierno del Perú.* 1567.

C. DE MOLINA, « el Cuzqueño. » *Ritos y fábulas de los incas.* 1575.

F. DE MONTESINOS. *Memorias antiguas historiales y políticas del Perú.* 1644.

M. DE MORUA. *Historia del orígen y genealogía real de los incas.* 1590.

B. DE OCAMPO CONEJEROS. *Descripción y sucesos históricos de la provincia de Vilcabamba.* 1610.

ANELLO OLIVA. *Historia del reino y provincias del Perú.* 1631.

P. J. DE ORICAIN. *Compendio breve . . .* 1568.

P. PIZARRO. *Relación del descubrimiento y conquista de los reinos del Perú.* 1572.

POLO DE ONDEGARDO. *Los Errores y supersticiones de los indios,* 1559.

―――. *Relación anónima . . .* 1539.

D. RODRIGUEZ DE FIGUEROA. *Narrative of the Route . . .* 1565.

P. SANCHEZ DE LA HOZ. *Relación para S. M. de lo sucedido en la conquista.* 1535.

J. SANTA CRUZ PACHACUTI YAMQUI SALCAMAYHUA. *Relación de antiguedades desde reino del Perú.* Circa 1613.

H. DE SANTILLAN. *Relación del orígen, descendencia, política y gobierno de los incas.* 1564.

P. SARMIENTO DE GAMBOA. *Historia general llamada índica.* 1572.

FR. DE TOLEDO. *Libro de la visita general.* 1570–1575.

C. VACA DE CASTRO. *Discurso sobre la descendencia y gobierno de los incas.* 1544.

―――. *Carta al emperador don Carlos.* 1542.

B. VALERA. *Relación de las costumbres antiguas de los naturales del Perú.* 1604.

VASQUEZ DE ESPINOZA. *Compendio y descripción de las Indias Occidentales.* 1628.

F. DE XEREZ. *Verdadera relación de la conquista del Perú.* 1534.

A. DE ZARATE. *Historia del descubrimiento del Perú y conquista.* 1555.

Among the great poets who have written about Machu Picchu, let us note:

MARTIN ADAN. *La Mano desaida.*

MARIO FLORIAN. *Machu Picchu de voces triunfales.*

ALBERTO HIDALGO. *Patria completa.*

PABLO NERUDA. *Alturas de Machu Picchu.*